WILLIAM E. BORAH

AND

AMERICAN

FOREIGN POLICY

WILLIAM E. BORAH
AND
AMERICAN
FOREIGN POLICY

Robert James Maddox

LOUISIANA STATE UNIVERSITY PRESS

BATON ROUGE

To Robert C. Maddox

CHIEFLY remembered today for his opposition to the League of Nations, his commitment to neutrality in the 1930's, and the prediction he made less than two months before Germany attacked Poland that there would be no war in Europe, William E. Borah in his prime ranked as one of the most famous and powerful figures on the national scene. Endowed with a singular talent for attracting attention, he constituted, in Walter Lippmann's phrase, "a host unto himself." He rarely lacked an opinion, whatever the subject, or a willingness to express it. Reaching the peak of his career during the Harding-Coolidge era, the Senator in those years wielded considerable influence over the shaping of American foreign policy. His significance declined under Hoover and sagged further with the coming of the New Deal, but he remained to the end a man difficult to ignore.

Borah's treatment at the hands of scholars rests largely upon his performance as a spokesman for causes. Unlike many other senators who made their contributions through legislative enactments, committee work, or organizational manipulations, the Idahoan conducted most of his operations as proselytizer and polemicist in full public view. Indeed, there is little evidence that a "private" Borah existed at all, as anyone who goes through his voluminous correspondence quickly learns. His letters to those closest to him, which was never very close, oftentime resemble paraphrases of his most recent Senate speech. To a great extent, therefore, historians have confronted the Senator on his own terms through his speeches and writings.

Several additional factors have contributed to this tendency. First, even his most vehement critics habitually acknowledge his "utter sincerity," thereby assuming the validity of interpreting the man through what he said at any given time. Second, when such a practice reveals a myriad of incongruities and contradictions, these are explained away by alluding to another of his alleged traits, his "bewildering and often grossly inconsistent views on foreign policy." As a result, although he is frequently accorded high marks for particular positions he espoused, the most pervasive interpretation of Borah portrays him as an incorruptible, outspoken, but muddled idealist —hopelessly naive, a utopian, a man who sought to attain world peace through formalized expressions of good will.

The present study, in part a reevaluation of his correspondence and public statements, represents an effort to go beyond textual analyses by examining closely his words in the context of his actions. This approach has unveiled no such startling disclosure as proof that the Idahoan secretly favored the League. It has, in the author's opinion, yielded a series of qualifications and corrections, the cumulative effect of which markedly alters the conventional view of Borah. Three themes stand out: that a deep and unshakable fatalism permeated his entire outlook; that his fundamental objectives never changed throughout his career; and that in pursuing these objectives, his honesty and integrity notwithstanding, he utilized whatever tactics served his ends—and the tactics rather than the goals often created the appearance of inconsistency where none existed. Whether such conclusions raise or lower Borah's place in history depends upon the reader's preferences.

The book's format roughly follows the Senator's own interests and activities. Heavy stress has been placed on the issues he devoted most of his time to or greatly influenced— the League, his peace plans during the 1920's, Russia, and neutrality—those matters, in short, upon which his reputation stands. Other areas have been slighted comparatively; having analyzed his opposition to interference in Latin American nations, the author has thought it unprofitable to treat in detail each of the many times Borah raised a protest. Nor has the attempt been made to work into the study every question he spoke about or voted on during his thirty-three years in the Senate. Coverage of this sort would require several volumes or result in a book other than that intended.

The author is indebted to L. Ethan Ellis, who supervised an earlier version of this manuscript, and to the Central Fund for Research at the Pennsylvania State University for financial aid. Grateful acknowledgment is also made for permission to reprint in revised form materials that were first published as articles in the following journals: "Borah and the Battleships," *Idaho Yesterdays*, IX (Summer, 1965), 20–27; "William E. Borah and the Outlawry Crusade," *Historian*, XXIX (February, 1967), 200–20; and "Keeping Cool with Coolidge," *Journal of American History*, LIII (March, 1967), 772–80.

ROBERT JAMES MADDOX

CONTENTS

E ARLY in 1907, William Edgar Borah presented his credentials to the United States Senate where he was to serve uninterruptedly until his death in January, 1940. He came to enjoy an enviable political situation over the course of his long career. Idaho had produced few men of more than local reputation thus far, and he represented a public asset through which Idahoans could be assured that the rest of the nation knew they existed. With another senator to press their state needs, Borah's constituents asked little more of him than to be controversial. He rarely disappointed them. Having no political organization and a minimal interest in state affairs, his senatorship more nearly resembled the position of Idaho's permanent ambassador to the outside world.

Borah's opponents within the state habitually claimed he ignored his local responsibilities—a charge whose validity failed to impress the voters as they returned him to the Senate every six years in elections which often amounted to mere formalities.[1] His electoral impregnability afforded him an independence he never hesitated to exploit, visiting untold grief upon Democrats and Republicans alike. Immune to most political pressures, he cared nothing at all for party regularity and supported the national ticket only when the spirit moved him, which was seldom. As a friendly critic said of him, he was "a comet visiting this system rather than a planet in it."[2]

Borah always had resisted placing himself in a fixed orbit.[3] His personality and character seem to have been molded immutably at birth. Recollections of his early boyhood in Illinois describe a lad resembling the mature Borah in every respect. He was moody, introspective, a loner by choice—one who endured youth rather than enjoyed it. Infatuated with the written and spoken word at a tender age, he is said to have recited verse to the farm animals, although with what effect is unknown. He could be witty on occasion, more often he affected a dignity of bearing which for a teenager verged on pomposity. Perpetually engrossed with his own moral rectitude, he was apt to defend it in the absence of a challenge. He wished above all to attract attention, to matter, to influence people by his own *rightness,* about which he seldom entertained doubts.

William's father, a devout Presbyterian, wanted the young man to enter the ministry where he could place his undeniable talents at the Lord's disposal. Borah later claimed, however,

[1] In 1936, for example, alluding to Borah's campaign for the recognition of Soviet Russia, his opponent ran on the slogan "From Idaho—For Idaho —Not Russia." Borah defeated him easily. Idaho *Statesman*, October 31, 1936.

[2] William Hard to Raymond Robins, December 12, 1922, Box 18, Raymond Robins Papers, State Historical Society of Wisconsin, Madison, hereinafter cited as Robins Papers.

[3] Detailed accounts of Borah's early life can be found in Claudius O. Johnson, *Borah of Idaho* (New York, 1936), and Marian C. McKenna, *Borah* (Ann Arbor, 1961). See also John Milton Cooper, "William E. Borah, Political Thespian," in the *Pacific Northwest Quarterly*, LVI (October, 1965), 145–53.

that he had dreamed of becoming a lawyer for as long as he could remember and never really considered another profession. His opportunity came through the intercession of an older sister whose husband was a practicing attorney. Aware of his aspirations, the couple invited him to live with them in Kansas where he could complete his secondary education, enroll at the state university, and eventually take his law degree. Since his father was neither affluent nor much inclined to help him attain his goal near home, Borah accepted the invitation.

The onset of tuberculosis interrupted his college education after two years. He had been a good student, excellent in most subjects, but the inordinate number of hours he spent working to keep himself in school ruined his health. He never went back to the university, but instead chose to read law the latter part of his convalescence. Borah passed the state's rudimentary bar examination in the fall of 1887, then for a time practiced with his brother-in-law. When the older man left Kansas for Chicago, Borah headed West. He landed in Boise, Idaho, according to his own account, for the very good reason that he lacked the money to continue any farther.

Scarcely more than a frontier community in the early 1890's, Boise had a population of sufficient contentiousness to ensure the young lawyer's gainful employment. Before long, Borah had built for himself a thriving practice and a reputation as a "comer." Entering local politics almost immediately, he soon achieved wider recognition and was named chairman of the Republican State Central Committee only two years after his arrival in Boise. His reputation increased even more when the Populist crusade and Free Silver issue shattered party lines, producing an emotional atmosphere the young exhorter knew instinctively how to exploit. He had found his true calling. As a lawyer he could influence the jury, perhaps even the gallery; as a politician he could work on the entire population.

Borah joined the Silver Republican bolt of the regular organization in 1896, declaring that the McKinleyites had perverted the Grand Old Party's true principles. He supported William Jennings Bryan—though not fusion with the Democrats—and was an unsuccessful candidate for a seat in the House of Representatives. He did not seek elective office again until 1902, when he ran for the Senate. By then the silver furor had died and he had returned to the party. Clearly the most popular choice for the Republican nomination, he was undone by the party caucus, many of whose members looked askance at his Populist-variety of rhetoric and his recent apostasy. That experience merely intensified his running battle with the state's Old Guard. He had accumulated sufficient strength by 1906 to make the regulars treat for peace; he received the Republican senatorial nomination by agreeing to accept the state machine's candidates for other offices. It was the last such bargain he ever had to make. A Republican victory that fall insured his election by the state legislature and he rarely encountered serious competition thereafter.

Borah attained national recognition even before attending his first congressional session. He had served as prosecuting attorney in a sensational murder trial involving "Big Bill" Haywood and other labor leaders who allegedly hired a demolition expert to ply his trade on the ex-governor of Idaho, Frank Steunenberg. With Clarence Darrow leading the defense, the combination of personages involved and the implications for organized labor centered widespread attention on the proceedings. That trial was still in progress when Borah himself came under indictment on charges of fraudulent dealings in timber concessions. Before his acquittal, as one biographer puts it, doubt existed whether he would go to the Senate or to jail. Thus Borah was elevated from the relative obscurity of being just another freshman senator, and his colorful personality and performance guaranteed his continued presence on the public stage. The Senator displayed but a modest interest in foreign affairs during his first term in office. Unmistakably a westerner, with his cowboy hat and Bryanesque haircut, he acted as though he were commissioned specifically to destroy "the interests." These "interests" might be particular ones such as banking and railroads; more broadly defined, they were the real power behind anything emanating from east of the Mississippi River. Once described as a man who "eats a magnate for breakfast every morning," the Idahoan believed that the shameless excesses of business groups threatened the nation's social and economic structure.[4] He excluded, of course, the silver and lumber interests from that category.

Convinced that the development of a corporation-dominated economy posed the nation's major problem, Borah hammered away at the need for confronting it squarely. "The great question of the century," he said in 1912, "is whether the combinations will control us or we will control the combinations."[5] Foreign affairs from this viewpoint were distractions, unworthy of the attention usually shown them— unless, that is, they impinged directly upon the domestic economy. The controversy over reciprocity with Canada during the Taft administration provides such an instance. Here, Borah accused the interests of conniving for reciprocity in order to fatten their own profits while subjecting farmers to the competition of cheap imported produce. More often

---

[4] Record of personal interview with Raymond Robins, prepared by Hermann Hagedorn found in Box 7, William Boyce Thompson Papers. In writing a biography of Thompson, Hagedorn collected ten boxes of Thompson's papers, recollections of those associated with him, etc. This material is included in the Hagedorn Papers, Library of Congress, hereinafter cited as Thompson Papers.

[5] *Congressional Record*, 62nd Cong., 2nd Sess., 6961.

than not he minimized the importance of external matters, contending that they were peripheral to the vital questions of the day.

Borah displayed a fairly consistent—and unexceptional— outlook insofar as he did express himself on foreign policy. Ever distrustful of the European powers, he advocated having as little as possible to do with them. He regarded Great Britain as especially dangerous because entirely too many Americans assumed a commonality of interests with the British which in his opinion did not exist. Harboring a chary admiration for the Japanese and their recently acquired world position, he feared their militance endangered legitimate American interests in the Far East. Though much more sympathetic toward China, he opposed immigration from both countries. The Idahoan persistently censured intervention in the affairs of Latin American nations, demanding equal respect for the sovereignty of all states, large or small. Finally, he thought the United States should rid itself of insular possessions without delay.

Despite his intense personal admiration for Theodore Roosevelt, the Senator refused to join the Bull Moose revolt of 1912. He informed Roosevelt that he would fight for the latter's nomination but declared his intention to abide by the convention's outcome. Reform must be achieved within the organization, he argued, or the Democrats alone would profit by a third party. Besides having a prudent concern for his political fortunes in Idaho—he had his own campaign to wage for reelection—Borah disliked parts of the Progressive platform, such as the plank on trusts, and loathed the party's financial angel, George W. Perkins.[6] Perkins' connections with International Harvester and United States Steel per-

---

[6] "There is only one way to do with a monopoly," he wrote, "and that is to destroy it." Borah to T. C. Mansfield, January 30, 1914, Box 165, William E. Borah Papers, Library of Congress, hereinafter cited as Borah Papers.

mitted no doubt in Borah's mind of the man's duplicity. Although they later reached a modus vivendi of sorts, in those years he regarded Perkins as a "thief" who "thinks everybody ought to agree to his system of theft."[7] Borah's heart was not with the Progressive Party.

The election bore out his prediction. Largely because of Roosevelt's personal popularity, the Progressives gouged deeply into Republican strength but attracted insufficient numbers of liberal Democrats. Woodrow Wilson, who received only 42 percent of the popular vote, scored a thumping victory in the electoral college. The entire affair disturbed Borah greatly. Not only had his relations with Roosevelt suffered, but supporting a man whom he freely admitted had secured the nomination fraudulently called into question his self-proclaimed devotion to principles over party. Roosevelt, who publicly embarrassed him over this on one occasion, later described the Senator as "entirely insincere," an insurgent whose only ability was to "insurge."[8] Perhaps. But it sufficed to get the Idahoan reelected in 1912 despite the party schism.

Although Borah never hesitated taking outspoken positions on domestic issues, he became increasingly involved with foreign affairs during the Wilson administration. The thrust of events themselves, rather than a deliberate shift in focus on his part, stimulated his actions at first. Indeed, since he believed "the interests" a potent factor in the determination of foreign as well as domestic policy, he merely carried his fight to a different arena. Without proper restraint, he thought, corporations could no more be expected to act in the national interests abroad than at home. He set about countering what he regarded as the unfortunate tendency among government officials to identify corporate interests with those of the United

---

[7] Borah to Mark Austin, March 28, 1914, *ibid.*

[8] Roosevelt to William Allen White, November 7, 1914, Box 323, William Allen White Papers, Library of Congress, hereinafter cited as White Papers.

States as a whole when, in fact, the two rarely coincided. But as his excursions into matters of diplomacy earned him ever greater adulation from various segments of the public, another motive emerged which at times strongly influenced his conduct. William E. Borah wanted very much to become President of the United States. His political ambitions, coupled with his personal prejudices and characteristics, produced in the Senator an often penetrating, often baffling critic of American foreign policy. If he provided few answers, he raised some interesting questions.

WILLIAM E. BORAH

AND

AMERICAN

FOREIGN POLICY

CHAPTER I

Borah and Wilsonian
Diplomacy

W_{HEN} the Sixty-third Congress met in the spring of 1913, William E. Borah received a place on the Senate Committee on Foreign Relations, a seat he occupied for the next quarter century. The appointment in itself signified no new departure for him, believing as he still did that the regulation of monopoly and related matters were of consummate importance. Growing involvements in Latin America and Europe during the administrations of Woodrow Wilson, however, persuaded him that badly conceived foreign policies threatened the nation directly and also indirectly because they diverted attention from crucial domestic questions. Leaving to others the construction of positive programs, the Senator devoted himself almost exclusively to combatting what he regarded as the subversion of traditional American principles. His variations on this theme enabled him in a few short years to become one of the Republican Party's leading spokesmen on foreign affairs.

Borah was already nearing fifty at the time of Wilson's

inauguration. His resolute unwillingness to modify or amend the corpus of ideas he had brought with him from Idaho emerges as the salient fact about his later career. Though in the decades to come he tried his best to cultivate the appearance of growth via numerous public "conversions," his fundamental conceptions about foreign policy remained impervious to changing times and circumstances. An examination of the issues with which he concerned himself between 1913 and the end of World War I reveals a pattern of responses which, in various combinations, characterizes his behavior until the time of his death.

Borah's earliest clash with Wilsonian diplomacy arose over the administration's handling of relations with Mexico. His conduct, influenced to be sure by political considerations, rested primarily upon his certain conviction that Wilson's policies threatened the national interests. His speeches and correspondence over the course of the dispute are illuminating, not alone for the light they shed on his thinking about the crisis at hand, but because they reveal some of his basic assumptions about foreign policy. An understanding of these assumptions helps to explain why it happened that the Idahoan, whose initial assessment of a given situation usually coincided with Wilson's, almost invariably disagreed with the President as to the appropriate course for the United States to follow.

Mexico, having recently emerged from the long, brutal regime of Porfirio Diaz, by 1912 appeared on its way toward establishing some kind of progressive system. But the revolution had unleased practically unmanageable forces with outside pressures complicating already staggering social and economic problems. Proponents of reform faced the concerted opposition of the landowners, the church, and foreign interests. Vast amounts of the nation's resources lay in the hands of Americans and Europeans who cared less for Mexican aspirations than for the safety of their own investments. Whether the man who tried to lead this revolution, Francisco Madero, could have surmounted these obstacles is unknown; his tenure ended when he died in a hail of bullets in February, 1913, just weeks before Wilson took office.[1]

The rise of Victoriano Huerta, following Madero's assassination, elicited mixed reactions in the United States. Some people welcomed the turn of events as a return to sanity; they saw it as an end to talk of nationalization and expropriation. To them Huerta appeared a strongman in the mold of Diaz, one who could control affairs and make Mexico once again safe for investment and business as usual. Those admiring stability above all else contemplated Madero's murder with equanimity, if not enthusiasm; Henry Cabot Lodge, for instance, expressed the wish that in addition Huerta would do "sufficient throat-cutting to restore the peace."[2]

Others, notably Borah and Wilson, looked upon the coup as a barbaric act which threatened to abort the Mexican revolution and, if allowed to go unpunished, might encourage similar attempts in other areas. Borah therefore supported the President emphatically when the latter refused to recognize a regime which had taken power in such fashion.[3] Neither had any difficulty suppressing indifference to the anguished cries of American investors, most of whom demanded that the administration accord Huerta's government recognition forthwith.

The Senator, who despised Huerta and what he represented,

---

[1] Arthur C. Link treats the Mexican situation exhaustively in both *Wilson: The New Freedom* (Princeton, 1956) and *Wilson: The Struggle for Neutrality* (Princeton, 1960). See also Charles C. Cumberland, *The Mexican Revolution: Genesis Under Madero* (Austin, 1952).

[2] John A. Garraty, *Henry Cabot Lodge: A Biography* (New York, 1953), 301.

[3] The Taft administration had not accorded Huerta recognition, but only in order to use it as a bargaining weapon in settling disputes. Link, *The New Freedom*, 348.

refused to countenance any steps beyond nonrecognition. When Wilson stated that Huerta must promise to hold elections and at the same time absent himself from those elections, Borah said he "announced a policy the inevitable logic of which was war with Mexico." A strident nationalist himself, Borah understood the situation more clearly than did the President who mistakenly thought the very benevolence of his wishes somehow would overcome Mexican resentment against outside interference. The Idahoan accurately predicted that if the United States insisted upon meddling there, "we must no longer expect to contend with the divided forces of Mexico, but we must expect to contend with the united forces of Mexico." Nonrecognition (which he soon discarded as a viable tool) was one thing; overt intervention in Mexican affairs quite another. He proposed instead complete abstention thereby allowing that unfortunate nation to work out its own "salvation."[4]

However genuine his solicitude for the fate of other peoples, Borah worried more about the salvation of the United States. He viewed Mexico and Central America as a perpetual lure for American expansionism, an impulse he believed constant and susceptible to deliberate manipulation by certain interest groups. The United States had enough on its hands, he wrote, to "masticate and assimilate and digest what we have."[5] Unfortunately, the easier alternative of foreign adventure appealed more to politicians who were unwilling to grapple with basic domestic issues. Borah said he entertained no doubts as to Wilson's sincerity in claiming that the United States disdained territorial acquisition, but "that is what we said while taking New Mexico and California, Hawaii, Puerto Rico and the Philippines." Warning that if the American

---

[4] All quotes in this paragraph from *Congressional Record*, 63rd Cong., 2nd Sess., 7121–22.

[5] Borah to F. J. Hagenbarth, April 29, 1914, Box 165, Borah Papers.

flag "ever went up in Mexico it would never come down," Borah prophesied a course which would go on and on until the United States had taken every square inch of soil all the way to the Panama Canal.[6] Citing recent developments in Nicaragua as an example, he wrote privately that to continue such activity meant placing the United States in a position comparable to that of Imperial Rome. "I would dread to see that," he added.[7]

Administration policies elsewhere in Latin America reinforced the Senator's misgivings. Although the President and Secretary of State William Jennings Bryan proclaimed their devotion to justice and high morality, interventions in the weaker nations to the south accelerated under Democratic auspices. Borah fought trespasses against Santo Domingo, Haiti, and Nicaragua as well, while continuing to urge forbearance toward Mexico. Repeatedly affirming his allegiance to the Monroe Doctrine, he insisted that his adherence was to the document as originally formulated. In recent years, he lamented, it had been perverted into an "instrumentality of imperial aggression."[8]

The Idahoan disliked imperialism on principle and because he believed it produced insoluble dilemmas. In his mind, only the Anglo-Saxon "race" possessed the traditions and temperament required for coping with the subtleties of republican government. Wherever the United States dominated foreign territory, it had either to treat the native populations as subjects or to incorporate them into the political structure. The first alternative he regarded unbefitting, the second an impossibility. Speaking of the Mexicans, Borah said that they had no better conception of representative govern-

[6] Cf. note 4 above.
[7] Cf. note 5 above.
[8] Borah to J. B. Hofflinger, January 9, 1914, Box 176, Borah Papers.

ment "than I have of the technical value of Beethoven's music."[9]

The Senator's fear of expansionism symbolized an even more fundamental article of his political faith. His reading of history had convinced him that every situation contained its own "logic of events," which the participants are often powerless to alter.[10] If the Senator had a motto, it might well have been "One Thing Leads to Another." Any action, however innocuous or well-meaning on its surface, could set off a train of consequences totally unforeseen at the start. Just as he questioned President Wilson's ability to control the forces his Mexican policy would generate, Borah regarded *any* positive step latent with danger. Able to predict catastrophic possibilities undreamed of by others, the Senator's deepest instincts invariably counseled against setting in motion that "logic of events" which might drag the nation into involvements beyond the scope intended and from which there could be no return. Thus Borah's pessimistic fatalism ineluctably made of him an isolationist; "western provincialism" merely determined his frame of reference.[11] It is no coincidence that his status in the Republican Party, toward which he was also an isolationist, coincided precisely with his views on the role of the United States in world affairs.

Borah's preoccupation with corporate influence represented

[9] Cf. note 5 above. Borah grounded his racism less on inherent inequalities than on traditions as well as geographic and climatic factors. Referring to the Philippines, for example, he stated that "neither the Anglo-Saxon race nor any other . . . has ever demonstrated capacity for self-government in regions and under environments such as surround the Philippines." Borah to Adam Aulbach, February 22, 1914, Box 176, Borah Papers.

[10] Borah used such terms endlessly. Elsewhere, he spoke of the "inner" or "irrefutable" logic of events.

[11] Walter Lippmann, in a perceptive article, "Concerning Senator Borah," *Foreign Affairs*, IX (January, 1926), 211-22, stated that Borah had written him a letter in which he approvingly quoted Buckle's dictum that "the most valuable additions made to legislation have been enactments destructive of preceding legislation."

another thread stitched prominently into the fabric of his thinking about foreign policy. His conduct during the Panama Canal tolls controversy, usually attributed to his belligerent nationalism and dislike of the British, furnishes an illustration.[12] Undoubtedly motivated by considerations of honor and a chance to twist the lion's tail, the Idahoan's behavior hinged largely on his undying suspicions of the "interests" and their pervasive ability to manipulate diplomacy for selfish ends.

In August, 1912, before the canal's completion, Congress passed legislation providing for its use without charge by American coastwise shipping. Other nations decried such action as discriminatory; Great Britain also claimed it violated the Hay-Pauncefote Treaty. Defenders of the exemption clause, on the other hand, denied discrimination or violation of any treaty as it pertained to transoceanic trade. Borah had urged a strong statement favoring exemption at the Republican National Convention, but opposition within the party prevented an affirmative stand. The Progressives had included a plank backing it in their platform and Wilson, heeding Perry Belmont's advice not to "let Roosevelt appear as the 'defender' of American interests," had agreed to go along with it as well.[13] Congressional action during the summer, followed by the Democratic victory in November, apparently settled the entire question.

Wilson had second thoughts on the matter even before his inauguration. Several elements influenced him: the opinions of certain individuals whom he respected, his "discovery" that coastwise shipping lay in the hands of a monopoly, and above all, his belief that Anglo-American cooperation would be essential in settling the Mexican situation.[14] Unwilling to

[12] McKenna, *Borah*, 229.
[13] Ray Stannard Baker, *Woodrow Wilson: Life and Letters* (7 Vols., New York, 1946), III, 396.
[14] *Ibid.*, 399–400.

jeopardize domestic legislation, the President delayed announcing his reversal until January, 1914. Then, meeting with the Senate Foreign Relations Committee, he told its members that repeal of the exemption clause would help secure vitally needed British help. Wilson publicly adopted the moral position that the tolls exemption compromised American dignity and violated the spirit if not the letter of the Hay-Pauncefote Treaty.[15]

The President's appeal left Borah unmoved. Contending that Great Britain incorrectly interpreted the treaty, the Idahoan said he resented implications that the United States had sought an unethical advantage in the first place. These were superficial considerations to him. Behind the facade of references to national dignity, the Senator thought he glimpsed the Mephistophelian conspiracies of his old enemy, monopoly. He was positive that the real strength for repeal ran back to the railroads. Pointing out that farmers would have to ship their goods at higher prices by rail, Borah perceived the campaign against exemption as a brazen effort to cartelize the nation's transportation system.[16]

If the Idahoan's suspicions—certainties in his own mind— smack of vestigal populism, perhaps it is significant that William Jennings Bryan voiced the same opinion, though not publicly in his capacity as Secretary of State.[17] To President Wilson's great embarrassment, however, he had as a candidate also put forward that interpretation. While he had discussed the tolls issue in only one campaign address, and probably gave it scant thought then, he had alluded specifically to the railroads as the force behind the repeal movement.[18] That Borah knew of Wilson's earlier stand is almost certain

[15] Link, *The New Freedom*, 308; New York *Times*, January 28, 1914.
[16] Borah to C. E. McCutcheon, March 11, 1914, Box 176, Borah Papers.
[17] Baker, *Life and Letters*, III, 414. Bainbridge Colby assured Borah his suspicions were correct. Colby to Borah, no date, Box 176, Borah Papers.
[18] Baker, *Life and Letters*, III, 397; Link, *The New Freedom*, 307.

since opponents of repeal quoted his speech freely and had had it read into the *Congressional Record*.

A repeal bill eventually was passed by Congress after several months of furious wrangling, and Borah's later attempts to reinstate exemption met with failure.[19] Of no great significance itself, the tolls dispute nevertheless impressed him. Wilson's performance during the affair, together with some of the domestic legislation he espoused, helped convince Borah that the President, far from being anti-big business, was in fact extremely friendly to the corporate world the Senator so heartily detested.[20] The moral was plain to see: the ability of the "interests" to shape events remained comparatively undiluted regardless of an administration's party affiliation or the degree of progressivism it boasted. The only possible remedy lay in the hands of truly independent public officials like himself, acting in behalf of the American people, to seek out and expose such chicanery where it arose. Borah through the years considered this function one of his most important senatorial obligations.

II

Germany's march through Belgium in the summer of 1914 temporarily relegated Latin American affairs to the back pages. Neither the American people not their leaders at first responded with anything more definite than expressions of shocked disappointment, but unaminity quickly developed over what the United States should do. Practically everyone endorsed President Wilson's announced policy of strict neutrality. Borah thought, as did most Americans, that whatever the war's causes and results, this nation would serve its

[19] Garraty, *Lodge*, 299; and Philip C. Jessup, *Elihu Root* (2 vols., New York, 1938), II, 262–70.

[20] Borah to F. J. Wilson, July 1, 1914; and Borah to the Ford Motor Company, September 14, 1914, both in Box 167, Borah Papers.

interests best by remaining aloof from what he regarded as an exclusively European quarrel. His opinion did not change over the following years. When he eventually voted for American entry, he did so reluctantly and with the greatest foreboding as to where it might lead. At the time, however, there seemed to be no responsible alternative. The results exceeded his direst expectations.

During the war's early months, Borah vacillated between two explanations of its origins. Sometimes he spoke disparagingly of it as the inevitable result of national hatreds and cynical power struggles which had plagued Europe for centuries. European diplomacy, carried on behind closed doors without regard for the wishes of the people, represented to him the essence of Old World depravity. Such diplomacy involved only the ruthless pursuit of interests as defined by a class of men steeped in the arts of treachery and deceit. His premise led him to simple, stark conclusions. There could be no "right" side in what essentially was a battle between competing imperial blocs, nor did the United States have a stake in its outcome.

In his more grandiose moods, Borah described the war as an evolution of "those inscrutable forces of humanity" which lay beyond mortal comprehension, much less control. The forces were scrutable enough for him to prophesy beneficial results, since he also counted himself among those believing in the "inexplicable philosophy" of human progress. He predicted that Old Europe would be swept away by the war, her people freed of the "accursed and infamous practices, trappings and burdens of royalty."[21] What would rise in its place he did not make clear—presumably stable republics resembling the American model. Stripping aside its veneer of mysticism, the Senator's forecast can be seen as another version of his "logic of events" theme—that situations move to

[21] Borah to George F. Harvey, August 30, 1914, Box 165, *ibid.*

inexorable conclusions only minimally influenced by the conscious decisions of individuals.

Neither of Borah's interpretations struck him as contradictory; he stressed whichever seemed most appropriate for the occasion. Both, happily enough, led to the same diagnosis: American entanglement in European affairs was unwarranted in the first instance, useless in the second. The Idahoan subsequently admitted that what happened elsewhere could affect the United States, but he never abandoned his practice of blaming existing conditions on the unscrupulous actions of policymakers while simultaneously subscribing to the "inscrutable forces" view of history.

The American neutrality policy might have achieved its goal had the war ended quickly. But the antagonists had to scrap strategies of movement when traditional military operations proved obsolete against modern artillery and the machine gun. After a brief period of maneuvering, the war settled into a pattern of immobility on the western front with huge armies facing each other along a line extending from the English Channel to Switzerland. The struggle resolved itself into an issue of which alliance could hold out longest against the terrible attrition of men and resources. Practically everything had to be subordinated to securing and distributing the vast amounts of materials necessary to wage total war. These requirements would involve the United States regardless of its intentions.

The Mexican situation meanwhile grew more chaotic. Huerta had abdicated in July, 1914, after which Venustiano Carranza had seized nominal control only to find himself confronting an insurrection headed by Francisco "Pancho" Villa. Wilson's continued efforts to pacify Mexican affairs earned him the enmity of almost everyone concerned, providing an excellent target for Republican criticism which soon erupted. Borah's contribution to the assault reveals an interesting metamorphosis on his part, and his attempt to play off Mexico against the European crisis foreshadowed a tactic he would employ frequently in the coming years.

Theodore Roosevelt opened the attack by accusing the President of having made a complete botch of relations with Mexico. Attributing all the real and imagined atrocities committed there to Wilson, he found the administration's past conduct without a single redeeming feature.[22] Diplomatic bungling had so endangered American lives and property, Roosevelt went on, as to require immediate and forceful action. Wilson's reply, in his Jackson Day address of January 8, 1915, advanced a remarkable thesis in view of his previous behavior. Pronouncing interference in the affairs of a sovereign state immoral, the President insisted that the Mexicans be left alone to work out their own problems. Since Wilson had tampered in their affairs almost from the day he took office, his comments left him extremely vulnerable. Mexico loomed as an excellent issue; Republican disunity over Europe made it all the more attractive.

Borah, chosen to make a rejoinder from the Senate floor, wielded an axe. He denounced Wilson's diplomacy in every respect and, like Roosevelt, held him personally responsible for everything that had happened or was rumored to have happened in Mexico. Recalling his own earlier observations, Borah claimed that the situation would not be in its present state had the President refrained from intruding. But Wilson had interfered; he had antagonized the Mexicans; and now, just as the fury of this antagonism descended upon helpless American citizens, the President proposed to abandon them. Borah said that since the administration had caused the troubles, it bore the responsibility for solving them—or, as he put it, "the flag which will not protect its protectors is a

22 New York *Times*, December 7, 1914.

dirty rag which contaminates the air in which it floats."[23] Suggesting no specific formula, the Senator strongly implied that he personally would not shrink from using force. The man who had prophesied apocalyptic results from intervention less than two years previously now stood at the head of those demanding aggressive action. Why the forces set in motion by such a policy would be any easier to control in 1915 than in 1913 he did not spell out. Borah's usual caution did evaporate at times over matters involving national "honor." Then too, he may have subordinated his apprehensions to political exigencies. His use of the issue in the following months strongly suggests a third and possibly crucial motive—a calculated effort to divert attention from the European war which, in his opinion, constituted the greater threat to American interests.

The Idahoan developed the practice of counterposing Mexico to Europe in what became a constant refrain—that the problems of vital concern to the United States lay south of the border rather than across the Atlantic.[24] Expressing wonder how anyone could become emotional about rights at sea while ignoring the infinitely more important humiliations in Mexico, Borah called upon the American people to recognize the priority of matters nearest home.[25] Perhaps he really believed this although elsewhere he left no doubt that he, too, counted maritime rights essential. Borah went on emphasizing Mexico to the day the United States entered the war,

[23] *Congressional Record*, 63rd Cong., 3rd Sess., 1502.

[24] Borah to Senator William S. Kenyon, June 1, 1915, Box 92, Borah Papers; Borah's speech at the Republican National Convention, New York *Times*, June 7, 1916; speech to the Friendly Sons of St. Patrick, March, 1917, Box 577, Borah Papers; and interview given to the Idaho *Statesman*, April 1, 1917.

[25] Before the war, Borah had wondered how anyone could become emotional about Mexico in view of the labor troubles in Colorado where "hell reigns from one end of the state to the other." Cf. note 5 above.

whereupon his belligerent attitude subsided as quickly as it had evolved.

Dismayed by what he construed as an excessive absorption with Europe—distinguished by widespread sympathy for Great Britain and France—Borah also grew disenchanted with the administration's conduct toward the war. He had backed the Wilson-sponsored resolution banning munitions shipments to any of the warring powers and applauded his refusal to sanction loans for the Allies. Borah said he thought Wilson's pronouncements the correct ones, but he began accusing the President of betraying them in practice. The decision to make credits available to France and Great Britain, for example, amounted to an unneutral act in the Senator's opinion because credits served the same purpose as loans. Reserving his most bitter scorn for the President's behavior toward the belligerents in the matter of neutral rights, Borah indicted him for compromising American dignity before willful, flagrant violations by both sides. Referring to Wilson's protests over the *Lusitania* sinking of May, 1915, the Idahoan wondered "just how long rhetoric will suffice," and said he hoped this was not "the only method left for the defense of the rights of American citizens."[26] He was equally truculent over British encroachments.

Borah can best be described as a militant neutral. Unlike many other western progressives, he believed in maintaining a large navy and in using the fleet to safeguard American privileges.[27] He urged the administration to inform the European nations that America would counter infringements by either side upon neutral rights with force rather than protests. Violations would cease only when the warring powers understood that Washington meant to enforce its demands. Wilson's lack of firmness, according to the Senator, encouraged by belli-

[26] Borah to Henry Cabot Lodge, May 28, 1915, Box 176, Borah Papers.
[27] Borah to F. Plaisted, November 16, 1915, Box 170, *ibid.*

gerents to take ever-greater liberties as they assumed he would restrict himself to sending notes. The argument for a belligerent posture was attractive. In obvious contrast to the painful and frustrating negotiations carried on by the President, it extended the promise of maintaining neutrality in a manner consistent with national honor. Borah undoubtedly thought it was the best policy—he put forward precisely the same views during the 1930's. At the same time, however, he appears to have doubted that the "logic" of the situation would permit the United States to stay out, whatever actions it took. In August, 1917, he wrote that he was "satisfied in my own mind that had we not gone in early, we should have gone in late."[28]

Beginning in 1915, Borah's name cropped up with increasing regularity as the best Republican candidate for the coming presidential election.[29] The proposal merited attention in view of the party's internal divisions. Wilson would win again by default unless the regular organization affected a settlement with the Bull Moose defectors. Assuming that the regulars would veto Roosevelt's candidacy, and the Progressives anyone the Old Guard designated, the Idahoan impressed many people as the one individual who could placate both sides. Obviously popular, he had voted with the Progressives often but not always, and his position on foreign affairs was satisfactorily patriotic without Roosevelt's excesses. Finally, Borah did not then have the reputation for inconsistency and obstructionism which in later years would be so damaging to his chances for the presidency.

Several factors worked against his being seriously considered. Conservatives found him only slightly less repugnant than Theodore Roosevelt—conceivably more dangerous,

[28] Borah to John D. Works, August 22, 1917, Box 180, *ibid.*
[29] See McKenna, *Borah*, 135; and K. Vieillard, "An Apostle of the Mean," *Nation*, CI (August 26, 1915), 257–58.

given his attitudes toward business—while his political irregularity scarcely endeared him to anyone believing in party loyalty. The Senator had not operated within an organizational framework since his days in Idaho, nor had he shown any interest in courting the party's rank and file. The situation would become a familiar one for him; the very outspokenness and independence which attracted a broad personal following and assured his senatorial longevity caused him to become a pariah to those who could nominate him. Borah likely told the truth when he said that he had no hope of receiving the nomination, although presumably he stood ready to answer if called.[30]

The Senator greatly desired to reorient the regular organization along progressive lines—a goal which the Bull Moose departure had rendered critical. Wilson occupied a stronger position than he had in 1912, which meant that the Republicans faced certain defeat unless they wooed back the recalcitrant Progressives. Borah announced his willingness to go to any lengths to achieve fusion, with a single exception. He insisted that the candidate take a firm stand on foreign policy, warning that if the nomination went to a "milk and water man," he would "do like Villa, I suppose, take to the woods and shoot at somebody's campfire."[31] The Idahoan never lost his taste for guerilla warfare in politics.

Two obstacles, Old Guard conservatism and Theodore Roosevelt himself, barred the way to unification. The former consideration mattered most since a liberal candidate and platform were the minimal prerequisites for ending the schism. Roosevelt could be troublesome, of course, especially because he commanded such personal loyalty among his followers. But his strength might be directed into constructive channels if handled shrewdly; Borah favored using it to extract conces-

---

[30] Albert Cummins to Borah, September 3, 1915, Box 92, Borah Papers.
[31] Borah to W. H. Remington, January 31, 1916, Box 176, *ibid.*

sions from the standpatters. The Senator did not insist that Teddy's nomination be one of the concessions. The ex-President looked upon the Progressive threat as a means of securing the Republican nomination for himself. Failing in that, he had little enthusiasm for conducting another third-party campaign. Borah, who had patched up their relationship since the 1912 debacle, appears to have nourished this dream although he must have known Roosevelt's quest was doomed. Had he really been interested in the Rough Rider's personal fortunes, the Idahoan might have tried persuading him to moderate some of his demands. Instead Borah urged him to stress the point that Progressive independence made reconciliation impossible unless the regular organization granted important capitulations.[32] The Senator obviously wished to use Roosevelt as a club against the Old Guard in hopes of achieving fusion on liberal terms.

Borah saw his ends partly accomplished. Their fear of the ex-President did move the party managers to get behind Charles Evans Hughes, for whom they had no real liking, and to accept a quasi-progressive platform. Roosevelt's minions proved more refractory when they spurned a compromise candidate. Borah served with members from both conventions on a reconciliation committee which tried to negotiate a truce, but nothing came of it. When the Progressives steadfastly refused to abandon their hero, the Senator proposed that the Republican convention proceed as though no third party existed.

The attempted reconciliation ended in a farce. At last persuaded to accept his lot, Roosevelt suggested Henry Cabot

[32] Roosevelt to Frank Knox, September 1, 1915, found in Box 91, Borah Papers (apparently forwarded by Knox since it is the original). Referring to a recent speech he had made, Roosevelt wrote, "Remember that Borah particularly wanted me to emphasize the fact that the Republicans could not count on the Progressives if they continued along standpat lines." See also Roosevelt to Borah, May 10, 1916, Box 684, *ibid.*

Lodge as a surrogate. If he was at all serious in view of Lodge's record on progressivism, the Rough Rider must have felt a bellicose posture on foreign affairs to be all-important.[33] Even Bull Moose loyalty had limits, however. The party thereupon collapsed. Some of the heretics crept back into the Republican camp, an important minority opted for Wilson, and others, shattered by the experience, simply went to the sidelines.[34]

Borah had enhanced his reputation substantially. Exuding patience and restraint, he avoided the more vicious infighting and received the plaudits of both conventions. Indicative of his growing stature as a critic of administration diplomacy, he delivered a key speech before the Republican convention and figured significantly in constructing the foreign policy plank. Both stressed the Idahoan's established theme: that while the United States should act more forcefully toward the European powers, Mexico remained the vital issue.[35] His references to Europe were at least palatable to most Republicans, while everyone recognized the desirability of concentrating on Wilson's patently assailable Mexican policies. Party leaders quite appreciated his talent for attack—against Democrats. Different opinions would prevail when he showed himself equally prepared to challenge a Republican administration, but this lay in the future.

Wilson's victory in November condemned the Grand Old Party to another four years in opposition. The Democrats, combining the appeals of peace and progressivism, had augmented their base of support since 1912. Hughes's campaign

[33] Henry F. Pringle, *Theodore Roosevelt* (Harvest Edition; New York, 1956), 408. Outmoded in many ways, Pringle's book shows rather convincingly that the European issue dominated Roosevelt's thinking at this time.

[34] Arthur S. Link, *Woodrow Wilson and the Progressive Era* (Harper Torchbook Edition; New York, 1963), 232.

[35] McKenna, *Borah*, 137-40; and see *Republican Campaign Textbook* (New York, 1916), 48–52.

proved inept for a variety of reasons. He became entangled in the treacherous question of "hyphenate" loyalties, Roosevelt's incessant war cries embarrassed him, and too many voters remained skeptical that the Republican Party had changed its inventory regardless of the window dressing conceded by the Old Guard. The Republicans managed to lose a close election despite the normal preponderance of Republican voters. Borah stumped energetically for Hughes—he collapsed from exhaustion while on a campaign tour in Wisconsin—but, to the Senator's chagrin, even the state of Idaho went Democratic for the first time in years.

The decision which culminated in American entry into the war had been made even before Wilson entered his second term. Germany's announcement, on January 31, 1917, that she would resume unrestricted submarine warfare removed all but the slenderest doubts about the ability to remain neutral. German military leaders, incorrectly it turned out, had argued for some time that such a move would destroy the Allies' capacity to wage war before American strength could be brought to bear. When the civilian government bowed to this strategy, it became only a matter of time before the United States retaliated.[36]

Loath to admit the nation had either to fight or abandon its previous claims to neutral rights, Borah without much conviction said he thought the possibility of staying out yet existed and went on belaboring the Mexican question.[37] Nonetheless, he supported the President when the latter broke off relations with Germany, asked for legislation to arm merchant ships, and finally, requested a declaration of war.[38] Seldom in the

[36] Ernest R. May, *The World War and American Isolation, 1914–1917* (Cambridge, Mass., 1959), Chap. 18.

[37] Idaho *Statesman*, April 1, 1917.

[38] *Congressional Record*, 64th Cong., 2nd Sess., 2748. Borah insisted his support was in defense of neutral rights and "not an indication of slipping to the side of the entente." Borah to Ed Dewey, March 29, 1917, Box 180, Borah Papers.

habit of giving his unqualified approval to anything, the Senator during these weeks contented himself with castigating Wilson's lack of consideration for the Senate. The methods employed by the President to get his proposals through, Borah said, constituted an obnoxious display of "executive arrogance."

The Idahoan justified his vote on the declaration of war in what was for him a brief and unemotional speech.[39] German actions, he stated, left the United States without recourse except to defend its rights by force of arms. Violations of neutrality alone warranted American entry; there existed no mutuality of interests between the United States and the Allies beyond that of defeating the Central Powers. "I join no crusade, I seek or accept no alliances," Borah said, "I obligate this government to no other power." Anticipating efforts to entangle America's fortunes with those of the Allied nations, as well as a natural tendency to view their goals with mounting sympathy, he added that he coud not endorse such notions "even tacitly." The Senator asked—demanded—that national interests be the sole criterion for American participation in the war.

Borah reiterated his admonitions frequently after the United States became a participant. American decisions, he argued, should be made without reference to British and French ambitions. This nation sought no territory, had no empire to protect, and should avoid venturing into the swamp of European imperial struggles. Contemptuously dismissing the idea that the Allies (the United States remained throughout the war an "Associated Power" rather than an Ally) fought for "liberty," "democracy," or any other abstractions, he belittled such claims as wartime propaganda utterly without substance. Certain revelations, only a few months after the United States declared war, bore out his most cynical remarks.

[39] *Congressional Record*, 65th Cong., 1st Sess., 252–53.

Exactly when reports of secret treaties among the Allies first began circulating is unknown. Fairly accurate descriptions of their contents appeared by the early summer of 1917. These treaties dealt with postwar territorial compensations for each of the Allied Powers, containing as well mutual pledges against separate negotiations with the enemy. The Russian Provisional Government—which had taken power in March—substantiated the treaties' existence in its appeal to the western powers for a redefinition of war aims.[40] By refusing even to discuss modifying them, Great Britain and France bared themselves to charges that the spoils of war mattered more to them than did ideals.

Borah thought the disclosures self-explanatory. Under the guise of a struggle against "Prussian militarism," the Allies in reality made war for national aggrandizement. The United States would lend itself to furthering British and French imperial designs should it defer to Allied strategy and goals. Accusing the administration of "waiting upon other powers which were directing the course of the war," the Senator urged a frank rejection of the premise that the United States must "fight on and on until captured colonies and certain territories are adjusted."[41] He denied that America had any interest in these adjustments, or that it should regard itself bound by treaties concluded among other parties. Calling for a "strong stand," the Idahoan asked the administration to define the "terms and conditions" under which the war was being fought and under which it would end. Anything less amounted to a confession that American diplomacy had as its basic purpose the wish to further Allied territorial pretensions.[42]

---

[40] See below, Chap. 2.
[41] *Congressional Record*, 65th Cong., 1st Sess., 5496.
[42] New York *Times*, July 27, 1917; and *Current History*, XXI (September, 1917), 465–66.

Although still referring often to the selfish aims of the Allies, Borah gradually abandoned his advocacy of a war for limited ends. He became particularly belligerent after American troops went into combat and no longer publicly criticized the war's justifications. The Senator moved eventually to the position he had earlier branded as hypocritical—that this was a clash between systems in which one or the other must prevail.[43] He stated, during the last few months of the struggle, that he favored continuing the fighting until peace terms could be dictated in Berlin.[44]

The Idahoan's enlistment to total war failed to inhibit his denunciations of both the administration and the "interests" for the way in which they guided the American effort. He railed at everything from the draft—calling it a "slur" on patriotism—to the methods used in financing the war. Often employing the terms "administration" and "interests" synonomously, he accused the latter of exploiting the war for their own purposes. Borah demanded higher taxes on war profits, strict control over private industry, and, understandably, an end to what he considered the unconscionable favoritism shown food processors as against food growers. The Idahoan did what he could throughout the war to expose and ridicule the administration's evermore oppressive attempts to limit freedom of speech and press.[45]

On January 8, 1918, the President issued his famous "Fourteen Points" message, part of which outlined what he believed were the requisites for lasting peace. Wilson at the time hoped that his formula would provide the basis for a

[43] *Congressional Record*, 65th Cong., 2nd Sess., 3655.

[44] New York *Times*, October 7, 1918. See also telegrams: Borah to National Security League, October 15, 1918; and to Charles Stewart Davison, October 26, 1918, both in Box 542, Borah Papers.

[45] See Borah to D. Anzer, July 10, 1917, Box 180; and Frank Harris, editor of *Pearson's Magazine*, to Borah, December 18, 1918, Box 194, Borah Papers.

negotiated settlement between the warring nations. Subsequent actions by the Central Powers had convinced him that no such compromises should be made with the German and Austrian governments as they were then constituted. So long as the military dominated these systems, he came to believe, enduring settlements lay beyond reach. When Berlin and Vienna, desperately trying to stave off complete dissolution, attempted in October to secure an armistice based on the Fourteen Points, Wilson replied that he could treat with unrepresentative governments solely on terms of surrender. His rebuff helped trigger in Germany a popular revolution which swept away the monarchy and led quickly to an armistice.

The Senator commended Wilson's diplomacy during the October-November negotiations.[46] Like the President's, Borah's talk of absolute capitulation had pertained to the regimes which governed the Central Powers through the war. Making a sharp distinction (again like Wilson) between the German and Austrian peoples and their rulers, the Idahoan advocated the most conciliatory kind of disposition for these nations under republican forms of government. Both men wished to prevent the total destruction of the Central Powers and the untrammeled domination of the continent by the Allies as well.

Borah proclaimed himself eager to help effect the reconstruction of a prosperous and stable Europe once the threat of German victory had ended. He knew the United States would assume a large part in writing the peace terms, a task presenting "questions far more complex and stupendous in many respects than did the war itself." Never as optimistic as Wilson that this war would end all wars, the Idahoan yet hoped that something durable would result. "Permanent

[46] William E. Borah, "No Peace with the Hohenzollerns," New York *Times*, October 13, 1918, Sec. 8; Wilson to Borah, October 17, 1918, Box 684, Borah Papers.

peace," he announced, "depends on how well we do the work of reconstruction."[47]

The Senator's ambitious rhetoric, unquestionably stimulated by end-of-the-war enthusiasm, implied a greater divergence from his former beliefs than actually was the case. As he would soon make plain, the American commitment he envisioned in no way abandoned the independence and freedom of action he had always deemed so important. What he had in mind involved scarcely more than the tendering of good offices by the United States—a one-shot performance as honest broker in laying the foundations for a resuscitated Europe. Having discharged this obligation, the nation could then devote its entire energies to improving and ennobling the conditions of its own citizenry, an undertaking he thought sadly neglected during the war years. The Idahoan approved of the United States acting as a mediator in European affairs, perhaps even an arbiter, but never as a partner. "No graver nor more far-reaching proposition," he said, "has been proposed to the American people since the adoption of the Constitution."[48]

Thus, Borah's outlook by the war's end remained essentially as it had been five and a half years earlier. Almost everything that had taken place during the interim merely strengthened his existing attitudes. Even so cataclysmic an event as the war itself did not, as some historians have claimed, radically alter his views—except to fortify an already deepseated distrust for the British and French. The "logic" of developments, moreover, amply justified the fears he had expressed in April, 1917. What he had predicted would happen was happening; a growing chorus of voices, conducted by President Wilson, demanding that the United States participate in continental affairs on an ongoing basis. To do so, Borah

[47] New York *Times*, November 12, 1918.
[48] *Congressional Record*, 65th Cong., 3rd Sess., 189.

warned, meant breaking away "from the fundamental principle upon which the foreign policy of this government was established more than a century ago."[49] Because he held that principle to be as valid as ever before, the Senator would resist violations of it in any way he could.

[49] New York *Times*, February 1, 1919.

CHAPTER II

Borah Discovers Russia

HE Russian revolutions of March and November, 1917, seized and held Borah's interest. Although at first he tended to relate these events almost exclusively to their impact upon the fighting in western Europe, the Senator came to believe that in some ways they were more portentous than the war itself. Unfamiliar with Russia's history and forced to rely upon secondhand information, Borah often based his conclusions upon flimsy evidence, and sometimes he lapsed into hazy rhetoric to explain matters about which he knew nothing. For all this, his understanding of the broader issues involved compared favorably with that of other American observers, in or out of the administration. And of one thing he became certain—that the Western Allies and the United States were unwilling or unable to respond appropriately. American policies toward the Provisional Government and the Soviet regime which succeeded it sooner or later violated practically every tenet of his code, especially his strictures against meddling in the affairs of another nation. More ominous still, in

Borah's mind, was the likelihood that such policies afforded a glimpse of America's role in the postwar world envisioned by President Wilson.

Borah's prediction, at the start of the war, that the "trappings and burdens of royalty" would be lifted from the heads of European peoples, must have seemed inspired when the Romanov dynasty collapsed in March, 1917.[1] Borah joined most Americans in welcoming the revolution, which at the time appeared to be another step toward universal liberation.[2] Militarily, however, Russia posed a grave problem because of the deterioration of both her economy and her armed forces. Her departure from the field would release large numbers of German and Austrian troops for campaigns in the west. The Allies and the United States faced the delicate task of trying to keep her in the fighting while at the same time helping the Provisional Government consolidate its position. These goals contradicted one another due to the war's unpopularity with Russian soldiers and civilians.

Americans outside the administration possessed little information concerning the extent of Russian weakness. Borah appears to have had no inkling that anything was amiss until midsummer. Government officials and the press consistently portrayed the Provisional Government as a stable middle-class group dedicated to a strong war effort.[3] Periodic declarations to this effect by Russia's leaders received wide publicity, stimulating confidence in her ability to keep open the eastern front. Presumably, the Russian people under democratic leadership would recover the militant spirit dissipated by the

[1] Borah to George F. Harvey, August 30, 1914, Box 165, Borah Papers.

[2] President Wilson acclaimed the revolution in his war message, hailing Russia a "fit partner in a leagues of honor." *Papers Relating to the Foreign Relations of the United States, 1917, Supplement I* (Washington, 1931), 200, hereinafter cited as *FRUS* with pertinent data appended.

[3] *Literary Digest*, LIV (March 31, 1917), 885–87. Christopher Lasch, *The American Liberals and the Russian Revolution* (New York, 1962), 44.

tsarist regime's corrupt, wasteful conduct.[4] That this optimism had no basis in fact became patent when the much-heralded Russian summer offensive ended disastrously, causing further dissolution of their will to go on fighting.

The campaign's abject failure unleashed great turmoil in Russia that forced changes in the Provisional Government's structure. Russian demands for the initiation of peace discussions based on the formula "No annexations and no indemnities" reflected the growing influence exercised by the Soviets. At this stage, before the Bolsheviks obtained control of the Soviets, most of the socialist parties supported continuation of the war as a defensive measure, though not in pursuit of territorial acquisitions.[5] Leaders of the Provisional Government believed its very life depended on a restatement of Allied war aims. Seeking desperately to force the issue upon their reluctant partners, they raised the threat of making public the secret treaties should their pleas go unanswered.[6] The facade of Russian-Allied unity threatened to give way at the worst possible moment.

These developments precipitated a public debate in the United States during which Borah, who had said little beyond commenting on the need for keeping Russia in the war, began urging a reevaluation of American policy. The overriding problem, he said, lay in retaining the eastern front as a means of dividing the Central Powers' forces. Since Russian armies refused to fight for tsarist war goals, they should be encouraged to fight in defense of their own revolution. The United States, Borah argued, having no commitment to secret wartime agreements, should regard itself free to act independently. To do otherwise meant endangering the lives of American soldiers who would have to face reinforced German armies in

[4] *FRUS, 1918, Russia*, I, 38–39.
[5] *Ibid.*, 101.
[6] *FRUS, 1917, II*, 144–46.

the west should Russia collapse. He called upon the President to take whatever action required to prevent such a debacle, despite the cost to French or British sensibilities.[7]

The administration had known for some time how critical the situation really was. Its official posture reflected neither Wilson's nor Secretary of State Robert Lansing's estimate of Russian affairs.[8] Although information received from regular American representatives in Russia often was inadequate, copious evidence existed which showed the Provisional Government's extreme frailty. Yet, alternating appeals to national honor with economic coercion ("No fight, no loans" as one American crudely phrased it), the Allies and the United States directed the floundering regime into a suicidal course.[9] President Wilson doubted the wisdom of such a policy but despaired of finding an alternative acceptable to the Allies. He did attempt, through commissions and inspirational messages, to assure the Russians of American friendliness.

Russian threats and increased domestic criticism confronted Wilson with a painful dilemma. The slogan "No annexations and no indemnities," he believed, struck a responsive note with the peoples of the world, which should be exploited. He knew as well that Russian leaders looked to the United States

[7] New York *Times*, July 27, 1917. *Current History*, XXI (September, 1917), 465–66.

[8] Lincoln Steffens, *Autobiography of Lincoln Steffens* (New York, 1931), 770–72. Returning from Russia in June, 1917, Steffens carried with him a Russian appeal for a restatement of war aims. Wilson was "very disturbed," according to Steffens who met personally with the President, and wished to satisfy Russia's demands. But, he remarked, "that I cannot very well do." Edith Bolling Wilson, in *My Memoir* (Bridgeport, 1938), 138, wrote that Wilson told her, in the summer of 1917, that he thought Russia would "soon be in a state of revolution." This surprised her, she recalled, because others seemed so optimistic at the time. For Lansing's equally skeptical view, see Lasch, *American Liberals*, 44; and William A. Williams, *American-Russian Relations, 1781–1947* (New York, 1952), 95.

[9] George F. Kennan, *Russia Leaves the War* (Princeton, 1956), 25.

as the power most likely to appreciate their difficulties.[10] But what of the Western Allies? The President had to bear in mind their implacable determination to achieve the goals set down in the secret treaties. Any unilateral stand aimed at negating these arrangements would sorely damage Allied-American relations for the duration of the war and in negotiating the peace. This latter consideration, together with the opportunities it presented, had by this time grown paramount in shaping Wilson's diplomacy.

After a period of agonizing hesitation, the President elected to maintain Allied-American solidarity at all costs. The French, responding to the Provisional Government's threatened exposure of war aims, had requested from Wilson clarification of his position on the matter.[11] Wilson drafted a reply stating he did not see how Russian demands could "wisely be rejected." World opinion, he wrote, made it imperative that the Allies show they fought not for territorial conquest "but the freedom of the peoples to secure independence."[12] Whether or not these phrases accurately represented the President's innermost feelings—and they probably did—he recognized their incompatibility with Allied objectives. The draft went unused.

Wilson's decision to remain silent was of fundamental importance for American foreign policy. Until the war's end the President, with deep misgivings, committed himself to close cooperation with France and Great Britain. His attitude underlined the basic difference between himself and Borah, both of whom shared a chronic suspicion of Allied motives. Wilson, who looked toward creating a new era in the postwar world, counted Allied-American unity as an absolute prere-

---

[10] Edward M. House to Wilson, August 19, 1917, in Charles Seymour (ed.) *The Intimate Papers of Colonel House* (4 vols., Boston, 1926–28), III, 157–58.

[11] Cf. note 6 above.

[12] Baker, *Life and Letters*, VI, 204.

quisite. Seeking to avoid controversy until the fighting stopped, he intended asserting forceful leadership at the peace table—a leadership made possible "because by that time they will, among other things, be financially in our hands."[13] Borah thought precisely the opposite. He would gamble on Allied cooperation because he believed the Allies had no choice given their reliance upon American military and economic asistance. The correct procedure, according to Borah, was to define American interests and then bludgeon the Allies into recognizing them whether they wanted to or not. This should be done at once, he said, because British and French dependence would cease at the war's conclusion.

The Idahoan shrewdly guessed that Wilson was being "led" by the Allies in his decisions. Probably unaware how seriously the President had contemplated taking an independent stand, Borah protested in vain. That an alternate course might have saved the Provisional Government is conjectural; it is certain, however, that the policies followed could not have been more destructive. Conditions in Russia grew progressively worse through late summer and fall and culminated in the Bolshevik coup of November 7. A bewildered administration went on purveying a version of Russian affairs it did not itself believe; as late as November 2, Secretary Lansing stated publicly that the Provisional Government, rumors notwithstanding, planned to "organize all Russia's resources in a wholehearted resistance and carry the war through to a victorious conclusion."[14]

Borah again suggested a reexamination of American policy soon after the November Revolution. In an article in the New York *Times* (December 7), he declared it high time the United States benefit from past mistakes and assume the moral

---

[13] *Ibid.*, 180.
[14] *FRUS, 1918, Russia*, I, 218.

leadership for which it was suited.[15] Reviewing the Provisional Government's brief history, the Senator attributed its downfall to Allied "particularism," which he defined as selfish national interests. Since this "particularism" had become "ingrained" in European powers, only the United States could translate the war to a loftier plane. Pointing out that Wilson already had tried to elevate the nature of the struggle, Borah predicted the President would receive wide approbation if he went further regarding Russia and the war aims. Sidestepping the issue, the Idahoan warned, meant that our noble appeals consisted largely of verbiage and "it would be well to modify our pretensions of making the world safe for democracy."

Instead of feeling betrayed, Borah continued, the Allies and the United States should have realized the priority of domestic needs in Russia. Rather than preventing or delaying these reforms, the most intelligent approach lay in convincing the Russians that German aggression threatened them. To accomplish this, the United States should take the lead in working with the revolution, not against it. The resumption of an offensive war now lay beyond hope but the possibility still existed that Russia could continue serving the Allied cause in however reduced a role. As to the kind of government she had, Borah said this was of no concern to France, Great Britain, or the United States.

Borah's proposals included sending a commission to Russia to assist whatever government it found there.[16] This commission should be composed of able men who could get things

[15] Borah, "Shall We Abandon Russia?", *New York Times Magazine,* December 7, 1917.

[16] Although this writer can establish no direct connection, Lincoln Colcord of the Philadelphia *Public Ledger* wrote to Wilson at the same time Borah's article appeared, outlining a program similar in every respect including the commission. Wilson replied he was "very much impressed" by the suggestion, but did not know "where I would find the men suited to the purpose." Baker, *Life and Letters,* VI, 396.

done but who, above all, should be in sympathy with the aims of the revolution, if not its methods. The American contingent, furthermore, should be prepared to stay in Russia as long as was necessary. More substantial assistance might follow, provided conditions became stabilized. At the very least, wrote the Senator, such measures would help to counteract German propaganda. Admitting that the situation looked bleak, he believed its importance demanded an effort. Whatever happened, he said, his proposals were preferable to sitting back "anathematizing the Bolsheviks."[17]

But the Allies had no intention of sitting back on the Russian question. Instead they concluded that the Bolshevik regime must be destroyed. In addition to nonrecognition and a cessation of economic aid, Allied leaders began discussing the possibility of direct intervention. They negotiated unofficially with Soviet representatives for the time being in order to prevent separate arrangements between Russia and Germany. The Allies sought to avoid antagonizing the Bolsheviks as long as Russo-German peace talks, initiated in December, foundered on extreme German demands.[18] Simultaneously they entered relations with anti-Bolshevik elements as a possible means of overthrowing the Soviet government in the future. Bolshevik leaders periodically hinted that they might take a more belligerent stance against Germany should the Allies grant firm promises of aid. Whether this alternative actually existed is uncertain, for both sides negotiated less than candidly, and their exchanges in the end came to

[17] That was precisely what Lansing proposed to do. At a cabinet meeting held December 4, he submitted a draft declaration of policy, expressing the "disappointment and amazement" with which the United States viewed the "rise of class despotism in Petrograd." Wilson said he agreed in principle but thought the time inopportune for such a statement. *Ibid.*, 391.

[18] David Lloyd George, *War Memoirs* (6 vols.; Boston, 1933–37), V, 114. Allied thinking followed the line that a "mere armistice" was preferable to a separate peace and they did not want to drive the Bolsheviks into German arms. See also Seymour, *Intimate Papers*, III, 281.

nothing. Unrecognized, unaided, and in desperate straits, V. I. Lenin secured for his government its "breathing space" when Russia left the war in March, 1918, under the terms of the Brest-Litovsk Treaty.[19]

President Wilson's Fourteen Points message appeared in January before the treaty's conclusion. As a response to Bolshevik peace propaganda, and as an effort to influence the Bolsheviks themselves, his statement contained some significant passages. Those sections of it pertaining to Russia implied a shift in American policy which greatly encouraged Borah and those of similar persuasion. At last, it appeared to them, the President had cast off the baneful influence of Great Britain and France. Wilson urged a policy of non-interference in Russian affairs, calling it the "acid test" of Allied goodwill. His reference to Russia "under institutions of her own choosing," moreover, signified acceptance of the Bolshevik regime although the administration still withheld official recognition.[20] The Senator believed this indicated a fundamental change in Wilson's thinking, an impression strengthened a few days later when he and several other congressmen met with the President at the White House. Bringing with them a plan for dealing with Russia on the basis of recognition and assistance, they received no commitment from Wilson but considered his reaction encouraging.[21]

The President had not "come around," however. Detesting the Bolsheviks as much as did France and Great Britain, he welcomed any opportunity to hasten their destruction. He opposed intervention at first, not because he disapproved in principle, but because he doubted its efficacy and knew such

---

[19] For opposing views on whether Brest-Litovsk might have been avoided, see Williams, *American-Russian Relations*, Chap. 5 and Kennan, *Russia*, Chap. 24.

[20] Point 6 of Woodrow Wilson, *The Fourteen Points, House Document* 765, 65th Cong., 2nd Sess.

[21] Baker, *Life and Letters*, VI, 475.

a move would arouse a storm of opposition in the Senate.[22] When, after ratification of the Brest-Litovsk Treaty, the Allies stepped up their demands for military action, he refused on the ground of its impracticality. In a note to Secretary Lansing, Wilson said he agreed with his military advisers who counseled against intervention because "no strong force" could be sent to Murmansk without subtracting this strength from the western front where it was badly needed. As to Siberia, "they [the military] believed . . . there is no sufficient military force, in Japan or elsewhere, to do anything effective."[23] The President left the door open, however, to other possibilities. As early as December, administration officials discussed aiding General A. M. Kaledin's anti-Bolshevik campaign in southern Russia, but it collapsed almost immediately. Wilson later asked Lansing to "follow" what General Gregori Semenov was "accomplishing" in Siberia to determine whether "there is any legitimate way in which we can assist."[24]

Borah mistakenly interpreted the Fourteen Points declaration and his interview with the President to mean that Wilson opposed interfering in Russia's domestic affairs. Guided by this assumption, the Senator espoused intervention by March and went on advocating it for several months.[25] The kind of intervention he had in mind, of course, was purely a military one to guard Allied stores in northern Russia and to prevent

[22] "Non-joining [intervention] because of Senate," Lansing noted in his desk diary, March 1, 1918. An entry made later the same day indicates Wilson's agreement with this view. Box 3, Robert Lansing Papers, Library of Congress, hereinafter cited as Lansing Papers.

[23] Baker, *Life and Letters*, VII, 153; and Wilson to Edward A. Woods, April 15, 1918, Case File 64, Series IV, Woodrow Wilson Papers, Library of Congress, hereinafter cited as Wilson Papers.

[24] Baker, *Life and Letters*, VIII, 153. Semenov was a Cossack leader who attempted to create an independent government in Siberia. He later fell under Japanese influence, becoming little more than a puppet. For Lansing's discussions with Wilson concerning Kaledin, see Lansing's desk diary, entries for December 10, 11, 12, 13, 17, Box 3, Lansing Papers.

[25] Borah to Wilson, March 5, 1918, Box 684, Borah Papers.

Japanese penetration of Siberia.[26] He grew even more ardent in favor of it when the Japanese let it be known that they might intervene regardless of whether the Western Allies or the United States participated.[27] Thus Wilson held back from intervention because he thought it would fail; at the same time the Idahoan, unaware of its purpose, continued to back the policy. "I believe we should have acted immediately after the revolution," Borah wrote, "I sincerely hope we may not much longer delay."[28] Ironically, when Wilson finally agreed to go along with Allied demands, Borah was in the process of reversing his position as well.[29]

It is tempting to diagnose Borah's about-face as an example of his congenital weakness for dissent. In his own mind the Senator acted for good reason. Until July, 1918, he had advanced a paradoxical view of the Russian situation. Insisting that the United States aid the Soviet government so as to extend American influence in its development, Borah neverthe-

[26] Borah to J. O. Holderman, March 12, 1918, Box 191, *ibid.*

[27] Kennan, *Russia,* Chap. 34. Kennan shows there was little real danger of unilateral Japanese action but Borah had no way of knowing this.

[28] Borah to editors of the *Christian Science Monitor,* July 11, 1918, Box 191, Borah Papers.

[29] Scholars have interpreted in several ways the President's decision to land American troops on Russian soil. Williams, in *American-Russian Relations,* sees intervention as an anti-Bolshevik measure. He has expanded his thesis in "American Intervention in Russia," a two-part article appearing in *Studies on the Left,* III (1963), 24–48, and IV (1964), 39–57. See also Robert James Maddox, "Woodrow Wilson, The Russian Embassy and Siberian Intervention," *Pacific Historical Review,* XXXVI (November, 1967), 435–48. John A. White, in *The Siberian Intervention* (Princeton, 1950), and Betty Miller Unterberger, in *America's Siberian Expedition, 1918–1920* (Durham, 1956), emphasize Wilson's fear of Japan and interpret his differences with the Allies as based upon his determination not to interfere with the internal affairs of Russia. George F. Kennan's *The Decision to Intervene* (Princeton, 1958) advances a multiple-causation interpretation and Lasch, in *American Liberals,* claims Wilson believed he was fighting the Germans through intervention. N. Gordon Levin, Jr., in a recent book, *Woodrow Wilson and World Politics: America's Response to War and Revolution* (New York, 1968), weaves together several earlier interpretations to argue that Wilson sought to create a liberal Russia in opposition to the Germans *and* the Bolsheviks.

less referred to the regime as a "phase" which soon would pass. He characteristically invoked "some higher law of human progress which we do not yet quite comprehend," describing Leon Trotsky as "an incident" and Lenin as "of no concern in the final adjustment of things."[30] The Senator apparently assumed that, given enough help, the Russian people themselves would overthrow the Bolsheviks and perhaps install some kind of liberal democracy. Although expressed within his "irrefutable logic" framework, Borah's "phase" interpretation of the revolution was commonly held at the time. He personally abandoned it late in the month—substituting the belief that eventually the Soviet government would evolve into something more "acceptable" by Western standards—after a series of discussions with Raymond Robins, a prominent reformer and chairman of the 1916 Bull Moose Convention, who recently had returned from Russia. Always partial to "inside" information, Borah changed his outlook after he heard what Robins had to say.

Robins had gone to Russia in August, 1917, as a member of a Red Cross Commission authorized by President Wilson. The group had the dual task of providing assistance to the Russian people and spreading the gospel of democracy—although the latter aspect seemed ill-fated from the start. Robins had taken an active but unsuccessful part in Russian affairs until his recall in the early summer of 1918.[31] He returned to the United States convinced that Allied and American policy, having destroyed the Provisional Government, was equally wrong as applied to the Bolsheviks.

Allied intrusion, according to Robins, had subverted the Provisional Government's chance to create a stable system.

---

[30] *Congressional Record*, 65th Cong., 2nd Sess., 9054–55.

[31] Williams, in *American-Russian Relations*, gives an interpretation extremely favorable to Robins. Kennan, in *Russia Leaves the War* and *The Decision to Intervene*, portrays the Colonel as a well-meaning but gullible amateur.

Its only hope for survival had depended upon its ability to satisfy the demands of laborers and peasants, since no broad middle class existed. The Allies, instead of aiding the regime, had pushed it into unpopular positions over the strongest protests. "Unless he [Alexander Kerensky, last premier of the Provisional Government] did what they wanted," in Robins' words, "they could at any time withhold funds from him and and his government would collapse."[32] The most serious blunder lay in forcing the exhausted Russian troops into the summer offensive. France and Great Britain had failed to realize that in the people's minds they were the tsar's allies, not Russia's.[33]

Robins had done everything he could to aid the Provisional Government during its short lifetime. Declaring his belief in "burying a corpse, not sitting up with it," however, he considered puerile all hopes of resurrection.[34] Neither a communist nor a socialist himself, he believed the Bolsheviks held a powerful attraction for the Russian people. Because of that appeal, he thought, the only sensible policy for the Allies and the United States was to acknowledge the regime and exert as much direction as possible upon its evolution. Robins undoubtedly overestimated the frankness which Soviet leaders had shown him, yet he felt sure they needed, and could be swayed by, American assistance. He said the United States ought to grasp the chance to be an important factor in Russian affairs, as well as the opportunity to penetrate that vast nation's economy.

Robins had returned to the United States carrying an appeal for American aid given to him by Trotsky. He had tried to influence American policy by presenting the appeal and his own case to the administration upon his arrival, but he found

[32] Interview with Robins by Herman Hagedorn, Box 6, Thompson Papers.
[33] William Hard, *Raymond Robins' Own Story* (New York, 1920), 35.
[34] *Ibid.*, 48–50.

he could get no serious hearing either from the President or the State Department.[35] Wilson, steadfastly refusing to see almost everyone with first-hand experience in Russia, developed an unaccountable number of head colds.[36] The State Department treated Robins as a subversive and, at Lansing's insistence, subjected him to a humiliating search of his possessions at the port of entry. More irresponsible people circulated the story that he was a Soviet agent; later, he was denounced in the Senate as the "minister plenipotentiary of the Soviet Union."[37]

Unable to convince—or, more precisely, even to see—administration officials, Robins turned to congressional leaders and others whom he considered "right" on the Russian question.[38] Borah and Senator Hiram Johnson, who had known him for years, proved especially receptive to what he told them. The three men planned a campaign to secure recognition of the Soviet government and to prevent intervention from becoming an invasion. As long as the war lasted, however, this group had to proceed carefully since the administration had successfully presented intervention as part of the war effort. In the emotional atmosphere of the time,

[35] William, *American-Russian Relations*, 146.

[36] Even Elihu Root, who had led an official American mission to Russia, received but a brief hearing from the President. William Boyce Thompson, having returned before Robins, tried to reach Wilson through Herbert Hoover, Bernard Baruch, and Thomas Lamont. None could get him an interview. See Box 1, Thompson Papers; and Thomas Lamont to Wilson, January 29, 1918, Wilson to Lamont, January 31, 1918, Thompson to Wilson, January 31, 1918, all in Case File 64, Series IV, Wilson Papers.

[37] *Congressional Record*, 65th Cong., 3rd Sess., 3338.

[38] See Robins to Lansing, July 1, Robins to Wilson, July 7, 9, 13, 1918, all in Box 14, Robins Papers. Robins received no reply to these letters although Wilson, commenting on the one of July 1 which Lansing had forwarded him, said Robins' suggestions were "much more sensible than I thought the author of them capable of. I differ from them only in practical details." Wilson to Lansing, July 3, Decimal Files of the State Department, National Archives, Washington, D.C. 763.72/10610½, hereinafter cited as State Department Decimal Files.

particularly after American troops went into the trenches, criticism was often equated with disloyalty.

Soon after the armistice, Johnson began to question Wilson's Russian policies from the Senate floor. He told Robins that he had "started something" with his speech which he hoped would force the administration into revealing its intentions.[39] Convinced by late December that "something rotten" lay within the War Department's demobilization program, Johnson thought "it might be Russia." He wrote that Secretary Newton D. Baker had assured him of a quick demobilization at the war's end but that he (Johnson) now had "dope" from several army camps revealing that nothing was being done to reduce the forces. The Californian mistakenly believed stronger intervention might be in the offing.[40] His apprehensions seemed warranted when administration spokesman Senator Gilbert M. Hitchcock gave what Johnson called his "Why Our Boys Are in Russia" speech on January 3, 1919. The Borah-Johnson-Robins group suspected collusion between the administration, the press, and certain interest groups to hide the real nature of intervention from the American people.[41]

Borah replied to Hitchcock in the Senate. There could be but a single justification for intervention, said the Idahoan, and that was the existence of the German military threat. Since that threat had ended, American forces should remain in Russia "only as long as it will take to get them out."[42] Referring to the President's policy toward Russia as stated in his Fourteen Points, Borah said he thought at the time, and still thought, that policy to be the correct one. "Through the persuasion of others," however, Wilson had modified his approach. "I have reason to believe that he modified it with a

[39] Johnson to Robins, December 13, 1918, Box 14, Robins Papers.
[40] Johnson to Robins, December 27, 1918, *ibid.*
[41] Johnson to Robins, January 3, 1919, Box 15, *ibid.*
[42] *Congressional Record*, 65th Cong., 3rd Sess., 1164.

great deal of reluctance,'" Borah continued, but "it is with the modification now that we are dealing and not with the policy the President originally outlined."[43] Succinctly put, the joint operation had as its goal destroying the Bolshevik government rather than helping the Russian people. The Senator criticized intervention both as bad tactics and bad principles. The forces then in Russia could accomplish little beyond antagonizing the Russian masses, and American participation had failed to check the Japanese. The presence of foreign troops allowed the Bolsheviks to appear as defenders of Russian sovereignty which, if anything, strengthened Red domination. Borah questioned the practice of differentiating between Bolsheviks and Russians. Those who talked of "shooting Bolshevism out of Russia" miscalculated badly if they believed this would gladden the Russian people.[44] When Senator Porter McCumber suggested that the Allies and the United States should try to organize a government of "law-abiding classes," or failing in that, to set up an autocracy again, Borah answered that "this is precisely what the Russian people are afraid of."[45]

The Senator protested against intervention on ethical grounds as well. He asked why everyone suddenly had become so exercised about "despotism" in Soviet Russia when few people had bothered themselves over despotism under the tsar. Their real antagonism, he said, derived from attitudes about the Soviet economic system and had nothing at all to do with social justice. He derided as contrary to American traditions tampering in the affairs of a sovereign state for the purpose of overthrowing a particular form of government. "I take the position," he concluded, "that the Russian people

[43] *Ibid.*, 1166.
[44] *Ibid.*, 1167.
[45] *Ibid.*, 3338.

have the same right to establish a socialistic state as we have to establish a Republic."[46]

As Borah and Johnson sniped away at intervention in the Senate, President Wilson employed almost similar arguments at the peace negotiations in Paris. Once more, however, he rested his case on ineffectiveness rather than on morality. Singly or collectively, the powers had shown themselves unwilling to commit enough troops to overthrow the Bolsheviks directly, he maintained, and an inadequate force had proven worse than none. He said it had become distressingly clear "that by opposing Bolshevism with arms they were in reality serving the cause of Bolshevism."[47] In a line paralleling Borah's, the President claimed that intervention thus far had enabled the Bolsheviks to argue convincingly that the Western powers really wished to reestablish the old regime. But Wilson did not insist that Allied and American forces should be removed. Indeed, there is cause to believe his posture represented less a genuine desire to pull out than a device to extract from the Allies promises that reform of the White Russian governments—all of them to some extent reactionary —precede recognition and wholesale military assistance.[48] Whatever his motives, he said he would "cast in his lot with the rest."[49]

Although the developing struggle over the League of Nations early in 1919 tended to subsume the Russian question, neither Borah nor Johnson diminished their efforts to influence administration policy. During debates over the League,

[46] *Ibid.*, 1167.

[47] *FRUS, 1919, Russia*, 21.

[48] Maddox, "Woodrow Wilson, the Russian Embassy and Siberian Intervention," 444–46. But see Arno J. Mayer, *Politics and Diplomacy of Peacemaking: Containment and Counterrevolution at Versailles, 1918–1919* (New York, 1967), Chap. 23; and John M. Thompson's *Russia, Bolshevism, and the Versailles Peace* (Princeton, 1966), Chap. 8, for contrary views.

[49] *FRUS, 1919, Russia*, 59.

they used intervention as an example of the kind of entanglements that membership would entail. Borah often alluded to the situation in Russia as a preview of things to come should the United States join the organization and foretold the use of American troops to settle the "57 varieties" of European problems.[50] Failing to bring about recognition or an immediate end to intervention, their protests did have some effect.

In January, 1919, Acting Secretary of State Frank Polk cabled the Commission to Negotiate Peace to report the "critical spirit in Congress" regarding Russia.[51] He stated that, in view of this opposition, he doubted the possibility of Congress appropriating money to carry out the administration's plans calling for a reorganization of the railway system in Siberia. This was considered necessary for maintaining a pipeline to Admiral A. V. Kolchak's anti-Bolshevik government with its headquarters at Omsk. Wilson initially responded to this news by suggesting that Polk arrange secret hearings before a congressional committee for the purpose of explaining the administration's position. With the President's authorization, Lansing cabled a number of arguments for Polk's use in facing the congressmen. It is perhaps significant that the first suggestion concerned economic aid to Siberia, "where the people are relatively friendly and resistant to Bolshevik influence."[52] Polk, after discussing the matter with other members of the State Department and several Cabinet officials, doggedly replied that it would be "very inadvisable" to go to Congress with a plan "having anything to do with Russia."[53] Wilson finally accepted Polk's advice and withdrew his request.

[50] *Congressional Record*, 65th Cong., 3rd Sess., 192.

[51] *FRUS, 1919, Russia*, 245.

[52] *Ibid.*, 246–48. Aid to Czech troops, developing American commerce, maintaining the "open door," and "watching" the conduct of German prisoners of war were also listed.

[53] *Ibid.*, 248.

Thus Borah, Johnson, and the others failed to achieve their maximum demands but did affect and help circumscribe the President's Russian policies. By mid-February a Johnson resolution calling for withdrawal of American forces was defeated only by Vice President Thomas Marshall's tie-breaking vote.[54] The Idahoan, making Russia his own special cause, continued advocating the resumption of diplomatic relations both publicly and in his personal correspondence. He launched in addition several peripheral attacks on the administration seeking to make known the inconsistency of American policy. The Senator used these forays, relatively unimportant in themselves, to keep the recognition issue alive and to embarrass President Wilson.

On March 18, 1919, a Mr. Ludwig C. A. K. Martens presented credentials to the State Department identifying himself as the official representative of the Russian Socialist Federal Soviet Republic. Besides requesting recognition of his government, he made a number of proposals for resuming trade relations between the two nations and notified several New York banks that all "Russian funds" on deposit should be disbursed only with his authorization.[55] Opening offices in New York City, Martens began discussing trade with private firms as well as appearing before public meetings to advocate recognition. His claims raised embarrassing complications

[54] By no means all those who voted for the resolution shared the Borah-Johnson position, many wished merely to strike at Wilson. See Mayer's *Politics*, 447–49. In June, the Senate unanimously approved Johnson's resolution that the State Department be directed to inform the Senate of the reasons for intervention, to which Wilson replied on July 22. Although repeating some of the points made in the earlier instructions to Polk, his emphasis greatly differed this time. Now he stressed the dangers presented by "hostile armies apparently organized by and often largely composed of enemy prisoners of war." This was patently untrue. The threat posed by prisoner of war "armies" was known to be mythical many months before Wilson's statement. *Congressional Record*, 66th Cong., 1st Sess., 4816.

[55] *FRUS, 1919, Russia*, 133, 142.

because the United States still disbursed funds to the "Provisional Government" which no longer existed.

The National City Bank of New York, for example, urgently requested clarification of the matter from the State Department. Having entered into transactions "of such great magnitude" with the "Provisional Government *since December, 1917*," bank officials feared recognition endangered these investments.[56] Also, inquiries from businessmen interested in trade led some members of the State Department to believe Martens' offers might bring about increased demands for recognition. Finally, military intelligence reported Martens' activities as being " the largest and most dangerous propaganda undertaking thus far started by Lenin's party in any country outside of Russia." Wilson and the State Department, agreeing that Martens must go, initiated efforts to deport him on the basis that, as an official of the Soviet government hence connected with the Third International, he belonged to a group advocating the violent overthrow of the American government.[57]

Senator Borah at first tried to prevent this move through congressional action, then sought advice as to whether the case could be taken into the courts. His efforts went for nothing. The Soviet government, instructing Martens not to appeal, had him recalled prior to deportation in the spring of 1921.[58] Victims of their ideology in this case, Russian leaders believed they stood a better chance of recognition from the incoming Republican administration because of its domination by the "interests," whose lust for trade would override all other considerations. Instead of having Martens become

[56] *Ibid.*, 143 (Italics mine).

[57] *Ibid.*, 144–46.

[58] Borah to George H. Moses, April 6; William Hard to Borah, April 18; Borah to Hard, April 19; all in Box 198, Borah Papers. See also Borah to Judge Thomas G. Hardwick, January 10; Hardwick to Borah, January 11, 1921; in Box 209, *ibid.* Moscow's action mystified the Senator, who believed the courts would uphold Martens' appeal.

involved in litigation, therefore, Moscow simply dropped the issue until after the inauguration.

While fighting to have Martens' status accepted, Borah started a campaign against the officially recognized "Russian Ambassador," Boris Bakhmetev. Bakhmetev, having represented the Provisional Government before its collapse, had gone into a sort of limbo until he became a representative of Kolchak's regime. During this time, and even after Kolchak's fall early in 1920, the United States continued to recognize him. Working through George Creel, chairman of the Committee on Public Information, Bakhmetev had persuaded Wilson to distinguish between the Russian governments and the masses (a not unusual practice for the President); Bakhmetev's official designation became "Ambassador of the Russian People."[59] His title lent an air of "legitimacy" to the financial transactions conducted with unrecognized governments, thus helping to maintain the fiction of "noninterference" in Russian affairs. Actually, the embassy headed by Bakhmetev served as a dummy corporation through which the administration could channel funds to anti-Bolshevik groups without having to approach Congress.

Borah tried to capitalize on Bakhmetev's ambiguous status as a lever to "expose" the entire tangle of the government's Russian policy. He began collecting information about the ambassador, his activities, and his associations with counterrevolutionary regimes.[60] Accomplishing little during the waning months of Wilson's administration, he managed to focus enough attention on Bakhmetev to help keep Russia before the public. The first stage of what was to be a lengthy

[59] Recording, *Boris Bakhmetev*, Oral History Project, Columbia University, New York City.

[60] See Box 214, Borah Papers, for the collection of letters, testimony, etc. Much of this information came from junior officers and government officials who had served in Siberia and wished to tell the "real story" of what had taken place.

campaign had ended; Borah, like the Bolsheviks, anticipated greater success when the Republicans came into office. The Senator's response to the Russian revolutions on the whole comported with his long-established principles. During the period before March, 1918, the overriding issue for him was the necessity of keeping Russia in the war. Uncharacteristic proposals, such as his suggestion that an American commission be sent to shore up the government, grew out of his concern for the military situation rather than from any desire to become involved in the domestic problems of a European nation. Even here, he carefully defined the nature of the mission in a way calculated to avoid entanglement. Borah opposed political intervention while the war lasted and intensified his protest at its end. Efforts to coerce revolutions throughout the world into forms Allied and American policy-makers considered acceptable he thought futile and extremely dangerous. In a broader sense, western diplomacy toward Russia confirmed all Borah's misgivings about the kind of world order that the victors meant to impose at the war's end.

CHAPTER III

The Postwar World

PPALLED though he was by the war's destructiveness, Borah did not at first identify himself with any formula for preventing conflicts in the future. He hoped a benign peace settlement would mitigate national rivalries, but beyond this he was unwilling to go. His aversion to American involvement in European matters caused him to look askance at the war-stimulated growth of organizations dedicated to establishing formal peace programs, the most popular of which called for some type of world association.[1] Prone to regarding war as an unwelcome intrusion upon the orderly conduct of international affairs, few Americans doubted that there existed a common interest to banish it forever. What could be more natural, therefore, than to endorse proposals designed to further this interest through collective action? The Senator came to look upon such reasoning as the greatest threat to its independence the Republic had ever known.

[1] For a brief discussion of these organizations, see John Chalmers Vinson, *Referendum for Isolation* (Athens, Ga., 1961), Chap. 1.

Fortunately for Borah and the relatively few like-minded individuals, the near consensus on the desirability of an association quickly disintegrated over questions of form and substance. Should it be limited to particular nations, the Allied and Associated Powers for example, or open to all? How could representation be made equitable for large and small states? Most important, what substantive resources, if any, should be granted the structure to compel adherence to its decisions? This latter question, and the degree of obligation assumed by a member nation, revealed fundamental differences among those supporting a world organization in general. Indications that these differences were deep and non-negotiable appeared well before the fight over the League of Nations.[2]

The Idahoan was one of the small number who had refused to embrace the idea of a league even in the abstract. Yet, in the days when the subject seemed academic, he had not become especially perturbed over it. Approached late in 1915 by one of the pro-world-organization groups, the League to Enforce Peace, the Senator merely stated that he would "defer" actual membership.[3] He replied to a correspondent asking for his views a year later that while he did not think he would favor such a proposition, the matter required "far more consideration than it has been my privilege to give it before arriving at a final conclusion."[4]

Within weeks, presumably having given it more consideration, Borah decided that "if it [a league] would work at all it would simply be almost fiendish in its results."[5] President Wilson's note of December 18, 1916, to the warring powers had crystallized his thinking. Part of the note, with which

[2] Ruhl J. Bartlett, *The League to Enforce Peace* (Chapel Hill, 1944), 36–42; Vinson, *Referendum*, 18–19.
[3] Borah to Alton B. Parker, December 28, 1915, Box 175, Borah Papers.
[4] Borah to H. B. Summers, December 6, 1916, Box 179, *ibid.*
[5] Borah to Roosevelt, January 18, 1917, Box 183, *ibid.*

he had no quarrel, asked the combatants to define peace terms which they would accept. In addition, however, Wilson proposed the creation of a "league of nations" to "insure peace and justice throughout the world."[6] When Senator Hitchcock of Nebraska introduced a resolution asking for senatorial approval of the note, Borah and others initiated a struggle which lasted into the 1920's.

That the President sanctioned the formation of a league came as no surprise. He had made known his support for such an organization as early as May and had campaigned on a platform containing a league plank.[7] Complications ensued when campaign pledges emerged as an official presidential statement. The matter took on an urgency hitherto lacking and raised important political considerations. Thus far the campaign for a world organization had been bipartisan; many stalwart Republicans had approved the idea—Elihu Root, Henry Cabot Lodge, and Charles Evans Hughes, to name a few, and William Howard Taft served as president of the League to Enforce Peace. Now, Wilson's actions evoked the specter of a major Democratic coup which began tormenting Republican leaders whatever their own preferences.

The debate over Hitchcock's resolution augured badly for Wilson's plans. Lodge and others first tried to explain away their previous advocacy of a league, then they proceeded to enumerate the reasons why membership would wreak disaster upon the nation. Borah, free of such an inconvenience, described the proposed organization as a scheme to place the

[6] *FRUS, 1916 Supplement*, 97–99. The President's original draft of the note used the term "enforce" rather than "insure," but he changed it on advice from Secretary of State Robert Lansing. This was undoubtedly an effort to avoid a premature controversy over the question of substantive power. Baker, *Life and Letters*, V, 399.

[7] Vinson, *Referendum*, 32.

United States in the "storm center of European politics."[8] Outside Congress, Theodore Roosevelt scathingly denounced Wilson, Taft, and everyone else who would countenance a program so flagrantly in violation of American traditions.[9] In this, the first skirmish over the league, the opposition blocked Hitchcock's resolution, forcing him to introduce a substitute calling for approval of the request for peace terms only.

Borah's attitude transcended party politics. His hostility toward a league would burn just as intensely when directed against Republican proponents. Indeed, during the fight against President Wilson, the Idahoan had to cooperate with men for whom he had little respect, personally or politically. Their participation tarnished what was for him a crusade to save the nation. However joyfully he engaged the Democrats, he became positively exhilarated when directing his fulmi-nations against his own party. For then he assumed the part most coveted by him—that of the lone gladiator, disdainful of odds and mundane political intrigues, struggling to pre-serve the heritage of the founding fathers.

Nor did personal feelings influence his conduct. He had that rare ability to divorce completely personalities and issues. By this time it is difficult to name any public figure for whom he had more esteem than the President. To Borah, Wilson towered as a giant among pygmies, and however wrong-headed the Senator thought his politics, he seldom concealed his admiration for the man. Never during the following con-test did he so much as hint that Wilson acted out of any but the most pristine ideals. Borah did not exaggerate when he later stated that he would have opposed a league had the

[8] *Congressional Record*, 64th Cong., 2nd Sess., 892. Borah to Roosevelt, January 18, 1917, Box 183, Borah Papers.

[9] Theodore Roosevelt, "The Election," *Metropolitan Magazine* (January, 1917), 42–45.

"Savior of mankind" revisited the earth to campaign for its adoption.[10]

Wilson unhesitatingly took up the challenge. On January 22, 1917, he delivered his "peace without victory" address before the Senate. In addition to reaffirming his belief that a vindictive settlement would engender future wars, the President elaborated his stand on an international organization. Denying that participation meant bartering away American traditions, he compared a league with extending the Monroe Doctrine throughout the world.[11] In reality Wilson spoke to the public, for his phrases scarcely reassured those senators who had already expressed their displeasure. If anything, he had shown himself committed to a program even more comprehensive than previously suspected

Preoccupation with the war thrust the league question offstage—for the time being. That it would become an issue of paramount importance when the fighting stopped, few could doubt. Though the European powers had reacted to the President's league proposals with but faintly concealed apathy, the final words had yet to be spoken. As a neutral the United States might appeal, propose, and offer advice, but little more. As a cobelligerent virtually financing the war's later stages, this nation could expect to exercise formidable authority at the peace table. Wilson anticipated such potency in his "Fourteen Points" message of January, 1918.[12] Outlining the bases upon which a lasting peace might be built, he repeated his call for a world organization, this time in more adamant terms. He also made clear his intention of including it within the framework of the peace settlement. To do this he meant to control, circumvent, or defeat the Senate, whatever the cost.

[10] New York *Times*, February 1, 1919.
[11] Ray Stannard Baker and William E. Dodd (eds.), *The Public Papers of Woodrow Wilson* (6 vols.; New York, 1927), IV, 407–14.
[12] Wilson, *The Fourteen Points*.

As the war neared its conclusion, the President and his opponents girded for the fight they knew must come. Wilson's October appeal for the election of a Democratic Congress, often interpreted solely as a tactical mistake, actually represented an admission that his program faced discouraging odds in the Senate as it was then constituted. The results of the election, in which the Republicans gained control of the upper house, meant that he would have to contend with forces stronger than those which had attacked the Hitchcock resolution back in December, 1916. Thus confirmed in his belief that he would have to ram his proposals through an unfriendly Senate, the President thought conciliation unlikely.

Wilson's decision to attend the peace conference himself, and his failure to include any prominent Republicans in the delegation, demonstrated further that he regarded cooperation futile.[13] He saw two possibilities for success. He first toyed with the idea of hurdling the Senate completely through concluding, by executive action, a preliminary peace with a league appended. His advisors soon disabused him of this notion. Second, if he could make the league an integral part of the final settlement, support for a treaty ending the war might overwhelm objections to the organization itself.[14]

Borah at this stage took no part in thrashing out Republican strategy. Flatly opposed to an association of any kind, he began abusing the proposed league well before its provisions became known.[15] His own position in Idaho as secure as ever—he had won reelection in November—the Senator espoused open warfare. Aware that Wilson intended to use peace sentiment as a means of steamrolling his proposition through, Borah thought the American public would spurn participation in a league once its implications became evident.

[13] Typically, Borah questioned Wilson's decision but wished him success. McKenna, *Borah*, 152.
[14] Vinson, *Referendum*, 48–49.
[15] *Congressional Record*, 65th Cong., 2nd Sess., 192.

In fact, he said, he had "yet to discover any person who is willing to follow the league to where they admit it will go if followed to its logical conclusion."[16]

Party leaders coud not afford to act on Borah's premise regardless of its validity. Republican views ranged from "irreconcilables" of the Senator's persuasion to those who unequivocally supported a league. The sole postulate on which all Republicans could unite was the aversion to having Wilson and the Democratic Party go into the 1920 campaign "with the prestige of having accomplished what will then be said to be the greatest world adjustment of all history."[17] To counter that prestige without touching off an internecine war called for astute management.

Republican majority leader Henry Cabot Lodge provided the direction for an adroit political campaign. His own thinking consisted of a genuine mistrust for a league endowed with coercive resources, an intense personal hatred of the President, and a passionate resolve that the Republican Party regain power. It is impossible to determine the exact proportions of this brew, but conveniently for Lodge they all blended smoothly. He performed almost faultlessly given the disparate elements with which he had to work.

Unlike Senator Borah, Lodge shrank from attacking the League of Nations head-on. He had many pro-league Republicans to cope with, and such a position meant exposing the party to charges of obstructing efforts to create a peaceful world. Lodge therefore counseled opposition, not to *a* league, but to Wilson's League, the terms of which became public in the middle of February, 1919.[18] Calling for guarantees to protect the "territorial integrity" of all signatories, it presented a choice mark for the criticism that adherence carried

[16] New York *Times*, December 7, 1918.
[17] Beveridge to Borah, January 26, 1919, Box 195. Borah Papers.
[18] Garraty, *Lodge*, 350.

with it the loss of both independent action and a substantial degree of national sovereignty. The proposed organization did in fact involve a more drastic break with traditional foreign policy than many Americans found themselves willing to accept.

Lodge's strategy was almost assured success provided he could keep his forces together. If, on the one hand, Wilson eschewed compromise with the Senate, he would incur a great deal of responsibility should his League proposal fail.[19] In the event he accommodated the Republicans and the League passed, the latter party could then boast of having protected American interests before giving its assent.[20] If there had to be an organization—it is moot whether Lodge wanted one of any kind by this time—the Democrats must not be allowed to take all the credit for its formation.

Borah and the other "irreconcilables" endangered Republican alternatives. The Idahoan, who manifested a wooden indifference to the question of party solidarity, already had begun denouncing *the* League or any league. Lodge must have outdone himself, therefore, when he met with Borah in April and persuaded him to cooperate.[21] For Borah to work

[19] Acting on the advice of Frank Brandegee, an irreconcilable senator from Connecticut, Lodge had shown he could muster the necessary one-third of the Senate to defeat the league as originally formulated. Through parlimentary maneuver, Lodge succeeded in reading the famous "Round Robin" into the *Congressional Record* on March 3. This document, in the form of a resolution, contained the names of thirty-seven senators and declared the proposed organization unacceptable. *Ibid.*, 353–54.

[20] Wilson did try to meet Republican objections insofar as he felt them compatible with a viable league. But he could not satisfy the irreconcilables, of course, and neither Lodge nor other Republican leaders made any commitments as to what would be necessary for their approval. It is entirely possible that no matter what changes Wilson might have made, the ante would have been raised just so much higher. Vinson, *Referendum*, 64–65.

[21] An account of the meeting, and the agreements reached, can be found in Henry Cabot Lodge, *The United States and the League of Nations* (New York, 1925), 146–47. The book as a whole is apologia and frequently unreliable; his recollections on this matter, however, appear accurate on

with anyone, much less the frosty Bostonian, is in itself evidence of how menacing he estimated the League threat. Their relationship, always touchy, came near breaking down completely on several occasions. Borah neither liked nor trusted Lodge, who fully reciprocated his feelings. The uneasy alliance held together long enough to accomplish what the latter had in mind.

Lodge first of all wanted to procrastinate. He believed that the wave of public enthusiasm for a world organization would spend itself with the passage of time. Borah entered no serious demurrer and, swallowing his impatience, consented to go along with the idea of protracted hearings as a means of delay. Above all, the majority leader needed the Idahoan's support to get Senate approval for the reservations he intended using to qualify or defeat the League in its present form. The tiny Republican majority in the Senate made irreconcilable votes necessary for the proper execution of Lodge's tactics.

A reluctant Borah agreed to abide with the reservations. He did so only because Lodge had convinced him it offered the best way to beat the League, or at least render it comparatively harmless. Making the point abundantly clear that he viewed this as a marriage of convenience, the Idahoan proclaimed his eagerness to vote against the organization with or without reservations when the time came. His arrangement with Lodge left uncurbed his anti-League activities outside the Senate.

Some distinction should be made between Borah's genuine opposition to the concept and his public exercises conducted during the heat of battle. His passion to defeat the League, combined with an addiction to soaring rhetoric, oftentimes led him to exaggerations which, if taken to be the substance

---

this point, see Garraty, *Lodge*, 321ff. See also Lodge to Beveridge, April 30, 1919, Box 216, Albert J. Beveridge Papers, Library of Congress, Washington, D.C., hereinafter cited as Beveridge Papers.

of his thinking, make it simple enough to portray him as a mere yahoo. He pandered to "hyphenate" groups, exploiting longstanding grudges against the British whom he pictured as the true beneficiaries of the League;[22] he likened collective security to Bolshevism alleging that both destroyed the spirit of nationalism;[23] and he magnified a very real concern over the role of the "interests" to the point where he could speak of a "Wilson-Hoover-Lamont" plan to control the world.[24] As a member of the organization, he claimed, the United States would become an armed garrison whose main export would consist of soldiers for never ending world conflict.[25] Beneath such extravagances—neither side understated its case—the Senator's objections rested on firmer ground.

For years Borah had complained against executive domination over foreign affairs. Important matters should be thrashed out in the senatorial forum, he had argued, since only in this way could the public be informed of both the questions and the choices as they arose. He expressed impatience with the view that the Senate was hardly the place to conduct intricate negotations with foreign powers. Given his assumption that the United States would adhere to the "right" position if public opinion determined its policies, Borah belittled the need for secrecy. When asked whether public debate might not intrude upon "delicate questions," he replied that generally these delicate questions were ones of "dubious righteousness."[26]

The more relevant problem, in Borah's opinion, was that policies which the Chief Executive or the State Department

---

[22] Selig Adler, in *The Isolationist Impulse* (New York, 1957), Chap. 4, deals with the role of "hyphenate" groups and Borah's activities with them.

[23] *Congressional Record*, 65th Cong., 3rd Sess., 2654.

[24] See Borah to Frank Munsey, November 21, 1919, Box 550, Borah Papers.

[25] *Congressional Record*, 65th Cong., 3rd Sess., 1383–84.

[26] Walter Lippmann, *Men of Destiny* (New York, 1928), 152.

initiated too often served the interests of particular groups rather than the nation at large. The least praiseworthy aspects of American diplomacy—the gunboats, the pacifications, and the "revolutions"—characterized the decisions made by men who were unwilling to submit them to the bar of public opinion. Russia stood as a perfect example of Borah's complaints. Now the President advocated a program which would remove diplomacy even further from popular control.[27] The same men who previously had sent Marine contingents to Latin American republics at the request of New York bankers would now huddle in closed sessions with their counterparts from other nations. And the Senate, robbed of its deliberative function in the area of foreign affairs, would have to accept the agreements made or be accused of bad faith.

Even in what was to him the unlikely event that American delegates accurately reflected public opinion, which to Borah meant his own opinion, they would have to contend with European professionals dedicated to manipulating the League in behalf of selfish national goals. Borah especially feared Great Britain and France, who would surely take leading roles in the proposed organization. Just as he minimized any mutuality of interests between the United States and those two powers, he emphasized the degree to which they would act together. Participation in the League meant to him, therefore, that the United States would commit itself in advance to policies over which it would exercise minimal control. The Senator had no doubts as to where these policies would lead.

League supporters stressed its potential for preventing a recurrence of a global war. Borah believed nothing of the sort. Any violations of what the great nations deemed their vital interests would result in withdrawal and counter-alliance. The Idahoan had written, years earlier, that the existence of a league in 1914 would have had no substantial effect upon

[27] Borah to Lenora Austin, September 3, 1919, Box 550, Borah Papers.

European affairs—had Germany and Austria believed themselves at a disadvantage in such a league they would have pulled out of it.[28] Skeptical of its capacity for solving disputes between the large nations, Borah thought the organization's real purpose would be to serve the aggressive designs of those powers controlling it. France and Great Britain had colonies and spheres of influence to protect; peace meant to them not merely the absence of armed conflict but the preservation through force of their global interests.[29]

Given British and French animosity toward the former Central Powers, as well as their abhorrence of Soviet Russia, could anyone expect that the latter nations would receive equitable treatment? Citing Russia, where Japanese, British, French, and American troops were working to overthrow the Bolshevik government, the Senator looked ahead to the time when such operations would become commonplace.[30] He anticipated that the League would be used as a cloak of respectability to protect the status quo everywhere. Denouncing efforts to "underwrite the world" as impossible and undesirable, Borah predicted that what had happened in Russia, Mexico, and China would occur, sooner or later, all over the globe.[31] He regarded emergent nationalism as the irresistible force of the twentieth century and despised the idea of placing the United States on the side he thought fated to lose.

Article 10 of the covenant, providing for guarantees of territorial integrity, confirmed the Senator's opinion that the organization portended a new Concert of Europe applied to the world.[32] Not that the article's excision would have made

[28] Borah to H. B. Summers, December 6, 1916, Box 179, *ibid.*
[29] Borah to Reverend Frederick Lynch, August 1, 1919, Box 550, *ibid.*
[30] *Congressional Record*, 65th Cong., 3rd Sess., 2261.
[31] Borah to C. George Krogness, August 13, 1919, Box 550, Borah Papers.
[32] *Congressional Record*, 65th Cong., 3rd Sess., 3748. See Robert Lansing, *The Peace Negotiations* (Boston, 1921), 93–95, for the omission of the territorial adjustment provision. Borah regarded this as one of the League's most ominous failures. In July, 1917, he had sent H. N. Brails-

the slightest difference to him. His assumptions about the motives of the British, the French, and American "interests," coupled with his "logic of events" outook, precluded his acceptance of an association regardless of the form it took. He once phrased his own feelings perfectly when he said he would oppose American entry into a league structured along the lines of "an old ladies quilting society."[33] Even the most guarded first step signaled to him the beginning of a journey which would "finally lead us into all kinds of entangling obligations and conditions with European affairs." Called by whatever name, Borah thought, the League would try to make the world safe, not for democracy, but for European imperialism.

The Senator found the treaty itself as repugnant as he did the League. Its terms shocked him. With the exception of a world organization, the Idahoan had strongly backed Wilson's Fourteen Points; he had said immediately after the war ended that Germany's new republican government should be given every chance for success.[34] Instead, the Treaty of Versailles seemed to him to be the distillation of vindictiveness. Acknowledging Wilson's efforts to obtain a generous peace, Borah thought the European powers had demonstrated beyond cavil their contempt for a "new era." He failed to see how

---

ford's *League of Nations* to Wilson. Brailsford, an English liberal, stressed the need for machinery providing for such changes. Efforts to preserve the status quo, he said, were doomed. See Wilson to Borah, July 25, 1917, Box 684, Borah Papers. Article 19 of the treaty did provide for "the considerations of international conditions whose continuance might endanger the peace of the world," without specifically mentioning territorial adjustments.

[33] *Congressional Record*, 65th Cong., 3rd Sess., 2425.

[34] New York *Times*, November 12, 1918. In February, 1919, Borah wrote, "I am in favor of giving Germany in view of her present effort to organize a liberal government, a fair opportunity in the commercial and industrial world. . . . The trouble of it is that most of the people who want them to pay want to put them in a position where they cannot pay." Borah to Z. W. Whitehead, February 4, 1919, Box 196, Borah Papers.

any peaceful reconstruction of the continent could take place when Germany and Russia were excluded. It would have been too much to ask that he sanction the President's compromises since he rejected the latter's belief that the League would compensate for them. As far as Borah could determine, Wilson had spent his strength in quest of an organization which, in effect, would be worse than useless. The Senator warned that the harvest of the Versailles Treaty would be war, not peace.

II

The sequence of events leading to the League's defeat has often been told.[35] Through the failure to vote necessary appropriations, Republicans forced Wilson into calling a special congressional session which they controlled as a result of the 1918 elections. In exchange for Old Guard control over positions on other matters, Borah and other anti-Leaguers managed to have the Senate Foreign Relations Committee packed with irreconcilables.[36] Lodge conducted his program of delay under this arrangement with notable success. Committee hearings, often farcical, at times verged on the bizarre. On one occasion, having temporarily run out of witnesses, Lodge commenced reading the entire treaty aloud to a room soon emptied of glassy-eyed legislators and spectators alike.

[35] The most detailed account, although based almost entirely on contemporary sources, is Denna Frank Fleming's *The United States and the League of Nations* (New York, 1932).

[36] Borah opposed Old Guard moves to name Boies Penrose chairman of the Senate Finance Committee, indicating he might make an all-out fight against the appointment. When he ultimately voted for Penrose, charges were made that it was in return for satisfaction on the Foreign Relations Committee. Borah himself later confimed the rumors. "My real purpose in making this fight," he wrote, "was to bring about a more favorable Foreign Relations Committee so when they agreed to put [Hiram] Johnson on . . . the matter was adjusted." Borah to Claudius O. Johnson, December 11, 1935, Box 392, Borah Papers.

At last even the committee clerk sidled out "to attend to some mail," leaving the chairman to drone on in solitude.[37]

Some of the testimony proved valuable for Wilson's opponents. Secretary of State Robert Lansing caused a stir when he disputed the view that Japan would have refused to join the League had the Shantung cession been denied them.[38] True or not, his statement delighted the irreconcilables because it tended to validate their allegations that the entire peace settlement represented a cynical division of spoils over which the President had needlessly compromised his stated ideals. Wilson's subsequent denial of Lansing's estimate merely added to the disorder. The President served his own cause badly when he met with the committee. He allowed himself to be drawn into a semantic quibble over the difference between "legal" and "moral" commitments in Article 10, which clarified nothing.[39] In a three-way exchange between the President, Borah, and Hiram Johnson, Wilson also made the shocking assertion that he knew nothing, officially or personally, of the Allied secret treaties before he reached Paris.[40] Few believed him—with good cause—for he had been advised of them as early as the spring of 1917, and the Bolsheviks had published the ones to which Russia had been a party.[41]

[37] Fleming, *League of Nations*, 294–95.

[38] *Senate Documents*, 66th Cong., 1st Sess., No. 10, pp. 145–46, 1161–1291. Lansing's testimony also revealed how little he had participated in League matters. A later appearance of William C. Bullitt was even more damaging. Bullitt quoted Lansing as having said that "the great powers have simply gone ahead and arranged the world to suit themselves." Somewhat irrelevant to the League itself, such testimony created an aura of "exposures."

[39] For an analysis of the confusion over Article 10, see Roland N. Stromberg, *Collective Security and American Foreign Policy: From the League of Nations to NATO* (New York, 1963), 28–39.

[40] *Senate Documents*, 66th Cong., 1st Sess., No. 10, pp. 520–27.

[41] Edward M. House told Breckenridge Long that Arthur Balfour, British Foreign Secretary, had informed Wilson orally of the treaties in House's presence. See Diary 7, p. 222 (Entry dated November 29, 1924,

The Senator by no means exhausted his energies at hearings even though the patience he showed toward the lengthy parade of witnesses was foreign to his temperament. Continuing his anti-League speechmaking and correspondence, in his spare time he began baiting members of his own party. Several times threatening to break his agreement with Lodge, the Idahoan sporadically interfered with and derided the latter's progress in constructing the array of reservations which was to be used against Wilson's League. In July, for instance, Borah flatly denounced the formulation of reservations as a fraud designed to "get votes." He said he agreed with the Democrats that reservations were superfluous; all that mattered was acceptance or rejection.[42] He was, as usual, burdensome to the party leadership.

Borah displayed an uncharacteristic personal ferocity in his relations with Will Hays, chairman of the Republican National Committee. Hays, for whom Borah's endorsement had been a key factor in acquiring his position, tried desperately to avoid a party split over the League.[43] His job's very nature required straddling, yet this seemed to incense Borah who bombarded him with demands to take a position against the organization. Hays tried to placate the Senator by writing him that the League was an "American question" rather than a party matter. All issues were "American questions," Borah scoffed, and he asked Hays "in the name of clean, open manly politics," to "say something."[44] He later referred to "such miserable, cowardly, white-livered, contemptible crawling" as incomprehensible, vowing to have no dealing with Hays until the latter placed himself "on the side

---

but inserted in 1919 diary), Breckenridge Long Papers, Library of Congress, hereinafter cited as Long Papers.

[42] *Congressional Record*, 66th Cong., 1st Sess., 3141–45.

[43] Seward W. Livermore, *Politics Is Adjourned: Woodrow Wilson and the War Congress, 1916–1918* (Middletown, Conn., 1966), 107–109.

[44] Borah to Hays, June 14, 1919, Box 550, Borah Papers.

of the American Republic." "Treason," he added, "is just the same to me whether it comes under the name of Democrat or Republican."[45] Borah approached true happiness when flagellating his own party.

Aside from his few apostasies, the Idahoan cooperated with Lodge as well as anyone could have expected. Temporarily abstaining from his repeated statements as to the hypocrisy of qualifying the League, he helped to formulate the Foreign Relations Committee majority report which contained forty-five textual amendments and four reservations. A condensed version of this document became known as the "Lodge reservations," and purportedly it safeguarded American interests jeopardized by the proposed League. Borah also campaigned actively. When the President embarked on an appeal to the people in September, the Idahoan and others followed in his wake denouncing the League. And, whereas Borah returned to Washington ready to engage in the final struggle, the rigors of public campaigning proved too much for the aging, always-frail President, who was stricken ill on the cross-country trip. Wilson's illness incapacitated him through the critical stages of the League fight.

Voting on the treaty began after several weeks of proposals and counter-proposals, during which time the "Lodge reservations" passed the Senate.[46] Borah, having supported the reservations as agreed, now began ridiculing them as he had in the past. He argued that the only question worthy of consideration was whether to go into the League or stay out. Reservations of any kind were worthless decorations, he said, and he openly implied the political purposes behind

[45] Borah to Beveridge, June 27, 1919, *ibid.*
[46] On November 10, Borah offered his own reservation on Article 10. Calling for a specific disavowal of any obligations, moral or legal, it lost by a vote of 68 to 18. Lodge, *The United States and the League of Nations*, 178.

them.[47] He spoke dramatically, if at excessive length. But it was unlikely that any speech could have altered a single vote by this time.

Later that day, November 19, two votes were taken on the treaty, one with the "Lodge reservations" attached and one on the unamended version. Both failed of passage. The irreconcilables—fourteen Republicans, two Democrats— joined with the opposition to each proposal. They also co-operated with Lodge in preventing consideration of the treaty with the "Hitchcock reservations," these last comprising an effort to attract moderates from both camps. An ecstatic Borah hailed the day's work as the greatest triumph for the United States since Robert E. Lee surrendered his sword at Appomattox Courthouse.[48]

No one understood more clearly than Borah, despite his gleeful proclamation, that the victory represented a battle, not the war. The Senate, which had adjourned after the voting, began its second session less than two weeks later on December 1. Talk of compromise abounded as many senators returned convinced that the earlier deadlock had gone over badly with the public. The irreconcilables excepted, every senator had spoken favorably of the League in some form, and members of both parties announced their determination to prevent personal and political biases from killing the treaty. Borah grew particularly apprehensive when pro-Leaguers initiated a series of bipartisan meetings aimed at clearing away the obstacles to accommodation.

In one of the first such instances during the treaty fight, mild-reservationist Republican senators began hectoring Lodge to do something constructive.[49] Having no interest in the majority leader's personal antagonisms and with their own

[47] *Congressional Record*, 66th Cong., 1st Sess., 8781–84.
[48] Thomas A. Bailey, *Wilson and the Peacemakers* (New York, 1947), Part 2, pp. 193–94.
[49] Garraty, *Lodge*, 384.

pro-League constituents to think of, they demanded that he participate in the search for a way out of the impasse. Lodge responded, although his purposes now seem obscure. Perhaps he was genuinely interested in compromise; it is just as likely, however, that he sought merely to avoid accusations of obstructionism. Two considerations seem to have dictated all his moves. First, whatever else happened, he wanted to keep the party intact. Second, if the League went through, he wanted the Republican Party to receive credit for "sanitizing" it; should it fail, he wanted the blame cast upon the Democrats. Lodge's actions suggest his readiness to do anything—provided that these demands were met.

Borah anticipated complications. Everlastingly suspicious of Lodge, he feared the majority leader would take whichever course appeared politically expedient. One might depend upon Lodge in his relations with the President, for the Bostonian's personal animosity offset his tendency to equivocate. But what if members of his own party subjected him to enough pressure? Unwilling to find out, Borah moved swiftly to head off any possible "arrangements." He intended playing upon Lodge's greatest worry, the threat of party schism.

The bipartisan committee had scheduled a meeting for the afternoon of January 23, 1920. After summoning the others irreconcilables, Borah notified the majority leader that he would find it more beneficial to meet with them instead of the moderates. Lodge, foreseeing something drastic, called off his planned session. Accounts of what happened in the confrontation between them differ only in emphasis.[50] Borah told Lodge that if he made any concessions beyond the origi-

[50] Lodge's account of the meeting, in *The United States and the League of Nations*, 194, is much less colorful than the one Borah gave Thomas A. Bailey in 1937. See Bailey's *Wilson*, 230–31. According to Borah's version, a frightened Lodge meekly submitted to the Idahoan's bullyragging. Lodge's biographer seems justified in writing that the meeting probably was "less dramatic than Borah described it, but rather more heated than Lodge indicated." Garraty, *Lodge*, 386.

nal reservations bearing his name, the irreconcilables would bolt his stewardship and demand his resignation as majority leader. The discomfitted Bostonian replied that he had no intention of conceding anything "essential." This may have been true.

Lodge's assurances carried little weight with Borah. On the next day, he wrote the majority leader warning him against appeasement. Lodge previously had said "his" reservations were the "irreducible minimum" his party would accept. If so, Borah asked, upon what basis were they now negotiating? Anything involving further compromise would result in his defection from the Senate leadership. Borah also stated, "I must refuse even by implication to seem to go along with an organization which according to its own announcement is now engaged in compromising American honor and security. I propose to appeal from the organization to the voters."[51] The Senator knew which of the organization-minded Lodge's nerves to pinch.

The Idahoan later wrote that he believed the treaty would have gone through save for his actions.[52] More likely, he simply confirmed what Lodge already assumed. All through the treaty fight the majority leader showed more deference to the irreconcilables than their numbers would seem to have warranted. Their strength lay in their determination to defeat the League, whatever the consequences. In contrast, Republican moderates, lacking real leadership or direction, muddled about, wavering between devotion to ideals and loyalty to party; in the end they counted for little. The outcome might have been different had the mild reservationists exerted anywhere near the grit and cohesiveness exhibited by the irreconcilables. As it was, only a handful of men, through

[51] Borah to Lodge, January 24, 1920, Box 198, Borah Papers.
[52] Borah to Pittman Potter, July 19, 1929, Box 720, *ibid.*

their willingness to carry out their threats, succeeded in pulling the entire weight of the party toward their side. Given Wilson's intransigence and the personal factors involved, Borah, Johnson, and the others dictated to the majority leader as though they were the majority. Borah as much as any man deserves the credit—or blame—for the League's defeat.

The final vote on the treaty, taken on March 19, 1920, was anticlimactic. Put forward this time with an amended version of the "Lodge reservations" affixed, it stood little chance as the administration strove feverishly to hold wobbling Democrats in opposition. Some defected, enough remained to combine with the irreconcilables in blocking approval.[53] Although no one knew it then, this was to be the last time that the Senate voted on the treaty containing the League of Nations covenant.

The campaign for League membership foundered because a particular set of circumstances existed. This alone permitted the irreconcilables to wield such influence. Had the President shown more flexibility, had Lodge really worked for compromise, had the moderates acted with greater determination, any of these factors or combinations of them might well have resulted in passage.[54] Instead of congratulating himself on a job well done, therefore, Borah immediately directed his attention toward the forthcoming election. Should the Democrats win, a more adaptable President might adjust the question, and it was by now obvious that Wilson's health precluded his candidacy. A Republican victory, certainly preferable to Borah, would carry no guarantees since the majority of Republicans had supported the League, albeit with "proper" reservations. Only the strongest administration

[53] Bailey, *Wilson*, 266–68.
[54] Differing interpretations of the League's defeat abound. A convenient sampling of the literature can be found in Ralph A. Stone (ed.), *Wilson and the League of Nations: Why America's Rejection?* (New York, 1967).

pressures had prevented enough Democrats from accepting these qualifications, a deterrent which would cease to exist under a Republican President. Neither prospect enraptured the Senator. As he said, treason was the same to him regardless of which party label it wore.

CHAPTER IV

New Directions

F OR eight long years denied the power to which they had become accustomed but encouraged by the congressional elections of 1918, the Republicans anticipated victory in 1920. Everywhere signs proclaimed the American public's disillusionment with the war, the peace, and "Wilsonism" in general. Only the threat of schism barred Republican paths. Although Roosevelt was dead and the old Progressives grown tame, the League issue might yet result in crippling defections if mishandled. Many regulars looked upon the League as a nuisance meriting attention solely in terms of how many votes it would gain or lose. Compared to winning an election such matters were "problems," to be avoided if possible, compromised if not.[1] With the memories of 1912 still vivid, the situation was ripe for exploitation and Borah intended making

---

[1] Boies Penrose, for instance, wanted to run on a foreign policy plank consisting of one word—"Americanism." He said he did not know what it meant exactly, but he promised it would be "a damn good issue to get votes in an election." Talcott Williams, "After Penrose, What?", *The Century* (November, 1922), 54.

the most of it. He and the other bitter-enders, greatly out-numbered, held as their trump card their apparent willingness to split the party during an election year.

For the first time in a long while, one of the Republican candidates commanded the Senator's unreserved loyalty. Hiram Johnson, the California progressive, held similar views on many domestic matters and was as irreconcilable an opponent of the League as Borah himself. Impetuous, eccentric, inclined toward demagogy, Johnson's popularity rested with German and Irish ethnic groups, anti-Leaguers in general, some of the former Bull Moosers, and the Hearst press.[2] Borah had written Johnson, early in March, that he would "go out at once under your orders to any field you suggest" to promote the latter's candidacy.[3]

While campaigning for Johnson, Borah set about destroying the reputations of two other Republican hopefuls, General Leonard Wood and Governor Frank O. Lowden of Illinois. He publicly denounced their excessive campaign expenditures and accused both of trying to "buy" the nomination.[4] Regarding Wood's conduct, Borah wrote to Edward C. Stokes, a former governor of New Jersey, that a man mutually known to them as reliable had told the Senator of having seen a check for $200,000 which had been sent to one state "for the purpose of being used with the press."[5]

Borah found Wood and Lowden objectionable, not only because of their financial indulgences, but more because neither would repudiate the League of Nations. He went all out to defeat them. Hammering away at what he grandiosely referred to as a "saturnalia" of corruption, the Idahoan called

[2] Mark Sullivan, *Our Times* (6 vols., New York, 1935), VI, 42–43.
[3] Borah to Johnson, March 2, 1920, Box 199, Borah Papers.
[4] See Willam T. Hutchinson, *Lowden of Illinois; The Life of Frank O. Lowden* (2 vols., Chicago, 1951), II, 430ff.
[5] Borah to Stokes, March 24, 1920, Box 200, Borah Papers.

for a Senate investigation of campaign spending.[6] Subsequent revelations proved extremely damaging to both candidates, especially to Lowden in whose case there were allegations of direct bribery. Harry M. Daugherty, Warren G. Harding's campaign manager who was to become Attorney General, later told journalist Mark Sullivan that he believed Lowden would have won the nomination except for the scandal over fiscal irregularities Borah helped expose.[7]

The first real struggle in the convention took place over the foreign policy plank. In the platform subcommittee designated to write it, the three senators, Borah, Frank Brandegee, and Medill McCormick, argued for rejection of the League, threatening to bolt should their demands go unheeded. Opposing them stood a faction equally determined to secure a commitment to the organization with "proper" reservations. Led by the former senator from Massachusetts, W. Murray Crane, the pro-League wing included among others senators Frank B. Kellogg, Porter McCumber, and Irvine Lenroot. Crane protested it would be a grave mistake either to reject the League outright or to straddle the issue. He favored membership on principle and believed it would help the party at election time. "Uncle Murray" Crane, in no mood to equivocate, scorned threats of a bolt. "If there is going to be a split in the party over the treaty," he said, "let it come now."[8]

In between the opposing factions scudded those Republicans chiefly concerned with preventing disunity. Most of them had sanctioned a league, with various degrees of enthusiasm, but recoiled at the thought of its jeopardizing an election victory. Henry Cabot Lodge, personally willing to trim in any direction, spoke for this group. Having worked long and hard to keep the party together through the fight

[6] New York *Times*, March 27, 1920.
[7] Sullivan, *Our Times*, 6, 45.
[8] New York *Tribune*, June 10, 1920.

against Wilson, Lodge did not care to have his achievement nullified at the conventon. As before, the bearded scholar thought he had more to fear from the "bitter-enders" than from League advocates. He veered in their direction accordingly, going so far on one occasion as offering to obstruct the convention's acceptance of the "Lodge reservations."[9]

An implacable Crane refused surrender. For once the pro-Leaguers were prepared to match the determination of the irreconcilables—or so it appeared. They contended that the party would gain more votes by endorsing the League than it would lose even if the irreconcilables bolted. Besides, what could the bitter-enders do? Support a Democratic Party solidly committed to League membership? Not likely. For three days the struggle went on with neither side conceding and the straddlers searching for a way out. At last the acceptance of a compromise plank presented by the New York lawyer and congressional candidate Ogden Mills broke the standoff. Written weeks earlier by Elihu Root, the plank was a masterpiece of ambiguity. Historian Thomas A. Bailey has accurately likened the document to a fraudulent contract in which the fine print retracts everything appearing before it.[10] Neither Borah nor Crane had achieved their aims.

Subsequent accounts present the Root formula as a kind of *deus ex machina* permitting both sides to save face.[11] Root's reputation and his facile pen notwithstanding, such an interpretation exaggerates his contribution. Almost all the individuals who took part in the discussions had survived many conventions where noncommittal planks were a stock-in-trade. Any of them could have written a similar, if less gracious, statement had he cared to do so. The agreement over Root's formula represented concessions already made.

[9] New York *Times*, June 11, 1920.
[10] Bailey, *Wilson*, 302.
[11] *Ibid.*, 301; Fleming, *League of Nations*, 452; Jessup, *Root*, II, 452; and McKenna, *Borah*, 169.

According to a political aide, Birch Helms, who accompanied Crane throughout the convention, the pro-Leaguers came near forcing their position over the irreconcilables' objections. Then Kellogg, who had promised to back Crane down the line, wavered and deserted him at a crucial moment. Other defections followed Kellogg's until an isolated Crane had to accept the compromise. Helms attributed Kellogg's retreat to Medill McCormick. Supposedly, the Minnesotan had buckled when McCormick began using his newspaper connections to initiate a vendetta against him.[12]

Helms' account is uncorroborated but plausible. Statements made at the time reinforce his assertion that Crane almost won,[13] and Borah's reaction to the affair adds further substantiation. Having outwardly suffered a defeat, since he had committed himself to unqualified rejection of the League, Borah greeted the results as a victory. Replying to Hiram Johnson's inquiry as to whether "something may have been put over on us," he wrote with unconcealed elation that had Johnson been there with Crane and "those behind him," he would agree with Borah that there could be "no doubt as to who won the fight."[14]

Next the convention began choosing a candidate. Borah tried to advance his friend's cause against disheartening odds; Johnson's popularity eluded most delegates. The convention manifested little discernible ardor for progressivism in the first place, and the Californian's personal vagaries further limited his appeal. Party regulars, distrusting his unorthodoxy, looked with disfavor upon a man who had once committed the unpardonable sin of bolting the organization. Johnson, at the

[12] Birch Helms to Calvin Coolidge, October 30, 1923, Series 1, CF 712, Coolidge Papers, Library of Congress, hereinafter cited as Coolidge Papers.

[13] Fleming, *League of Nations*, 452.

[14] Johnson to Borah, June 22, 1920 and Borah to Johnson, June 24, both in Box 199, Borah Papers.

peak of his strength, ran a very poor third behind Wood and Lowden.

The two front-runners nullified one another. Wood took an early lead in the balloting but fell short of obtaining the votes necessary for the nomination. Then, when Lowden began moving up, the convention headed into deadlock. Party leaders began casting about for a compromise candidate. The Idahoan had little to do with subsequent bargaining beyond insisting that the party nominate a man with "clean hands." He sent men equipped with megaphones into the hotel lobby at one point to announce a meeting for the purpose of "preventing the sale of the United States."[15] But his voice was of small consequence at this stage.

The story of Warren G. Harding's emergence as the party's choice is a complex one. Recent scholarship has dispelled the myth of a monolithic cabal, smoothly pulling strings from a "smoke-filled room," foisting its choice upon an unsuspecting convention.[16] The party captains, the senators, and the "bosses," disagreed among themselves as violently as had the delegates on the convention's floor. Nor did they pull him out of a hat; he and the men around him had peddled his "availability" for years.[17] His chances at first remote, the impressive-looking, affable Harding profited from the inability of the leading candidates to reach accommodation. He was indeed a compromise—in some ways compromised—candidate.

Borah surveyed the outcome with mixed emotions. His

[15] McKenna, *Borah*, 170.

[16] Wesley M. Bagby, *The Road to Normalcy* (Baltimore, 1962), Chap. 3. See also Andrew Sinclair, *The Available Man; The Life Behind the Masks of Warren Gamaliel Harding* (New York, 1965), Chap. 9.

[17] "Standpatters are still fussing around somewhat with Harding of Ohio," wrote Harold L. Ickes in 1919, "but I think they are having difficulty in cultivating Harding sentiment." Ickes to Chester N. Rowell, June 5, 1919, Box 7, Harold L. Ickes Papers, Library of Congress, hereinafter cited as Ickes Papers.

efforts in behalf of Johnson and rejection of the League had failed, of course, and he thought Harding a sorry presidential aspirant. But the Idahoan had fared reasonably well under the circumstances. Compromise over the League spared him from carrying out his threat to bolt the party, while even Harding's nomination had its cheerful side. Though conservative on most domestic affairs, Harding had vacillated between the strong reservationists and the irreconcilables on the League question. The ambiguity of both platform and candidate in truth meant that little had been settled one way or another. Harding's paucity of strong convictions left the problem now turning on which individuals or groups would influence his campaign and, hopefully, his administration. Borah tried to affect the situation by withholding his support until the candidate established a satisfactory position.

From the standpoint of party solidarity, Harding could not have been a better nominee had Root created him along with the League plank. Vague, amiable, but possessing what Hiram Johnson described as an "infantile cunning," Harding by nature was a straddler and a nonpareil at delivering pompous speeches unembarrassed by content.[18] The candidate immediately began condemning "Wilson's League," yet he purposely remained unintelligible as to where he stood on a league with "proper" reservations. He developed the practice of referring favorably to an "association of nations" as the campaign went on, although no one knew just what he was talking about (including perhaps Harding himself).[19]

Friends and enemies of the League grew ever more frustrated over the candidate's equivocations. Each side prayed that he dissembled out of concern for party solidarity but would declare eventually the "right" position. Visitors coming away from Harding's side invariably believed he shared their

[18] Johnson to Raymond Robins, January 9, 1921, Box 17, Robins Papers.
[19] New York *Times*, August 29, 1920.

sentiments, whatever they might be. Speculation mounted through the summer of 1920 as Borah received frequent though conflicting reports about where the nominee's "real" sympathies lay.[20] The Senator privately had reason to think that in the end he would come out against the League. Frank Brandegee notified him soon after the convention that Harding had made a statement assuring his opposition at a meeting at Lodge's house. Besides the host, those present were Senator Reed Smoot of Utah and Brandegee. The candidate had said to them, "As to foreign relations, I suppose we can regard the treaty and the covenant as dead." "To this we all agreed," the senator from Connecticut told Borah in what may be construed as a significant commentary on Lodge's attitude at the time.[21]

Harding's deference to Philander C. Knox on foreign policy also gave cause for optimism. Borah trusted the irreconcilable Knox would immunize the candidate against pro-League heresies. Harding had written Knox late in June, that he would call upon the ex-Secretary of State for "suggestions and advice." On August 10, Knox received the first of several invitations to confer with Harding at the latter's home in Marion, Ohio.[22] Borah, in subsequent months, tried to secure for Knox the post of Secretary of State.

Good omens aside, the Senator found himself in an increasingly awkward predicament. Johnson and the other

[20] Harding possessed an ability, little short of amazing, to convince his listeners that their views were in complete accord. In July, Hiram Johnson reported that Herbert Hoover, a League advocate, believed Harding's position exactly the same as his own. Weeks later, Johnson said Albert D. Lasker had informed him that the candidate was "100 percent" opposed to a League. Johnson to Borah, July 1 and August 26, 1920, Box 199, Borah Papers.

[21] Brandegee memorandum, dictated on June 18, 1920, to Borah's clerk M. P. McCall, *ibid.*

[22] Harding to Knox, June 24 and August 10, 1920, Letterbook 21, Philander Chase Knox Papers, Library of Congress, hereinafter cited as Knox Papers.

bitter-enders had joined the campaign, despite their misgivings, to better influence the candidate. This policy had its own shortcomings—Harding's maddening vagueness had brought Johnson to the verge of apoplexy—but had the effect of isolating Borah.[23] Collectively formidable, the irreconcilables had to be treated cautiously. Alone the Idahoan could expect to exert no measurable influence on the election returns, and he personally doubted the League issue would make very much difference.[24] Persuading himself, therefore, that Harding's ambiguous statements about the organization constituted the rejection he sought, Borah announced he could support the candidate in good conscience.[25]

Pro-League Republicans, who themselves drew little comfort from Harding's balancing act, tried pulling him into their camp. On October 14, the famous "Appeal of the Thirty-One" appeared. This was a manifesto advising the public that a vote for Harding would "most effectively advance the cause of international cooperation to promote peace."[26] Drawn by Root (certainly the appropriate one to decipher the convention plank he had written), signed by a group of prominent Republicans, the "Appeal" blamed the League's defeat on Wilson's rigidity and the controversial Article 10. It implied

[23] In response to Johnson's demand for a statement of his position, the Ohioan replied that he would "maintain perfectly safe ground on which all Americans who want to be Republicans may find it possible to stand." Johnson to Robins, August 24, 1920, Box 16, Robins Papers. See also Harding to Beveridge, September 20, 1920, Box 221, Beveridge Papers.

[24] Borah to Munsey, October 24, 1920, Box 200, Borah Papers.

[25] New York *Times*, October 8, 1920. Harding's Des Moines speech, in which he stated "it is not interpretation but rejection that I am seeking," ostensibly led to Borah's approbation. As usual talking about "Wilson's League" and Article 10, Harding did not preclude a "Republicanized" organization. In the same address, he repeated his promise to work toward an "association of nations" after consulting the "best minds" available. For Borah it was clearly an interpretation of convenience inasmuch as he had consistently maintained that *any* version of *any* international organization was unacceptable.

[26] *Ibid.*, October 15, 1920.

that a victorious Harding would lead the United States into a "safe" league after excising the covenant's objectionable features.[27] Harding failed to confirm or deny this contention openly.

Borah responded placidly to the "Appeal." He had known all along that many Republicans favored membership in a qualified league; their current gesture merely confirmed his fear that the matter would remain unsettled no matter who won. The Idahoan wrote that should the Democratic candidate, James M. Cox, stress the idea that both parties favored a league with the choice being whether "we shall have a Wilson league or a league drawn by Root, [Paul] Cravath, and [George W.] Wickersham and a few other Wall Street attorneys," it would make a "considerable" dent in Harding's majority.[28] That Harding would obtain a majority Borah took for granted.

The Senator interpreted the elections correctly. Wilson had appealed in January for a "solemn referendum" on the League, but nothing of the kind resulted. The reaction to postwar economic dislocations, labor troubles, race troubles, the effects of the "red scare," Wilson's alleged pro-British views, and countless other factors contributed to the Republican landslide. Cox, whose platitude count almost matched Harding's, damaged his own cause by trying to walk half-in, half-out of Wilson's shadow. All these elements would have muted the election as a referendum had the Republicans run in flat opposition to the League. As it was, Harding's inscrutability, the "Appeal," and Cox's steady retreat from a

[27] Herbert Hoover had extracted a promise from Harding to stand behind the "Appeal." Elihu Root to Robert S. Brookings, October 23, 1920, Box 138, Elihu Root Papers, Library of Congress, hereinafter cited as Root Papers. See also William Allen White to Borah, March 31, 1922, Box 224, Borah Papers. Harding himself continued beclouding the issue by failing to distinguish between *the* League with reservations and an entirely new "association of nations."

[28] Borah to Munsey, October 24, 1920, Box 200, Borah Papers.

firm stand on the League as originally drawn rendered the voters' alternatives practically meaningless.[29]

The election left unclarified the Republican attitude toward a world organization. Borah and Johnson naturally interpreted the returns as an emphatic rejection, but pro-League Republicans maintained the opposite. They argued that the public simply had indicated it preferred a "Republicanized" version to the one Wilson advocated. Harding proved just as elusive after the election. Though he declared *the* League "dead," he refused to say whether he meant the covenant unamended or the organization in any form.[30]

Harding had promised to consult the "best minds" in constructing his administration's foreign policy. Aside from the implication that he lacked definite views personally, the idea of thoughtful deliberations with leaders representing all shades of opinion had about it an air of reasonableness in refreshing contrast with Wilson's pious certainties. The President-elect did in fact confer with purveyors of every conceivable outlook during the months before his inauguration. Whether he derived anything from these consultations is uncertain; as a result the League issue hovered in susupension. He refrained from divulging anything even remotely approaching a commitment.[31]

Well-known for his "flexibility," Harding over the years had shown a fitful interest in foreign affairs. An unusual amount of speculation arose, therefore, over his appointing a Secretary of State. A vigorous Secretary, many people believed, might well dominate the making of foreign policy. Though unverified, stories spread that only two men, Philander C. Knox and Charles Evans Hughes, received serious consideration. The choice between them appeared crucial

[29] But see Vinson, *Referendum*, Chaps. 8 and 9, for an opposing view.
[30] New York *Times*, November 5, 1920.
[31] See New York *Times* and New York *Tribune*, December 7, 11, 14, 1920.

because of Knox's irreconcilability and Hughes' pro-League sentiments.[32] Borah almost certainly made a case for the Pennsylvanian in a meeting with Harding on December 6.[33] He seemed under the impression several days later that the question was whether Knox would accept the offer when tendered him.[34] The President-elect's naming of Hughes sorely discouraged the Senator, and Herbert C. Hoover's inclusion in the cabinet meant that two of its strongest members had endorsed a qualified League.

It is clear in retrospect that Borah attributed too much importance to the matter of cabinet selections. Because he and Hughes seldom agreed on foreign policy, the latter's appointment did represent a distinct loss. Regarding the League, however, Borah exaggerated Hughes's significance. Harding, forewarned by the irreconcilables, stood completely firm on one subject; he had no intention of beginning his administration with the kind of destructive fight which had taken place in 1919–20.[35] Should this occur, it would be impossible to maintain the facade of party unity forged in opposition to the Democrats. However much men like Hughes and Hoover might have wished to join the League, this could be accomplished only by a strong executive at the cost of a bitter struggle. Neither Harding nor other party leaders were anxious to pay the price.

The Senator probably realized that Harding lacked the will

[32] Root, mentioned as a possible candidate, apparently eliminated himself when he took issue with Harding's statement that the League was dead. New York *Times*, November 23, 1920.

[33] *Ibid.*, December 7, 1920.

[34] Salmon O. Levinson to Borah, December 13, and Borah to Levinson, December 14, 1920, Box 208, Borah Papers.

[35] Henry C. Beerits, "The Separate Peace with Germany, the League, and the Permanent Court of International Justice," Box 172, Charles Evans Hughes Papers, Library of Congress. Under Hughes's supervision, Beerits in the mid-1930's prepared a number of memoranda on various phases of Hughes's career. This collection will hereinafter be cited as Beerits Memorandum, with specific title.

to risk such an encounter, yet his anxieties remained acute. He now feared that the pro-Leaguers, operating by indirection, would lead the nation in through what he referred to as the "back door."[36] With a zeal bordering on obsession, the Idahoan kept a constant watch to guard against this danger. Any move by the new administration so much as hinting of the League's existence—to Borah that fatal "first step"—automatically would bring down his considerable ire. As a further precaution, he set about erecting positive safeguards to make certain the door could not be breached.

II

During the treaty fight, Wilson had warned that the alternative to the League would be a chaotic world in which every nation must remain armed and ready for the next conflict. A sobering prophecy, coming as it did at the conclusion of "a war to end wars," yet subsequent events seemed to bear out its validity. Japanese-American relations had deteriorated steadily since the peace conference, raising the possibility of a confrontation in the Far East. The war-heated friendship of the United States and Great Britain had cooled to the point where talk abounded of a naval race between them. That Great Britain and Japan were allied by the Treaty of 1902 (renewed in 1911) further complicated matters. The postwar world in general sorely disappointed the American public. Still unfocused, the demand arose that something, anything, be done to check the drift toward international anarchy.[37]

Borah and the other irreconcilables, who had scoffed at Wilson's apocalyptic visions, could not ignore what was happening. Arguments that the League *caused* heightened ten-

[36] Borah to Gustave Hiller, December 13, 1920, Box 550, Borah Papers.
[37] For a detailed discussion, see John Chalmers Vinson, *The Parchment Peace: The United States Senate and the Washington Conference* (Athens, Ga., 1955), 43–49.

sions became progressively more untenable, whatever the organization's defects. The bankruptcy of the irreconcilable position lay in its failure to offer any constructive program at all, apparently depriving the United States of any alternative to preparedness for future struggles. Their hostility to all proposals offered justification for the complaint that they were irresponsible as well as irreconcilable.

The League's activities grew especially forboding. Bitter-enders had said it would be a superstate destructive of national sovereignty and a cause of incessant warfare. These allegations thus far had proven baseless. Indeed, by the fall of 1920, the organization had begun discussing arms limitation, a subject which the American people found extremely attractive.[38] The Chinese and Japanese delegates at Geneva claimed that America's absence posed the greatest deterrent to arms reduction. How, they asked, could other nations undertake to diminish their strength when the world's leading power spurned cooperation? President Wilson underlined their grievance when he refused an invitation to sit in a consultative capacity, explaining that he lacked authorization to send a representative.[39]

The onus settled directly upon the irreconcilables. They had taken a vital part in blocking acceptance of the League which now loomed as the one viable approach to world peace. Granting all its drawbacks, what had they to offer in its stead besides obstructionism? Borah supplied the answer on December 14, 1920, when he introduced a Senate resolution calling on the President to invite Great Britain and Japan to a conference on naval limitation. The goal of this meeting would be an agreement reducing naval construction over the next five years to "50 percent of present estimates."[40]

[38] *Ibid.*, 45–46.
[39] New York *Times*, November 20 and 21, 1920.
[40] *Congressional Record*, 66th Cong., 3rd Sess., 310.

His proposal created an uproar. Borah's usually keen perception of the public mood had not failed him. He was afraid that discontent over foreign affairs might be channeled into a broad base of support for the League, less through the organization's attractiveness per se than because it proffered a way out of the arms competition cycle. He put forward an infinitely more alluring substitute, one which promised great rewards without concomitant obligations or responsibilities. His plan precluded entanglement; and if Great Britain and Japan were serious about arms limitation within the League, they ought to be equally serious outside of it.

The Senator had kept his own counsel before offering his resolution. He always had a fondness for the dramatic gesture and the resulting headlines. More important, shared authorship would serve his purposes badly for he had designed his proposal, at least in part, to repudiate accusations that he was a sterile wrecker. Whatever its fate, his resolution enabled him to appear as a constructive statesman, unopposed to collective action providing it entailed no alliances or binding commitments.

Borah's resolution also served notice on Harding that some elements of the Senate meant to initiate foreign policies as well as to offer advice and consent.[41] The President-elect had pledged himself to international cooperation of some sort, but understandably he held reservations about triggering a factional struggle. Given enough popular support, promoting a naval conference might be a way out of his dilemma—a way acceptable to Borah and the rest of the "battalion of death." Finally, the simple fact of debating his proposal would divert attention from the League and, perhaps, an "association" as well. The Senator in the past had employed

[41] It was, of course, obvious that President Wilson would take no action and everyone understood Borah directed his resolution toward Harding. Vinson, *Parchment Peace*, 59.

one issue to divert attention from another; this marked the first of many times he would devise positive alternatives for the same purpose.

Although the tactical consideration of overshadowing the League is clear, Borah's espousal of a naval conference nevertheless indicated a greater awareness of the need for abandoning unilateralism. The Idahoan, having compiled a record of consistent nay-saying, now appeared committed to the search for constructive solutions. Scholars have regarded his disarmament resolution as marking a turning point in his career, an interpretation strengthened by programs he endorsed later in the decade such as international economic conferences, the movement to "outlaw" war, and the Kellogg-Briand Pact.[42] Actually, Borah had experienced no conversion, for *at the time* he predicated his conduct on the assumption that a naval conference would not succeed and very likely never would convene.

The Senator assumed Great Britain or Japan, or both, would refuse to countenance naval reduction. Over the years he had reserved his greatest contempt for the two nations he proposed inviting to the conference table. Seldom passing up an opportunity to denounce them as symbols of greed and aggression incarnate, he had referred to Japan as "the most militaristic nation now in existence."[43] Borah hinted that his attitude prevailed unsoftened when he said his resolution "would develop whether Great Britain and Japan are sincere in their talk or reducing armaments" (the wording of his proposal implied that he doubted they were).[44] He wished to

[42] Borah's most recent biographer credits this "important shift in emphasis" to his disillusionment with the postwar world, see McKenna, *Borah*, 176. John Chalmers Vinson, in *William E. Borah and the Outlawry of War* (Athens, Ga., 1957), 48–49, offers a more sophisticated analysis, but accepts the idea of Borah's conversion. Both authors refer to Borah's "utopianism."

[43] Borah to Lynch, August 1, 1919, Box 550, Borah Papers.

[44] "Whereas . . . the world is informed and *expected to believe* that

offer a challenge disguised as an invitation, a challenge he thought would go unmet.[45] Convinced that both nations used the absence of the United States from the League as an excuse for rearming, he sought to expose what he considered their fundamental hypocrisy.

Borah would have attained an important victory for the irreconcilable cause if Great Britain or Japan appeared reluctant to attend a conference or attached qualifications to their participation. Anticipating that such would be the case, his first interest lay in assigning culpability. When a substitute resolution was offered which would have broadened the conference to include France and Italy, and another to extend invitations to any interested nations, he argued publicly that such proposals would diminish the chance of accomplishment.[46] He explained his true purpose in a letter to Herbert Bayard Swope. Should additional powers be called in, he wrote, there would be more chance for "delay and jugglery, and *the less opportunity to fix responsibility for delay or for defeat.*"[47] This statement provides the key to Borah's thinking.

One of the Senator's basic criticisms of the League was that the governments dominating it were imperialistic and warlike.[48] He could score his point dramatically if he could "fix

Japan sincerely desires to support a program of disarmament. . . ." (Emphasis added.) Cf., note 39. The New York *Times* reported on December 15 that other senators regarded Borah's proposal as no more than a test of good faith.

[45] Daniel F. Cohalan, a strident Anglophobe who had worked with him during the League struggle, wrote Borah that he thought "you are right in the belief that they [the British] will not at present consent to disarm." Whether Cohalan referred to a letter Borah had written him or a personal conversation is unknown. The Senator replied, in any event, that "my opinion is that you have correctly interpreted the situation." Cohalan to Borah, January 27, and Borah to Cohalan, January 29, both in Box 206, Borah Papers.

[46] *Congressional Record*, 66th Cong., 3rd Sess., 4141–45.

[47] Borah to Swope, December 31, 120, Box 215, Borah Papers. (Emphasis added.)

[48] Some contemporary newspapers noticed this apparent inconsistency.

responsibility" on those nations for the failure of disarmament. In the unanticipated event that a conference did meet and achieved results—Borah certainy did not oppose disarmament —he could then fall back on the argument that such programs rendered the League superfluous. His situation appeared impregnable whatever the outcome; all that remained was to persuade the new administration to take up his proposal.

The Idahoan's resolution encountered strong resistance in Congress despite immediate and widespread popular support.[49] Almost everyone spoke in behalf of disarmament; the matter bogged down over questions of how and when to begin the program. The incoming administration disliked being placed on the defensive even before taking office, especially since Harding purportedly had in mind a plan of his own. Most Republicans consequently extrolled the virtues of arms reduction while protesting Borah's "usurpation" of executive authority.[50] Democrats complained, accusing him of dragging a red herring across the League's trail.

Some people decried initiating a conference before the United States had attained a navy "second to none." Those advocates of a large navy who did not reject limitation altogether said that action should be deferred pending completion of the naval program begun in 1916. Once the United States

---

How, they asked, could he trust Japan and Great Britain in a disarmament program in view of his long conviction as to their treachery? C. Leonard Hoag, *Preface to Preparedness: The Washington Disarmament Conference and Public Opinion* (Washington, 1941), 35–36.

[49] For a full account of the period between introduction of the resolution and its passage, see Vinson, *Parchment Peace*, Chaps. 5–9.

[50] As to the charges of "supererogation" Borah reminded his colleagues that they had only recently concluded a long struggle to assert the Senate's independence. He professed bewilderment, tongue in cheek, that those who had so roundly condemned Wilson's arrogance, could now argue that the Senate should trail meekly along behind Harding, fearing to act "until the President-elect nods." Borah said Harding would "still be free to suggest a better and wiser program." *Congressional Record*, 66th Cong., 3rd Sess., 3320–21.

had reached naval superiority, according to this view, a proportionate reduction of all fleets would pose no threat to national security. The probability that other powers would react accordingly failed to prevent navy buffs from claiming that the best way to disarm was to rearm. Harding apparently subscribed to this position. He displayed his usual impenetrability when discussing the matter, but he seemed to favor completion of the naval program and had been a large navy proponent in the Senate.[51]

The requirements of the 1916 program called for three more years of building—an odious prospect to the Senator. It would substantiate British and Japanese contentions that the United States bore the responsibility for the arms race and disinter Wilson's case that the refusal to enter collective security arrangements meant perpetual military competition. The fact that the Naval Appropriations Bill also lay before Congress vividly posed the choice between disarmament and continued building.

Seeking to head off the appropriations bill, Borah introduced another resolution on January 25, 1921, proposing that the United States suspend its building program for six months pending an investigation as to what constituted a "modern fighting navy."[52] He based his request on recent disputes over the relative value of capital ships compared with submarines and aircraft. A number of critics had expressed doubt that capital ships (under construction at an estimated cost of $40 million each and slated to consume the greater part of appropriations) were worth the price in terms of effectiveness. Borah hoped to scuttle the building program by raising questions about the relevancy of these ships for the future. Although his resolution got nowhere, it muddied the

[51] Vinson, *Parchment Peace*, 73–74.
[52] *Congressional Record*, 66th Cong., 3rd Sess., 1996.

debates in Congress and furnished more grist for the disarmament advocates.

Borah's second resolution adds substance to the theory of an "important shift" on his part because he had voted for the building program in 1916.[53] He denied this interpretation at the time, asserting that he believed an adequate navy as important as ever before. His interest in "modern" weapons *was* more than just a ruse. The Senator during these months had conducted an extensive but clandestine correspondence (all his letters were forwarded through a third party) with Admiral William F. Fullam, an ardent exponent of airplanes and submarines.[54] And, of course, a temporary suspension in the American program furthered his plans, for no results, propagandistic or otherwise, could accrue if the United States locked itself to the 1916 formula. Strategy, rather than a change of heart, dictated his moves.

When the final session of the Sixty-sixth Congress ended inconclusively on March 4, the likelihood of getting Harding to support a conference in the near future seemed remote. Although receiving some Democratic support, Borah had to conduct one of his rare filibusters to prevent last-minute passage of the Naval Bill. And nothing Harding said or did could be construed as favoring the Senator's disarmament proposal. All seemed lost, therefore, as the new President announced a special session of Congress to convene in April. Borah prepared to reintroduce his resolution, but the additional burden of an antagonistic administration threatened to overwhelm what forces he could gather.

The Senator, meantime, had shown more effectiveness with

[53] See McKenna, *Borah*, 178, and Vinson, *Parchment Peace*, 65.
[54] Borah promised Fullam that his identity would be "kept from the public." Borah to Fullam, January 28, 1921, Box 202, Borah Papers. Later, when disarmament seemed a reality, Borah would refer to the submarine as a "hideous, hellish, barbarous instrument of warfare." Borah to C. E. Elliott, November 10, 1921, *ibid.*

the public at large. He did not create popular sentiment, surely; yet his resolution came to symbolize the desire for peace. Easily understood and apparently practical, it appeared far more tangible than the "association" Harding continued to speak about. Borah used every means at his disposal, including a vast personal correspondence, to cultivate support.[55] Usually impressive leading a cause, he doubtless enjoyed being for, rather than against, something. His image changed in a few short months from that of a truculent obstructionist to one of an aggressive champion for peace. While the administration fumbled and hesitated, he led. The groundswell of discontent he had recognized in December turned into a roar of enthusiasm for decisive action.[56]

The President momentarily showed no sign of retreating. Just the opposite. In an unusual display of lucidity he had stated his disinclination to proceed with disarmament before completion of the naval program.[57] More characteristically, he went on obfuscating about an "association" while doing nothing to implement one. But the administration found itself on the defensive by the middle of May. Public clamor grew stronger instead of abating. What could Harding do? To follow through on an association meant a repetition of the League embroglio; to stall on disarmament could prove equally damaging.

The administration forces crumbled when Harding withdrew his opposition to the Borah resolution except on the matter of "usurpation." Without his backing, Republican leaders began to waver on what was becoming a steadily more unpopular position. When it developed that enough Republicans would join with the Democrats (some of whom were simply trying to embarrass the administration) to insure pas-

[55] See Boxes 202–204, Borah Papers.
[56] Hoag, *Preface*, 103.
[57] New York *Times*, April 23, 1921.

sage, the President, realizing the uselessness of further delay, instructed the regulars to vote for it.[58] The resolution cleared the Senate on May 25 by a vote of 74 to 0.

Harding tried to salvage something from the wreckage. Administration spokesmen minimized the importance of Borah's resolution by denigrating it as superfluous, perhaps even a hindrance to steps already taken.[59] Ignoring the President's earlier statement that he opposed a conference in the near future, they affected the attitude that "supererogation" alone had been at issue. In the House, when administration managers unsuccessfully tried substituting another resolution in place of Borah's, Harding once again had to make the best of an embarrassing situation.

Immediately before the House vote, Representative Frank W. Mondell read a letter from the President stating that the administration, recognizing Congress' favorable attitude on the question, had no serious concern about "the form of expressing that attitude."[60] Unable to defeat Borah's resolution, Harding implied its irrelevance. He professed to see the proposal merely as a gesture of concurrence with present administration policy—exactly which policy he neglected to identify. Released from the onerous task of seeming to oppose disarmament, Republican regulars joined with practically everyone else in passing the Naval Bill, with the Borah Resolution appended, by a vote of 332 to 4.

The Senator's assumption that neither Great Britain nor

---

[58] Vinson, *Parchment Peace*, 90–91.

[59] *Ibid.*, Chap. 10. Vinson explores these contentions thoughtfully and is not convinced they were wholly false. Whether a conference would have been called had it not been for Borah's agitation, Vinson concludes on page 97, "is a question of motives—a field beyond the historian." Borah believed then and later that Harding was totally insincere and had simply wilted under the pressure. See exchange of letters between Borah and Frank Cobb for June, 1921, Box 203, Borah Papers. Years afterward, the Senator said Harding absolutely opposed a conference "as late as June, 1921." Borah to J. O'Brien, June 16, 1924, Box 237, *ibid.*

[60] *Congressional Record*, 67th Cong., 1st Sess., 3223–24.

Japan would consent to naval limitation had rested on sturdy foundations when he introduced his proposal. The British then were discussing resumption of construction under the capital ship "replacement program"; Japan already had begun to accelerate building.[61] During the interim, however, popular movements for limitation had made great headway in both nations and, more recently, indications of approval had appeared on official levels.[62] Borah's dislike for the governments of the two powers burned steadily, but he now came around to the opinion that disarmament could succeed if correctly guided. He sensed no danger as yet, for he thought the admininstration had capitulated. And a successful conference bid fair to push the League into obscurity as an American issue.

The Idahoan hoped that popular crusades in Great Britain and Japan would force their leaders to acquiesce, as he believed had happened in the United States. "Governments are inherently against disarmament," he wrote, "the people are unalterably for it." He warned, though, that failure was assured should Harding attempt to negotiate through "quiet, diplomatic channels." Only bold and dramatic action could capitalize on the "driving power of public opinion."[63]

Borah misplaced his concern over Harding's intentions. When the President issued invitations on July 11 to what would become known as the Washington Conference, the occasion received suitable dramatization. What Borah had not suspected was that the administration would go far beyond anything contemplated by the recently passed resolution. For months the Senator had resisted every effort to broaden the

---

[61] Harold H. and Margaret Sprout, *Toward a New Order of Sea Power* (Princeton, 1940), 123–24. See also American Ambassador to Secretary of State, January 8, 1921, State Department Decimal Files, 711.0012 *anti-war*/1044.

[62] Vinson, *Parchment Peace*, 100–102.

[63] Borah to William Allen White, July 5, 1921, White Papers.

proposed conference, whether in terms of the nations invited or the questions to be discussed. Now Harding virtually ignored the limitations of Borah's resolution. He not only extended invitations to France and Italy but enlarged the agenda to include Far Eastern matters and, implicitly, land disarmament.[64] All these additions were an anathema to the Idahoan.

Borah's initial plunge into constructive statesmanship, his so-called "conversion," had lasted almost precisely six months and ended on the day Harding announced the conference. Expressing gratification over the stress placed on arms limitation, the Senator protested, as he had all along, against widening the conference's scope. "It seems to me that the suggestion of settling the Far Eastern question in the same conference is to subordinate the question of disarmament to the settlement of the Far Eastern question," he wrote a friend, "and that question will not be settled within your time or mine." That which he had begun as a multipurpose strategic move threatened to boomerang. Although "a little embarrassed myself in view of the fact that I was the author of the resolution," he now resumed his more familiar role as critic.[65]

[64] Vinson, *Borah and the Outlawry of War*, 40.
[65] Borah to Robins, July 22, 1921, Box 17, Robins Papers.

CHAPTER V

The Washington Conference

PRESIDENT HARDING's announcement that he had sent
out informal invitations to an arms conference predictably
aroused Borah's apprehensions. He had never placed a great
deal of faith in Harding and Secretary of State Charles Evans
Hughes and their perversion of the Borah Resolution substantiated his distrust of their motives. Once again, in his
mind, sinister forces lurked at the "back door" to the League;
this time they possessed a key which he, more than anyone
else, had helped to fashion. Borah would find the Washington
Conference instructive as a fresh confirmation of the need
for eternal vigilance against those men—Democrat or Republican—who planned to subvert the national interests in
the name of world peace.

Given the information available to him, the fact that the
President had gone beyond the original resolution lent itself to two interpretations, both disturbing. Harding at best
may have been prompted exclusively by the wish to seize the
limelight. His timing suggested as much. The Borah Reso-

lution was scheduled to be signed on July 12 and yet, in what seemed a deliberate rebuff, the President had refused to wait. Borah echoed journalist Frank Cobb's hope that Harding's decision grew out of "nothing more serious than his personal vanity."[1] That was serious enough. Doubting the likelihood of naval disarmament when he had introduced his resolution, the Senator had opposed inviting other powers in order to be able to fix the responsibility for failure. Now, with arms limitation a possibility, Harding's move threatened to bury it under a welter of problems Borah thought insoluble. If the conference degenerated into a confusion of claims and counterclaims, as he believed it would, even the virtue of assigning culpability would disappear. League advocates then could use an unsuccessful conference to show that international cooperation required formal machinery.

The question which seemed even more unpropitious from Borah's standpoint was: Did the administration look upon the conference as a stepping stone to the formation of an "association of nations"? Both Harding and Hughes suggested they had some such program in mind. Since it could be assumed they had no wish to see the conference fail, why else would they invite France and Italy? And if they seriously contemplated creating an organization, however informal, they could expect to capitalize on the public support for disarmament which Borah himself had done much to create. The pressure would be intense to accept almost anything coming out of the conference, providing it accompanied even a modicum of arms limitation. As Raymond Robins warned the Senator, "You should not be forced into the position where you either lose disarmament or agree to an 'entangling alliance.'"[2]

Borah's predilections dictated his choice between inter-

---

[1] Frank Cobb to Borah, July 12, 1921, Box 203, Borah Papers.
[2] Robins to Borah, July 19, 1921, Box 202, *ibid.*

preting Harding's actions either as a blunder or as a conscious "back door" maneuver. Positive that eminent figures within the administration conspired to lead the United States into an alliance system, he announced that he would pay most careful attention to the proceedings so as to safeguard American interests.[3] This amounted, of course, to a vote of no confidence in his own party's leadership; it meant in fact that any agreement which he could construe as forming the basis of an organization or alliance would incur the Senator's disapproval. Borah hung like an albatross around Hughes's neck throughout the negotations, and on at least several occasions, the Secretary pursued tactics designed almost solely to appease or head off the Idahoan.

Borah supposed the administration's conduct to be much more calculated than it really was. What status the idea of an association of nations enjoyed in Harding's mind at the time is uncertain, but his distaste for a confrontation with the irreconcilables had not diminished appreciably. In view of the circumstances imposed by passage of the Borah Resolution, calling a conference took precedence in any case. Whether the President and Hughes intended using the meeting as a point of departure for an organization probably depended upon its outcome. Fully aware that any efforts along this line would summon the "Battalion of Death" into opposition, they most likely planned to improvise as they went along. Considerable speculation arose on this point since Harding had spoken of an association so often, but the administration restricted itself to wafting a few trial balloons which Borah invariably shot down.[4]

In contrast with Borah, who believed disarmament should be approached independently, Harding—and more particu-

[3] William E. Borah, "Snags in the Way of Disarmament," *Literary Digest*, LXX (July 30, 1921), 12.

[4] Vinson, *Parchment Peace*, 140–44; New York *Times*, November 28, 1921.

larly Charles Evans Hughes—thought that arms competition merely symbolized the deeper conflict of national interests and had to be treated in such a context. The heart of the matter was the continued Japanese expansion which endangered America's position in the Far East. Unless Japan agreed to curtail her activities or unless the United States frankly abandoned "Open Door" principles, the Secretary regarded naval disarmament as a delusion, perhaps a costly one. American-Japanese relations had reached a stage already where the chance of open hostilities could not be ruled out.

Hughes played from a weak hand. Assuming that Japan "would go to war" to assure "untrammeled access" to the mainland, he assumed as well that the United States was unprepared to present a direct military challenge.[5] At most, he could hope to attain a modification of Japanese pretensions through diplomacy and, if that were possible, a disarmament program based upon mutual recognition of each other's interests. He never supposed diplomatic exchanges alone could dissuade Japan from policies she considered vital, but the removal of "outside" pressure might lead her to "pursue her economic objectives by peaceful means."[6] Always the realist, Hughes said in effect that since the United States would not or could not prevent Japanese expansion, at least it might be rendered less obnoxious. Whatever interests the United States retained would be preferable either to war or to total exclusion from the Far East.

By itself the United States could have accomplished little

[5] Memorandum "E. L. N." (Edwin L. Neville) to Hughes, April 8, 1922, paraphrased in Hughes to Secretary of War John W. Weeks, April 11, 1922, State Department Decimal Files, 500A4/182–83. This memorandum reviewed the assumptions under which Hughes operated in constructing American policy. The United States could not hope to exert pressure against Japan, "without making Guam a first class naval base." Hughes thought this impractical; there was little chance of Congress authorizing it and even the attempt might bring on war.

[6] *Ibid.*

through mere protests; these had proven unavailing over the previous five years. Great Britain brightened the horizons, however, by indicating that she, too, found the Japanese actions tiresome and desired cooperation with the United States in the Far East.[7] The Anglo-Japanese alliance had grown increasingly uncomfortable to the British, especially in view of Japanese friction with the United States. From the American point of view, the alliance's termination would isolate Japan and conceivably render her more amenable to accommodation. In a discussion held late in June, Secretary Hughes and the British Ambassador, Sir Auckland C. Geddes, explored the potential for destroying the alliance without offending Japan.

Hughes had to proceed cautiously. Fearing the drift of events might in time lead to war, he sought to reduce the threat of a collision by assuring the Japanese that the United States understood their position. He wished simultaneously to weaken that position by ending the alliance.[8] The British, sharing these goals in the main, expressed reluctance over having it appear that they were "slapping her [Japan] in the face."[9] Since the Japanese preferred renewing the alliance and said so, Hughes and Geddes concluded that some kind of an agreement had to be offered in its stead. Ever mindful of the Senate, the Secretary flatly rejected Geddes' suggestion of a tripartite pact by explaining that the United States could not consider any arrangement even resembling an alliance. He did agree on the need for an "understanding" both to as-

[7] H. C. Allen, *Great Britain and the United States* (New York, 1955), 736.

[8] *FRUS, 1921*, II, 314–15.

[9] George F. Harvey (Ambassador to Great Britain) to Hughes, July 8, 1921, State Department Decimal Files, 500 A4/1. The phrase is from Harvey's recollection of a conversation with the King. Prime Minister David Lloyd George and Foreign Secretary Lord Curzon had told him substantially the same thing. This portion of the message not included in *FRUS, 1921*, I, 19–21.

suage Japanese feelings and to protect American interests.[10] Only after reaching such an agreement could disarmament be pursued with any reasonable hope of achievement.

For the purpose of curbing the Japanese, Hughes would have found no more ardent ally than Borah. The Senator, a long-time critic of Japan, had called repeatedly for destruction of the Anglo-Japanese alliance. He would have gone even farther than the Secretary in some ways, for he also proposed cooperation with Soviet Russia in the Far East as an additional lever.[11] But Hughes knew the Idahoan would deplore any "understanding" despite British insistence on it, lacking a formal pact, as being the price necessary for terminating the alliance.[12] Throughout the preliminary negotiations, the Secretary showed as much deference to the wishes of senators—especially Borah—as to those of any foreign power.

Hughes would have preferred arranging a conference to deal solely with disarmament had he been able to do so, while handling the problem of severing the alliance on a more informal basis. Furthermore, he had intended waiting until Harding signed the Borah Resolution before issuing invitations.[13] Independent developments within the British empire

[10] Vinson, *Parchment Peace*, 108–109.

[11] Hughes could not utilize this tool because of the administration's failure to recognize the Soviet regime. See Chap. 8 below.

[12] This was borne out when Borah criticized suggestions of a tripartite agreement as "fundamentally wrong in principle." *Literary Digest*, LXXII (September 3, 1921), 9. The Senator's objections stemmed from more than just a dislike for commitments. When the conference opened, he wrote of a "powerful influence for practically establishing a suzerainty over China," and he did not restrict his accusation to Japan. Borah to John Spargo, November 16, 1921, Box 202, Borah Papers.

[13] Hughes to Harvey, July 8, 1921, State Department Decimal Files, 500 A4/a. Hughes's message, superseded a few days later, requested Harvey to make an informal inquiry concerning the British government regarding a conference restricted to arms limitation. "For your confidential information," Hughes added, "formal invitations will probably not be sent until after Naval Bill with Borah resolution has been passed by Congress." (Since the bill had already passed, Hughes undoubtedly referred to its promulgation by the President.)

ruined the Secretary's plans and forced him into actions which undermined his efforts to conciliate potential critics.[14] The desire to achieve a successful conference more than anything else shaped his decisions, not the wish to chastize the Senate nor an overweening commitment to an association.

On a deeper level, however, Borah's fears were justified. Hughes did look toward substituting an agreement for the Anglo-Japanese alliance. Although this fell considerably short of an association, it was no coincidence that the nations originally invited were the Allied and Associated Powers of the World War. Called by whatever name—Hughes scrupulously avoided the term "alliance"—the anticipated result would be maintenance of the status quo in Asia; this was a goal Borah thought unworthy with or without a disarmament program. The Secretary wanted Japan to play according to rules; the Senator disliked the game altogether.

Hughes performed superbly, given the narrow limits within which he operated and the rise of unforeseen contingencies. By emphasizing disarmament and by including senators in the American delegation, he left Borah and others grumbling but "unable to voice effective criticism."[15] Refusing British suggestions for preliminary conferences on the specific grounds

---

[14] A sense of urgency prevailed in Great Britain because the Anglo-Japanese alliance was due for renewal and the Imperial Conference, then sitting in London, showed no appreciation of the need for delicacy. At the insistence of the Canadians, who were concerned over the implications of the alliance for themselves, the conference instructed the British Secretary for Foreign Affairs to arrange a meeting between the powers "to consider all essential matters bearing upon the Far East and the Pacific Ocean." This decision and "importunate inquiries" from the House of Commons led Prime Minister David Lloyd George to inform the American ambassador that the British had to act no later than July 11. *FRUS, 1921,* I, 18–21. Since British and American diplomats agreed on the necessity of having it appear that the conference was American inspired (to placate both the Japanese and the Senate), Hughes combined the terms of the Borah resolution with the Imperial Conference's directive and issued preliminary invitations on July 10.

[15] Hughes to Harvey, July 13, 1921, *FRUS, 1921,* I, 28.

of senatorial opposition, he continued baffling his would-be tormentors throughout the negotiations.[16] An impotent Borah's only recourse lay in trying to arouse public opinion in favor of an "open" conference so as to prevent secret consummations of the arrangements he dreaded.[17]

The Senator published an article on the eve of the first session, warning that the "cloud" of Versailles hung over the conference.[18] That treaty, he wrote, had "Balkanized" Europe. Now that the powers responsible for it had focused their attention on the Far East, could anyone expect their actions in that area to be less cynical? Borah thought not. Although the administration referred to a "peace conference," he believed it had as its ultimate purpose to divide the spoils of China on a rational basis. His attitude resembled that of the *Nation*, which branded the conference as "essentially another attempt to substitute an imperialist trust for competitive imperialism."[19]

Borah protested futilely. The overwhelming enthusiasm for anything promising peace and an end to the arms race obliterated criticism. Just as Robins had predicted earlier, danger existed that the issue could be presented in such a way as to make the choice between losing disarmament or agreeing to an "entangling alliance." The Senator did foreshadow the strategy he would employ in following months. By pairing the conference with the rejected Treaty of Versailles, he sought to arouse once again the variety of forces which had defeated the League. This time the Idahoan battled a movement whose paternity he had once claimed for himself.

[16] *Ibid.*

[17] Vinson, *Parchment Peace*, 123–24, and Borah to David Starr Jordan, October 27, 1921, Box 202, Borah Papers.

[18] William E. Borah. "The Ghost of Versailles at the Conference," *Nation*, CXIII (November 9, 1921), 525–26.

[19] Unsigned editorial, *Nation*, CXIII (September 21, 1921), 310.

II

Hughes left nothing to chance. The conference, originally scheduled to open on November 11, was held off a day while the delegations took part in an impressive ceremony at the Tomb of the Unknown Soldier.[20] President Harding spoke at the tomb, proclaiming his and his nation's dedication to peace. Observers noted the depth of emotion shown by the participants and crowd—an atmosphere which carried over to the conference's first session. William Allen White described the opening day as "the most dramatic moment I had ever witnessed."[21]

President Harding, speaking first, couched his sentiments in the same general terms he had used the previous day at the tomb. After welcoming the delegations, he reiterated his desire for permanent peace. Secretary Hughes, permanent chairman of the conference, followed. Hughes restricted the first part of his address to the bromides everyone expected him to deliver. Then, to the astonishment of his audience, he made a number of specific proposals on arms limitation which included a ten-year holiday in the construction of capital ships, the destruction of numbers of existing vessels, and the maintenance of a ratio in battleships of 5-5-3 among Great Britain, the United States, and Japan.

The manner in which Hughes presented the American program surprised all but a tiny group of insiders.[22] It had been anticipated that opening-day remarks would be limited to statements of broad purposes and that discussions of actual plans would take place later. The Secretary instead effected a coup making him the dominant figure at the conference. He had boldly asserted America's readiness to assume active

[20] New York *Times*, November 12 and 13, 1921.
[21] William Allen White, *The Autobiography of William Allen White* (New York, 1946), 598.
[22] Beerits memorandum, "Treaty for the Limitation of Naval Armament," Box 170, Hughes Papers.

leadership. His proposals, containing no subtleties open to misinterpretation, appealed deeply to the longing for real measures of disarmament. Although some of the delegations (Japan's especially) were scarcely pleased, and even though Hughes's program underwent considerable revision before its acceptance, he had made a stunning debut.

The Secretary acted as he did for several other reasons. If his plan became known before the conference opened, Borah might try regaining the initiative for himself and the Senate. Well aware of the effective use Borah had made of resolutions in the past, Hughes wished to stymie the unpredictable Idahoan. If, for example, Borah introduced a resolution embodying the administration's program or something more drastic, he could place Harding and Hughes once again in the position of tagging along behind the Senate.[23]

In a broader sense, Hughes's deportment undermined the opposition before it could mount an attack. By advancing his program in open session, by dealing exclusively with arms limitation, and by leaving no doubt as to the plan's origin, Hughes had gone far to disarm his critics. His move generated a climate of favorable opinion which helped moderate the less popular results of the meeting. Even Borah had to admit the conference "is starting off in most splendid fashion."[24] He maintained his reservations about taking up "so many [other] questions," however, because he thought they might purposely be used to obstruct progress on disarmament. And he continued to have doubts over what would be done to China as well.

The stage had been set; now the major powers turned to the more complicated task of reaching satisfactory arrangements about the Far East. Out of these deliberations, con-

[23] Merlo Pusey, *Charles Evans Hughes* (2 vols., New York, 1951), II, 464–65.
[24] Borah to Spargo, November 16, 1921, Box 202, Borah Papers.

ducted largely in closed sessions or at Hughes's home, came the most controversial settlement—the Four Power Pact.[25] The treaty provided for the maintenance of "insular possessions and insular dominions in the region of the Pacific Ocean" and for "consultation" and "communication" between the signatory powers in the event the rights of any one of them were threatened.[26] At Hughes's insistence, the treaty specifically terminated the Anglo-Japanese Alliance and included France so as to allay complaints that the United States would have to confront alone the two former allies. Borah and the other irreconcilables thought they saw in this agreement elements of an alliance which they had anticipated.

Senator Lodge presented the treaty to the Fourth Plenary Session of the conference on December 10. Reaction among senators and the public at large was almost universally favorable, with a few dissents coming from the professional irreconcilables.[27] Borah, at first claiming he needed time to study the pact before making a statement, very quickly dubbed it a "war breeder."[28] He based his opinion, he said, on the fact that the treaty carried with it the threat of military force, regardless of the nomenclature the administration employed. He did indicate that he would reserve his final judgment until such time as it became clear what would be done for (or to) China.[29]

Borah knew the Four Power Treaty's fate depended upon

[25] Vinson, *Parchment Peace*, 149–58.

[26] For the complete text of the treaty, see *Conference on the Limitation of Armament*, Senate Document 126, 67th Cong., 2nd Sess., 1614–15. The Secretary was also responsible for limiting the pact to "insular possessions" because he did not wish to have it seem that the administration either recognized or countenanced Japanese activities on the mainland.

[27] New York *Times*, December 19, 1921.

[28] Committee on General Information Report dated December 13, 1921. This committee collated press reports and surveys which it presented to the American delegation almost daily. The origins and operations of the group are treated in Hoag, *Preparedness*, Chap. 7.

[29] *Congressional Record*, 67th Cong., 2nd Sess., 231.

the results of the conference as a whole. Correctly managed —and he never doubted the political acuity of Hughes and Lodge—the issue could be put forward in such a way that detractors of any specific agreement would have to bear the onus of threatening the conference's overall work. Since part of that work included a disarmament program, there would be a great deal of sentiment for ratification of the entire package whatever its defects. To stave off such a dilemma, the Senator began questioning the adequacy of capital ship reduction by arguing that "real" disarmament went ignored.

"It is all right to scrap battleships and I am delighted that we have even made a start," he wrote, "but let us not be misled into taking a stone when we have asked for bread." Completely reversing his earlier demand that arms limitation be restricted to naval matters, Borah now complained that "submarines, poison gas and the things with which the next war will be fought and the things which will tend to bring on the next war are not being touched."[30] What he would later refer to as "sinking some obsolete battleships," he insisted, offered paltry compensation for the other arrangements being fobbed off under the cloak of disarmament.[31]

Given Borah's frame of reference, his actions displayed a certain consistency. Had disarmament been approached independently, as he insisted it should, any diminution of fleets would constitute a step forward. As only part of a series of settlements which to him included an entangling alliance and "selling out" China, capital ship reduction appeared less commendable. Two considerations intensified his feeling of being offered a "stone" instead of "bread." First, since he adhered

---

[30] Borah to Reverend E. A. Orr, December 15, 1921, Box 214, Borah Papers. It should be remembered, however, that the Borah Resolution included overall building programs. Hughes tried to extend limitation to other classifications but France, insulted by the ratio proposed for her, blocked this effort except in the case of aircraft carriers.

[31] Borah to William M. Swain, May 26, 1922, *ibid.*

to the "modern"navy concept in which battleships per se were obsolete, he felt that the United States stood to gain nothing it should not already be doing in the name of efficiency. Second, he believed Hughes and the State Department, exaggerating the threat of war with Japan, had been overly inclined to compromise American interests. "There are bureaucrats here," he wrote, "who expect to wake up any morning and hear the Japanese guns battering away at the capitol."[32]

Although Borah did his best to show that the conference was manufacturing "dynamite," Hughes had performed his work too well to provide the Senator with a plausible case.[33] Disarmament was disarmament, after all, and was it not better to accept limited progress than none whatever? The Four Power Treaty, moreover, *had* replaced the Anglo-Japanese Alliance, and the administration stoutly denied it encompassed any commitments. Borah suffered an especial disadvantage among the irreconcilables because the original disarmament resolution bore his name. The tendency prevailed to interpret his attitude as stemming in part from resentment over having been shunted aside by Harding and Hughes. Fortunately, the President came to Borah's aid, albeit unwittingly.

The affairs of state rested uneasily upon Harding's shoulders. Combining an appetite for recreational activities (he had been "cruising" during that nerve-wracking first week in July when Hughes struggled to get the conference off the ground) with a stolid indifference to most aspects of foreign affairs, the President possessed but a dim awareness of what was going on at the conference. His saving grace lay in giving Hughes pretty much of a free hand thus far, while limiting himself to "bloviating" at official ceremonies. During a press conference held on December 20, however, Harding permitted himself the luxury of answering a question about

[32] Borah to Jordan, October 27, 1921, Box 202, *ibid.*
[33] Borah to Arthur H. Vandenberg, December 19, 1921, *ibid.*

the Four Power Treaty which gave Borah and the other irreconcilables the break they had been seeking.

One of the outstanding virtues Hughes had assigned the Four Power Treaty was that it meant just what it said; he admitted to no ambiguous interpretations. Harding destroyed this claim with one poorly chosen remark. Asked whether the term "insular possessions" applied to the main islands of Japan, the President replied that it did not.[34] Since the Secretary and other members of the American delegation had stated the opposite, a position confirmed by the State Department previously, Harding's pronouncement ignited a minor furor. Despite Hughes's efforts to rectify the damage, the irreconcilables gleefully distorted the matter out of all proportion.

If the President and the Secretary of State disagreed over the treaty's meaning, critics asked, how could the Senate approve such a document? And if Hughes's assessment prevailed, did this mean, as Hiram Johnson charged, that the United States had agreed to underwrite Japan?[35] How many other parts of the treaty later would prove susceptible to differing interpretations? Perhaps there was substance in the charges that the pact involved far greater ramifications than appeared on its surface. In any event, Harding's gaffe threatened to undo Hughes's patient work as the initial enthusiasm over the treaty began dissipating. "Senate Foes Want Treaty Made Clear," the New York *Times* announced, and while it is doubtful that clarity was all they wanted, prospects for an easy passage for the first time became uncertain.

[34] State Department Decimal Files, 500 A4A/160.
[35] Committee on General Information, January 5, 1922. Johnson was ever willing to pander to anti-Japanese feelings, a popular pastime in California. Japan immediately indicated that she did not care to have her home territory included under the pact as this would imply that she occupied the same status as some nondescript island. Instead of resolving the issue, the Japanese protest added to the confusion. A compromise was reached ultimately which satisfied Japanese pride.

Criticism leveled against the Four Power Treaty opened everything to question. Though Borah's distinction between capital ship reduction and "real" disarmament aroused little interest, even the seemingly innocuous Treaty for the Limitation of Armaments (Five Power Treaty) began receiving fire. Made public on December 15, the treaty provided for the 5-5-3 battleship ratio Hughes had proposed, but this had been achieved only by compromise.[36] In return for dropping their insistence on 10-10-7, the Japanese extracted the pledge that no fortifications or naval bases would be constructed in western Pacific island possessions. Hughes had assented to this provision because he thought Congress would refuse to fortify the islands anyhow, but opponents argued that the United States had thereby surrendered its position in the Far East.

Attacks on the negotiated treaties were noisy but limited, for the most part, to such disparate groups as the irreconcilables, the advocates of a big navy, and some disgruntled Wilsonian Democrats. Still, the two-thirds rule made the situation potentially hazardous. Memories of the League's defeat lingered, and Hughes had no intention of allowing a repetition of that shambles. Prepared to debate the merits of what already had been done, he looked askance at having the administration's reputation hinge on senatorial caprice. Instead the Secretary sought to bury his antagonists under an avalanche of "achievements."

Although few senators joined Borah in advocating the restoration of complete autonomy to China, there existed a general feeling that something should be done to reaffirm Ameri-

---

[36] *Conference on the Limitation of Armament*, 1581–82. The ratio was waived in special instances, such as that of the Japanese *Mutsu*. Due to be destroyed under Hughes's program, this nearly completed ship stood as the pride of the Japanese Navy and Tokyo insisted it be retained. Italy and France accepted a 1.75 ratio each.

can concern for that much-despoiled nation.[37] With the active help of Great Britain and the acquiescence of the other delegations, Hughes negotiated the Nine Power Treaty providing for a multilateral declaration of Open Door principles. Partially designed to offset criticism that the Western powers ignored Chinese aspirations at the conference, the treaty had little practical effect other than to elevate a previously unilateral American policy to the status of an international agreement.[38] Most Americans, regarding the Open Door policy as "enlightened" in contrast to European imperialism, greeted the treaty as a victory for American diplomacy.

Hughes strove to gain other settlements for Far Eastern probems. He prevailed upon the Japanese and Chinese to reach a compromise on the Shantung question, working out an arrangement whereby Japan agreed to turn over nominal control of the area while retaining important concessions there.[39] The Secretary negotiated a treaty between Japan and the United States ending the long controversy over the island of Yap. Insignificant except as a cable station, Yap became a Japanese possession with the provision that both powers would enjoy equal rights to its facilities. Finally, resolving another dispute of long standing, the Japanese agreed to evacuate their troops stationed in Siberia since the joint Allied intervention of 1918.[40]

Hughes had amassed an impressive array of settlements with which to face the Senate. From the administration's point of view, it had made a great stride toward disarmament, destroyed the Anglo-Japanese Alliance, and relieved all the outstanding points of tension in the Far East. Best of all,

[37] Cf. note 29 above. See also Vinson, *Parchment Peace*, 171.

[38] Yamato Ichihashi, *The Washington Conference and After* (Stanford, Calif., 1928), 178–201, 248–66.

[39] Hughes had to exert considerable pressure on the Chinese to get them to agree to the Shantung settlement. See *FRUS, 1922*, I, 945.

[40] Ichihashi, *Washington Conference*, 306–39.

this had been achieved without abandoning China and without sacrificing American independence in foreign affairs. Except for Harding's unfortunate lapse, Hughes had amply covered his every move. With one ear always tuned in to senatorial rumblings, he had won formulations relatively safe from frontal assault.

The results of the conference appeared as anything but praiseworthy to Borah. He regarded the Four Power Treaty as an alliance with commitments every whit as binding as the League's, and no amount of semantic "jugglery" could convince him otherwise. More ominous still, what if this pact were only the first in a series of agreements leading to an "association"? As for Hughes's "sweeteners," Borah dismissed or downgraded them. He considered the Nine Power Treaty a meaningless sop to those wanting to do "something" for China but who were unwilling to insist upon it. Borah complained that other settlements, perhaps desirable in and of themselves, were being used to sandbag the Senate into approving the Four Power Treaty. He deemed this latter agreement sufficiently dangerous to warrant killing all the rest along with it. "I think there is only one thing to do, if it is possible to be done," he wrote, "and that is to defeat the Four Power Treaty."[41]

As the administration made ready to place the treaties before the Senate, leadership passed from the hands of Secretary Hughes to the equally capable hands of Majority Leader Henry Cabot Lodge. The man who had been instrumental in defeating Wilson's efforts to achieve world peace now endeavored to guide his own party's more modest program through the same gamut.[42] However, Lodge had much more

[41] Borah to Norman Davis, March 9, 1922, Box 215, Borah Papers.
[42] There was concern that Wilson might use what was left of his influence to defeat the Republican program, whether on principle or out of personal vindictiveness. There is no evidence to indicate that he in any way attempted to affect the voting. See Vinson, *Parchment Peace*, 189–91.

working for him, not the least of which was the dwindling number of hard-core irreconcilables. Philander C. Knox had died while others, such as Frank Brandegee, proved less intransigent as long as the League of Nations was not involved. Those who remained shouted as loudly as before but found few to listen.

Because the Four Power Treaty had aroused the most controversy, Lodge introduced it first. His strategy was simple but effective. By indicating that the failure to ratify this pact would preclude acceptance of the other settlements by Great Britain and Japan, he hoped to play upon the vast sentiment for disarmament and an end to trouble in the Far East.[43] Lodge knew many senators held reservations about the treaty itself, yet even Democrats showed an understandable reluctance to place themselves in a position where they could be charged with obstructing the administration's peace program. The Majority Leader subsequently claimed he sloughed off Democratic votes he could have gotten in order to prevent the opposition from claiming Senate approval as a bipartisan effort.[44]

The Senate spent a great deal of time debating the Four Power Pact. Little emerged either for or against it which had not received a thorough airing during the negotiations. Those denouncing the treaty repeated their charges that it represented an alliance, that it placed the United States behind Japanese aggression, and that approval would constitute a betrayal of the priceless heritage left by the Founding Fathers. The irreconcilables pictured the treaty as little more than a regional or, as Senator A. O. Stanley christened it, a

[43] One of the major sources of aggravation between Japan and the United States went all but unmentioned. Hughes had insisted from the start that immigration be excluded from negotiations because it was a "domestic" matter, see *FRUS, 1921*, I, 22. The Japanese, naturally, took this as an insult. Borah and Johnson could not exploit this very real weakness because both firmly opposed immigration.

[44] Alan Cranston, *The Killing of the Peace* (New York, 1945), 280.

"baby" League of Nations.[45] In answer to the administration's protest that the pact involved no commitments, the bitter-enders cried that its very ambiguity made it the more dangerous. Borah, comparing Article 2 of the treaty with the League's famous Article 10, found no appreciable difference. He disinterred the old argument that the "moral" commitment implicit in such a provision bound the nation in chains.[46] Indeed, had a visitor wandered into the Senate gallery while the Idahoan or one of the other irreconcilables held the floor, he might have thought they were debating the League of Nations all over again.

Lodge and other administration stalwarts, trying to head off efforts to link the treaty with the League, indulged in some fuzzy arguments for approval. On the one hand they presented it as an epochal step in international relations, while on the other, they denied it meant anything in terms of obligations and responsibilities. They even had to soft-pedal the fact that the treaty replaced the Anglo-Japanese Alliance because this assertion invariably brought up the question as to what compensations the Japanese had received. Their most telling point was that it provided the foundation upon which the other settlements rested.

From the start, some Wilsonian Democrats and the irreconcilables collaborated in trying to destroy the image of "open" diplomacy the administration had cultivated. Knowing the Four Power Treaty had been worked out in closed sessions and private meetings, Senator Hitchcock introduced a resolution asking that the Senate be given access to all material pertinent to the negotiations. Hitchcock, alluding to Harding's unfortunate misinterpretation of the treaty as an example of its ambiguity, said that clarification required an

[45] Committee on General Information, December 12, 1921. See *Congressional Record*, 67th Cong., 2nd Sess., 3232 ff., 3555 ff., 3776 ff., 3787 ff.
[46] *Ibid.*, 3613.

inspection of the collateral documents.[47] This gambit caused the administration some embarrassment; Harding felt called upon to reassure the Senate and the public that the treaty contained no secret clauses or understandings, while at the same time admitting the impossibility of complying with Hitchcock's request. Except for the pleasure of watching Lodge and Senator Oscar W. Underwood trying to explain how the negotiations could be open yet secret, opposition senators derived little mileage from the situation.[48] The public did not seem especially interested.

Borah fared somewhat better with his allegation that, dangerous though the pact appeared to be at face-value, the most important understanding reached appeared nowhere in its pages. He had secured a stenographic report of an address given before the Council on Foreign Relations by the prominent attorney Paul D. Cravath. According to the notes, Cravath had stated that members of both the American and British delegations told him that the truly significant result of the conference lay in securing an "understanding" between Great Britain and the United States directed against Japan. In view of the mutuality of British-American Far Eastern policy, this "understanding" provided for "cooperation" in preventing Japanese aggression. Now the Senator had two alliances to criticize instead of one.[49]

Borah's "revelations" caused a brief flurry of interest in the Senate and press and provided some additional fodder for the Anglophobe groups. Cravath's bumbling denials that he had ever made any such assertion, or at least could not remember any, rang hollow before the evidence.[50] That he

[47] *Congressional Record*, 67th Cong., 2nd Sess., 2587, 3233.
[48] New York *Times*, February 17, 1922; and *Congressional Record*, 67th Cong., 2nd Sess., 3547, 3715.
[49] *Congressional Record*, 67th Cong., 2nd Sess., 4119–20.
[50] Lodge read Cravath's denial of Borah's version to the Senate. *Ibid.*, 4157–58. Norman Davis wired Senator Joseph Robinson that he was

had said what Borah reported seemed incontrovertible; that he had any justification for saying it was another matter. Lodge and Underwood denied they even knew Cravath and, in any case, protested they had uttered none of the statements attributed to them. Hughes also rebutted the charge of unwritten understandings and expressed his hope that the delegates would be spared the embarrassment of such accusations in the future.[51] Considering the weakness of his case, Borah had done about as well as he could have expected.

Despite the attacks and dire warnings directed against the treaty, it passed the Senate handily.[52] Borah was one of only four Republicans to cast dissenting votes on March 24. "With the failure to defeat this treaty," Hughes exulted, "the whole opposition crumbled," and the remaining settlements went through without cavil. Except for Hearst's papers and a few others, the press commended the Republican administration for having achieved a resounding victory in the struggle for world peace.[53] And, as Harding and Hughes eagerly proclaimed, it had been gained without sacrificing American traditions.

From a longer perspective, the results of the Washington Conference seem less deserving of adulation. Described by a noted historian as a "face-saving retreat of the United States from active diplomacy in the Far East," the conference scarcely represented the dawn of a new era.[54] At best, it simply reflected public longing for peace (and of the administra-

---

"astonished" at Cravath's position and suggested that the Secretary or manager of the Council on Foreign Relations be summoned to testify as to exactly what Cravath had said. "Also, there were at least forty witnesses," he added. Copy of telegram, Davis to Robinson, March 21, 1922, in Box 215, Borah Papers.

[51] *Congressional Record*, 67th Cong., 2nd Sess., 4158.

[52] Vinson, *Parchment Peace*, 191–92.

[53] *Literary Digest*, LXXVII (April 8, 1922). The magazine's poll of 803 newspapers found that 723 favored the treaties.

[54] Samuel Flagg Bemis, *A Diplomatic History of the United States* (4th ed., New York, 1957), 696.

tion's wish to appeal to that longing); at worst, it resulted in an illusion of security which ultimately would prove expensive. Perhaps the soberest estimate came from Hughes himself, when he wrote later that they had merely provided "that for the next fifteen years we should not do what everyone knew we would not do."[55]

The outcome disgusted Borah. To him the conference's net effect was to abandon the Far East to Japan in return for a disarmament gesture. He dismissed as arrant nonsense the allusions to a "new spirit" of cooperation among the powers. "Ever since the adjournment of the Conference," he wrote in May, "there has been a determined effort in certain quarters to start these nations upon another race of competitive armaments."[56] His feelings, if they had changed at all, toward "these nations" had grown stronger than ever before. What he had conceived out of cynicism ended with his cynicism confirmed.

The Senator might justifiably have concluded that international conferences posed more threats than solutions. The administration's claim to innocence failed to satisfy him, and Hughes had demonstrated what could be accomplished through careful planning and manipulation. Immediately after the Senate passed the treaties, William Allen White had written Borah that "there is no doubt that Mr. Harding feels we are going to have conference follow conference, and lead us gradually into an association." This is precisely what the Idahoan feared.[57] As far as he could see, Republican leaders had revealed themselves perfectly willing to abandon tradi-

---

[55] Hughes to C. Bascom Slemp, secretary to President Coolidge, December 20, 1924, State Department Decimal Files, 500.A4/321. For an excellent critique of Hughes's approach to the Washington Conference, see Betty Glad, *Charles Evans Hughes and the Illusions of Innocence* (Urbana, 1966), 269–303.

[56] Cf. note 31 above.

[57] White to Borah, March 31, 1922, Box 224, Borah Papers.

tional American foreign policy, whether out of conviction or from the desire for political income.

Borah had one consolation amidst the gloom. Their reluctance to incur senatorial wrath had forced Hughes and Harding to suspend for the moment further talk of an association.[58] And, in trumpeting the conference's unalloyed success, they inadvertently strengthened Borah's hand over the long run. If individual conferences achieved such important results, did the need really exist for a permanent organization? By stressing the gains made and denying they involved any commitments or responsibilities, the administration itself helped to convince the American public that a day-to-day participation in world affairs was unnecessary. This was what the Senator had said all along.

Borah emerged from the affair chastened but unrepentant. The mutation of his disarmament resolution merely indicated the need for greater caution in the future. Although Hughes had outflanked and outgunned him this time, his use of "positive" alternatives as a substitute for bald obstructionism remained valid in principle. Desirable from a political standpoint, more effective than saying "no" to each and every other proposal, the practice would now become an integral part of Borah's repertoire over the years.

[58] See Vinson, *Parchment Peace*, 145–47.

CHAPTER VI

Reparations and the Genesis of Outlawry

ALTHOUGH disarmament and the Washington Conference dominated the headlines, Borah kept sight of the fact that the most important complex of issues—relations with postwar Europe—remained unsettled. These questions had gone into a state of suspension since the defeat of the Versailles Treaty, but their resolution could not be put off indefinitely. The League of Nations existed, as did its subsidiary commissions. Therefore, how could the United States, short of becoming entangled with the newly formed institutions, protect its interests in matters such as debts, reparations, and the resumption of peaceful intercourse with Germany? Borah found himself confronting dilemmas which, because of the suspicions he harbored for the nations involved and for the policymakers in his own government, defied solution. His conduct in this area deservedly solidified his reputation as an obstructionist, prompting him once more to retaliate with allegedly constructive proposals.

The Idahoan's response to European problems can be appreciated only within the context of his disabling "logic of events" doctrine. Any positive action in foreign affairs, regardless of origin or apparent safety, might become the harbinger of total commitment to the League. If the past had lessons to offer, and Borah thought it had, the most obvious was that involvements never liquidated themselves; they led to greater involvements. The Senator would have counseled extreme caution had he assumed the best intentions of everyone concerned. Certain as he was that powerful forces within the administration, the major political parties, and the business community stood ready to exploit the slightest misstep, Borah saw little in any proposed course save the possibility of twisting it in such a way as to forge a bond between the United States and the major powers of the League. Once their affairs became American affairs, he believed, no one could prevent alignment with the organization.

Borah looked upon the Reparations Commission as the handiest key to the "backdoor." Membership, he wrote, could involve the United States "in every conceivable question which can arise in Europe," and he thought the pro-Leaguers conspired sleeplessly to bring this about.[1] If they could link American interests to reparations, protection of those interests would require utilization of available League machinery and American formal participation would surely follow. The danger posed by the commission—that "Senegambian in the woodpile," as he put it—influenced Borah's every move.[2]

The separate treaty with Germany provided a case in point. First suggested by Philander C. Knox, though actually put together under the guidance of Charles Evans Hughes, the proposed agreement amounted to scarcely more than an abstract of the Versailles Pact with objectionable parts such

[1] Borah to Beveridge, October 3, 1921, Box 202, Borah Papers.
[2] Borah to Beveridge, June 20, 1921, Box 225, Beveridge Papers.

as the League covenant excised.[3] Its ratification would grant
the United States all the rights and privileges provided for in
the Versailles Treaty without its obligations or responsibilities.
Indeed, it contained no reference to German rights except
those which the United States saw fit to recognize. Signed on
August 25, 1921, the treaty was submitted to the Senate for
consideration several weeks later.

The irreconcilables, still powerful within the Senate Foreign
Relations Committee, found portions of the treaty unacceptable. As originally drawn, it provided that the United States
might participate in the Reparations Commission although
stipulating no obligation to do so.[4] The bitter-enders balked
at granting the administration such discretion, divining in it
a bridge to full cooperation with the League. As reported
from committee, the treaty went before the Senate with a
reservation providing that there should be no representation
or participation on any commission "unless and until an act
of the Congress of the United States shall provide for such
representation or participation."[5] The reservation seemed to
represent yet another victory for the irreconcilables as the administration accepted it without complaint. To Borah, however, even this did not suffice; together with eighteen Democrats and Robert La Follette, he voted against approval on
October 18.

Borah defended his action by claiming it would be immoral to enjoy the advantages of the Versailles Treaty unless
the United States also submitted to its obligations. More to

[3] See New York *Times*, March 10, 1921, for Knox's proposal; *FRUS,
1921*, II, 29–33 for text of the treaty. See also Beerits memorandum,
"The Separate Peace," Hughes Papers.

[4] Article 2, Part 4 reads as follows: "That, while the United States is
privileged to participate in the Reparation Commission . . . and in any
other Commission under the Versailles Treaty . . . the United States is
not bound to participate in any such commission unless it shall elect to
do so."

[5] *Congressional Record*, 67th Cong., 1st Sess., 5769.

the point, he contended that in fact the treaty granted merely the privilege of conferring with other powers as to what rights the United States should have. Already suspicious of the "unofficial observers" sitting on the commissions, he warned that frequent conferences would lead ultimately to *de facto* membership.[6] He regarded the reservation as inadequate because he trusted his fellow senators only a bit more than he did the administration.

Well before the vote on the treaty, Borah had become convinced it was a trojan horse. He said his first inclination was to vote for it but a careful scrutiny led him to realize it would tie the United States too closely to the Versailles Pact. His suspicions were confirmed, he wrote privately, by a statement he attributed to "one of the most influential members of the Cabinet," who supposedly observed that, "Borah is correct in his position. The ratification of this treaty takes us automatically into the Reparations Commission. We are already sitting practically as members of the Supreme Council, and we cannot avoid going into the League if the League continues in existence. And this, of course, is where we ought to be."[7]

The Senator's efforts to prevent the United States from having anything to do with the commission left him in an ungainly situation. Contemporaries and more recent critics have pointed out that he advocated a program the means of accomplishing which he would not condone.[8] He had argued since the end of the war that the reconstruction of Europe hinged on German economic recovery. The imposition of

[6] *Ibid.*, 5777–78 and 5791.

[7] Borah to A. J. Dunn, October 5, 1921, Box 206, Borah Papers. His letter does not name the cabinet member. It is presumed to have been either Hoover or Hughes.

[8] *Congressional Record*, 67th Cong., 1st Sess., 6410–11; Denna Frank Fleming, *The United States and World Organization, 1920–1933* (New York, 1938), 138–43; McKenna, *Borah*, 186.

huge indemnities, he believed, not only impeded the resumption of normal commercial relations in which America had a stake, but contributed as well to war-breeding national hatreds. Since it had been clear for some time that France employed reparations to crush Germany, it would seem to follow that the United States should participate in the commission to modify her demands. Complaining that Europe could not recuperate without a "reasonable, sane" reparations program, the Senator blocked efforts to create one.[9]

Borah's premises prohibited him from acting otherwise. Although the prospect of entanglement with the League figured most importantly in his aversion to the commission, he also doubted that representatives who might be named would act in the best interests of the United States.[10] He appeared to believe, for example, that the American "unofficial observer" R. W. Boyden had supported French policy thus far instead of trying to soften it.[11] Charging that Boyden acted as a participating member in fact if not in name, Borah questioned whether the administration seriously wanted a "reasonable, sane" program despite its public announcements to that effect. He perceived, behind this betrayal of the national welfare, the fine hand of his old enemy "Wall Street."

During the fight over the League, Borah had accused the bankers of a willingness to "sell our common country to make safe their foreign bonds and make secure their foreign invest-

[9] Borah to Bernard M. Baruch, April 5, 1922, Box 215, Borah Papers. And see Bernard Baruch, *Baruch: The Public Years* (New York, 1960), 157–58.

[10] Even if they did, the United States might be outvoted, hence obligated to support policies it considered harmful. Thus far, the British had been forced to "deal alone" with the intractable French, having received little help from the other members of the commission. Anglo-American collaboration, however, would have undercut French strength. *FRUS, 1921*, II, 51, and Fleming, *World Organization*, 137–38.

[11] Borah to Beveridge, September 6, 1922, Box 215, Borah Papers. As late as 1934, Borah still castigated "unofficial observers" likening them to international spies. See New York *Times*, January 9, 1934.

ments," an evaluation he saw no reasaon to qualify.[12] They would manipulate reparations to underwrite their schemes just as they had anticipated using the League to the same ends. Positive that banker influence was greater than ever before, the Senator fulminated against having an administration appointee represent the United States in matters of such vital interest. It was difficult for him to be cooperative when suspecting the motives of everyone.

The reparations question, which he regarded as the major deterrent to a stable Europe, plagued Borah throughout 1921 and 1922. Although he preferred scrapping the Versailles Treaty entirely, especially the guilt clause justifying reparations, it was the conscious use of indemnities as a political weapon upon which he poured his scorn.[13] France served as his favorite target. He remained indifferent to arguments that the French had legitimate cause to dread a resurgent Germany. Opposed to gratifying their security demands through an alliance or league, he professed to see their economic policy as stemming only from inherent greed and militarism.[14] One could expect little more from European powers, but the recent war had shown that the United States could not escape the effects of such madness.

Until the end of 1922, Borah's total contribution to the reparations dilemma consisted of issuing periodic broadsides against Gallic militarism and cupidity. His diatribes did little to better relations with the French; if anything, he helped con-

[12] Borah to San Francisco *Bulletin*, June 16, 1919, Box 552, Borah Papers.

[13] Borah, "The Ghost of Versailles at the Conference," 525–26; New York *Times*, January 26, 1922; and McKenna, *Borah*, 183–87.

[14] However superficial his characterization of French motives, many people believed Germany had been shattered for a long time to come. Borah shared Beveridge's view that French security was "a very flimsy pretext" for imperialistic schemes. "Lloyd George declared in Parliament," Beveridge wrote, "that 'Germany is powerless' and everybody who knows the facts knows that this is true. Germany is down and out." Beveridge to Borah, November 24, 1919, Box 550, Borah Papers.

vince them that the United States represented an unreliable factor in world affairs. The Senator capped this approach in November, 1922, by ostentatiously refusing to serve on a committee to welcome the visiting Georges Clemenceau, accompanying his refusal with a stern lecture on the immorality of France's reparations policy.[15] The recipients of his counsel proved singularly ungrateful and not at all moved to accept his advice. What he hoped to accomplish, aside from twisting the tiger's tail, is difficult to imagine.

Still, within his definition of permissible involvement, Borah felt something had to be done to prevent Europe's descent into chaos. The present state of affairs made a resumption of the war seem just a matter of time. But how, short of a wholesale commitment, could the United States ameliorate the situation? Barring participation on existing councils with the responsibilities thus entailed, American influence would be minimal without some effective vehicle. Hesitantly at first, then with growing conviction, Borah embraced the thesis that the United States had to utilize its only bargaining tool, the Allied debts. Manipulation of these debts, he thought, might be used to further American interests without a concomitant political entanglement.

Granting the premise of achievement through debt adjustment, he had to consider the matter of rounding up support for the idea. The administration maintained an unbending attitude on the sanctity of debts; prospects within Congress looked equally bleak. The only alternative seemed to be going to the public. By late July, Borah began contemplating such a move. Together with J. G. McDonald, chairman of the Foreign Policy Association, Frank Cobb, and Walter Lippmann, he explored the possibility of mounting a public campaign to force changes in the American debt policy. The

---

[15] *Congressional Record*, 67th Cong., 3rd Sess., 55, and Vinson, *Borah and the Outlawry of War*, 50.

ultimate goal would be an international economic conference to setttle the entire financial complex and, perhaps, ease other tensions as well.

In the midst of these discussions the British, on August 1, issued the so-called Balfour note.[16] This message, officially directed to those nations indebted to Great Britain, "with the greatest reluctance" requested them to begin funding operations immediately. Favoring a general cancellation herself, the note went on, Britain nevertheless intended meeting her obligations to the United States. She perforce had to act as creditor as well as debtor to do so. As long as the United States insisted upon debt collection, she had no choice but to follow suit. The contrast between English magnanimity and American greed clearly outlined, Britain, with an added twist of the stiletto, announced that she would collect sums only in the amount necessary to satisfy American claims since she "did not in any event desire to make a profit."

McDonald, Cobb, and Lippmann went into a hurried conference when the note appeared in the American press. Because Borah rarely displayed much tolerance of foreign criticism, especially from the British, they feared his response would upset all their plans. McDonald wired the Senator requesting that he "postpone statement on Balfour note" until the four of them could discuss it together.[17] He appealed in vain. Later the same day, however, Borah did wire back saying the statement he had released "does not confiict with any conference program." This news the grateful McDonald relayed to Cobb and Lippman by telephone.[18]

The Idahoan's comments on the Balfour note were surprisingly moderate. He denied British contentions without

[16] H. G. Moulton and L. Pasvolsky, *War Debts and World Prosperity* (Washington, 1932), 111–13.
[17] J. G. McDonald to Borah, August 3, 1922, Box 218, Borah Papers.
[18] *Ibid.*, August 4, 1922. (McDonald quoted Borah's wire to confirm the message.)

engaging in the kind of invective he usually reserved for perfidious Albion. Thus far, Borah admitted, the United States had stood immovable on the debt question and rightly so. There was no reason to believe reduction would benefit anybody under present circumstances. With armament programs underway in practically every European nation, debt reduction simply meant making more funds available for destructive purposes. The responsibility for the situation, therefore, rested with those powers and not the United States. They would find Americans much more sympathetic to their appeals for debt adjustment if and when they reversed the trend toward militarism. Thus, in Borah's opinion, the question was negotiable only if it could be used to advance the cause of peace.[19]

Borah proposed no method, such as a conference, for dealing with the problem. Still, he had indicated that the Balfour note left unaltered the trend of his thinking. A heartened McDonald urged him to seize the initiative. "Is not the time opportune now," McDonald asked, "when a suggestion for an international conference in Washington to discuss these interrelated problems would be welcomed and supported by American public opinion?" Alluding to the Washington Conference, McDonald said he believed that Borah, appealing to the same elements of public opinion, "could again induce the Administration to take another and larger and really epoch-making step."[20]

The Idahoan temporarily deferred action on McDonald's proposal. He now believed debt manipulation could be a potent force; implementation was something else. Disagreeing with McDonald's assessment of the popular mood, Borah thought it unlikely that the public would be receptive to another crusade following so quickly on the heels of the Wash-

[19] New York *Times*, August 4, 1922.
[20] Cf. note 18 above.

ington Conference. Violent and widespread labor disputes, moreover, had all but thrust foreign affairs from the headlines.[21] Borah's attitude toward the administration also caused him to hold back. Harding and Hughes would direct American policy at any called conference, regardless of its origins. Remembering what had been done to his disarmament resolution, the Senator understandably shied away from fathering another monster.

Borah's reluctance to sponsor a conference in succeeding months did not mean he thought the situation was improving. Far from it. He believed Europe to be traveling down the road to war and that the United States shared the blame. Speaking of the "unofficial observer," the Senator wrote that he "takes part, counsels, advises, and while he may not technically vote—I do not know about that—his vote is expressed and counted." He added, "I think this is a sleazy, cowardly way to do business."[22] He told another correspondent that Europe "is persisting in her own suicide." What was worse, American policy "connived" to the same end.[23] Although the possibility of forcing an economic conference remained dim, Borah grew frustrated with the alternative of doing nothing.

Several new developments affected the situation by late fall. First, Franco-German relations had reached a state of crisis bordering on open hostilities. Second, although agricultural prices had improved over the immediate postwar years, farm groups began showering Borah with letters beseeching him to do something about economic conditions in Europe. They

[21] Coal and rail strikes had reached such proportions as to cause speculation that the government would step in and take them over. See telegrams, *Outlook* to Borah, August 10, and Borah to *Outlook*, August 11, 1922, in Box 219, Borah Papers. The Senator withheld his views at this time saying they "would likely be construed as a criticism" of the administration.

[22] Borah to Beveridge, September 6, 1922, Box 215, *ibid.*

[23] Borah to Henry M. McCracken, September 26, 1922, *ibid.*

THE MISDIRECTED PACKAGE

contended that prices would recover fully only when the European markets resumed absorbing American farm surplus. Finally, the November elections had revealed a definite trend away from Old Guard Republicanism thus reawakening the Senator's dream of reforming the party. A dramatic stand on foreign policy would do a great deal to insure that leadership of such a movement devolved upon him rather than upon La Follette, for example, who already was making gestures in that direction. The year 1924 was not so far away.

On December 21, Borah introduced a proposal requesting an international conference such as he, McDonald, and the others had discussed the previous summer. The contents of his plan, however, and his conduct in the ensuing debates strongly point to another multipurpose strategic move rather than to a crusade. "I offered amendment to naval bill calling an economic conference," he wired McDonald, "if we can have good support believe we can do something."[24] The "something" he intended doing was not exactly what it appeared.

The Senator's amendment cast an exceedingly wide net. Open to all nations concerned, the proposed conference would deal with means of restoring international trade and sound financial conditions (debts and reparations), land disarmament, national naval limitations, and the abolition of military aircraft.[25] Borah's most recent biographer understates the case when she writes that "in its staggering totality, his plan was impractical."[26]

There is little reason to assume the Senator himself thought his suggestion practical, violating as it did almost every one of his own criteria for a successful conference. He had long insisted that such meetings be restrictive, both as to partici-

[24] Borah to McDonald, December 21, 1922, Box 230, *ibid.*
[25] *Congressional Record*, 67th Cong., 4th Sess., 810.
[26] McKenna, *Borah*, 188.

pating nations and the issues discussed. This had been his criticism when the administration expanded his disarmament resolution. Now he ostensibly favored inviting everyone to negotiate a spate of the most complex problems imaginable. More specifically, his proposal on its face was unacceptable to France, a fact which the Idahoan appreciated as well as anyone. The French conceivably may have agreed to modify their reparation demands, given the proper incentive; asking them to do so, and at the same time to disarm, verged on the incredible. However much Borah detested their attitude—his recent outburst against Clemenceau showed his feelings had not changed—he knew they would never consent to German recovery without adequate protection. He had predicted, before the Washington Conference met, that the French would rebuff efforts to promote land disarmament, which they did. Nor was it any secret they had vetoed Hughes's attempt to extend naval limitation beyond capital ships. As an indictment of Gallic militarism, Borah's resolution touched every base. As a serious project standing any chance of realization, it smacked of fraud.

He intended his program as more than a gesture though it was partly that too. Genuinely alarmed at the drift of events, Borah wished to influence them by using his resolution as a lever against the administration. If he could get the "good support" he spoke of in his wire to McDonald, he might force Harding and Hughes to move on the debts and related problems. The very attractive feature of his strategy was that whatever they did, Borah still would appear "ahead" of them in his willingness to solve world problems. Anything within the realm of possibility would come off as foot-dragging compared with his pretentious resolution.

Borah's conduct after introducing his proposal bears out this interpretation. Administration spokesmen criticized him for interfering with executive functions much as they had during the debate over naval limitation. They assured him that the President already had sent out feelers on the pertinent issues thereby rendering Borah's action unnecessary and confusing. The Senator, after indulging himself in some verbal horseplay over the proper definition of a "feeler," politely agreed to withdraw his resolution since he did not wish to "embarrass" the President.[27] He rarely displayed such consideration. Privately, Borah explained his tactic. "Of course," he acknowledged, "they [administration leaders] had the votes to defeat the measure." In defending their opposition, however, they had made some fairly definite statements about entering negotiations. Therefore, Borah said, "I felt the strategy was to leave them there and put the responsibility on them. I do not see how they can avoid moving forward."[28]

His proposal served yet another purpose. Except for his disarmament proposal two years earlier, Borah's reputation rested on his ability to obstruct the policies of others. This may have delighted his constituents in Idaho, but it hardly strengthened him as a presidential aspirant. Now, posing as a constructive statesman once again, he used the debates as a forum to show he had been misunderstood all along. His attempt to disassociate himself from the by now discredited "bitter-enders" revealed an interesting recollection of past events which, if nothing else, succeeded in alienating several of his one-time comrades.[29]

Borah led off by denying that he was, or ever had been, an "isolationist."[30] He had opposed plans which would en-

[27] *Congressional Record*, 67th Cong., 4th Sess., 1059–60; New York *Times*, December 30, 1922.

[28] Borah to Levinson, December 30, 1922, Box 230, Borah Papers.

[29] Hiram Johnson, particularly incensed, called Borah's proposal more dangerous than the League of Nations which at least had "some rules of procedure." *Congressional Record*, 67th Cong., 4th Sess., 926. This marked the beginning of an alienation between the two men which resulted in their complete estrangement.

[30] Since the term had become one of opprobrium, Borah of course

tangle the United States with Europe politically, but he had no qualms about cooperating with other nations as the need arose. He pointed out that European problems *were* American problems, a fact which any intelligent foreign policy presupposed. He personally had understood this for years, his critics notwithstanding; furthermore he had translated his perception into good works whenever possible. He cited his conduct in 1920 at the Republican National Convention as proof of his assertion. There he had tried to secure a commitment to an "association of nations" in order to facilitate international conferences. His allegation probably caused some of his auditors to wonder whether he had taken leave of his senses or they of theirs.

Having established himself as a leading exponent of international cooperation, Borah went on to defend the effectiveness of independent conferences such as he now proposed. He traced the history of these meetings from the Portsmouth negotiations of 1905 to the recently concluded Washington Conference and professed to see an unbroken string of successes. Apparently forgetting that he had opposed almost all the results of the Washington Conference, he unblushingly included it in his roster of triumphs. He went further. The greatest tragedy of the twentieth century, the World War, might not have taken place had there been a conference to compose the issues.[31] The Senator staged one of his grandest performances.

As a means of nudging the administration into reconsidering its policy on debts and reparations, Borah's short campaign must be adjudged a failure. Secretary of State Hughes

wished to disavow it. He did so by interpreting it to mean a person who advocated severing all relations with other powers, rather than one who merely stood against political commitments. Using his definition, the word did not apply to him nor to anyone else then active in politics. For the full texture of his remarks, see *ibid.*, 844ff., 926ff., 990ff., 1051ff.

[31] *Ibid.*, 930, 1052–57.

bestirred himself to comment on America's interest in German recuperation and to publicly suggest an independent reparations commission, but this hardly qualifies as an achievement.[32] The administration itself adhered to its pronouncements on the inviolability of the debts and denied they were in any way related to reparations.[33] Borah undoubtedly overestimated the degree to which debt adjustment could have influenced the French. As things stood, however, official policy consisted solely of platitudinous appeals to which the French paid no attention whatever.

Borah enjoyed more success on a personal level. Whatever its merits, his attractive proposal served notice that he was a man with a dynamic approach to foreign affairs, an appearance he did nothing to discourage. Though brief, the debates received wide attention and provided an excellent opportunity to launch another "new" Borah. A few skeptics doubted his "conversion," but generally he came off well with the press.[34] The Senator liked to claim he knew how to get the greatest return for the smallest investment, and he surely proved it on this occasion. His second venture into constructive statesmanship, having ended far more pleasingly for him than the first, served as a model for his conduct throughout the decade.

II

In addition to periodic outcries for adherence to the League, there appeared during the 1920's an enormous num-

[32] Hughes's suggestion ultimately resulted in the Dawes Plan of 1924 which alleviated Germany's reparations payments but had nothing at all to do with Allied indebtedness to the United States. Glad, *Hughes*, 222–23.

[33] See Harding's letter to the Senate, printed in the *Congressional Record*, 67th Cong., 4th Sess., 982.

[34] McKenna, *Borah*, 189, and Vinson, *Borah and the Outlawry of War*, 55–56. On January 30, 1923, he reintroduced his measure as a Senate resolution but went no further, see *Congressional Record*, 67th Cong., 4th Sess., 2681.

ber of programs designed to prevent war. Borah regarded most of these schemes as a bit potty at best, and in some cases dangerous.[35] But in order to avoid perpetual naysaying, to advance his political fortunes, and sometimes to head off projects he disliked, he suported a few of them himself. The way in which he advanced these causes—particularly his timing—casts serious doubt as to whether he ever really accepted any of them.

A plan had to meet one of two criteria to gain Borah's approbation. Like the economic conference, if it was so comprehensive as to defy fruition, he might bestow upon it his blessings. The other prerequisite for favorable consideration was the absence of provisions for applying sanctions or coercion as a means of punishing violators. An example of the latter type program can be found in the movement for the "Outlawry" of war, which culminated in the Kellogg-Briand Pact of 1928. The Senator's role in shaping the contents of Outlawry, and his willingness—or lack of it—to actively promote the scheme, indicate that he used it rather than believed in it.

Borah became acquainted with Outlawry during the height of the controversy over the League of Nations. He spent a few hours one evening in December, 1919, listening to a Chicago attorney, Salmon O. Levinson, who tried to enlist his support for a plan to abolish war. Alternately reading and defending a paper he had written with the help of Philander C. Knox, Levinson sought to convince the Idahoan that the program was practical in and of itself and would provide a positive alternative to the League. When he had finished his presentation, according to Levinson, Borah called

[35] "They can roll up their peace plans," he observed in 1927, "and tie blue ribbons around them for a quarter of a century." Borah to Daniel Cohalan, May 27, 1927, Box 284, Borah Papers.

the plan "masterly"; their conference began a relationship which was to endure for two decades.[36]

Levinson, an able and successful lawyer, possessed a crusading spirit which demanded more than his profession could offer.[37] He was, as he put it, "merely trying to make some contribution to civilization before I croak," but the prodigious efforts and substantial amounts of money he expended belied such modesty.[38] Deeply shocked by the outbreak of the world war, he had worked furiously, if futilely, to head off the ensuing carnage. Since then he had evolved a specific formula through which he hoped to banish war from the face of the earth. He modified his plan several times, to suit Borah among others, but not his fundamental proposition that the way to achieve lasting peace was to outlaw war among civilized nations.

The question of war's legality dominated Levinson's thinking. The problem, as he saw it, was that tradition and the present body of international law implicitly sanctioned the institution of war. So long as this remained true, heads of state would continue to regard it as an extension of diplomacy despite their pretenses to the contrary. Even worse, the very men who brought on war might well be lionized instead of punished by fellow citizens acting through a misguided sense of patriotism. Such conditions inevitably would produce international violence.

Viewed in this light, war became partially a question of semantics—organized slaughter masquerading as an obliga-

[36] Levinson to Borah, February 21, 1921, Box 202, *ibid*. The term "relationship" is used deliberately, where Borah was concerned. The Senator's regard for Levinson often bordered on contempt as he vacillated between mild amusement and not so mild annoyance at the latter's attempts to ingratiate himself.

[37] For a thorough, but favorably biased account of Levinson, see John E. Stoner, *S. O. Levinson and the Pact of Paris* (Chicago, 1943).

[38] Copy of letter, Levinson to Miss Frances Kellor, December 7, 1927, found in Box 21, Robins Papers.

tion to flag and country. Only one solution existed. By stripping away its glory and placing it beyond the pale of international law, war might be exposed for what it actually was. If future generations remembered it with loathing rather than as being inspiring, it would no longer be deemed a reasonable method of settling disputes. Simply stated, war would become obsolete.

In trying to explain his program as well as to offer an historical justification for its potential, Levinson repeatedly drew an analogy with the practice of duelling as an extinct social custom. Individuals once had vindicated their "honor" through the duel, just as nation states presently reacted to real or supposed insults and threats by going to war. Recognized by law, regularized by custom, duelling had existed as long as the community sanctioned it. The practice lost its function among honorable men and disappeared from civilized society when branded as a socially reprehensible act. War, hopefully, would meet the same fate.[39]

Although his response to the Outlawry plan had "warmed the cockles" of Levinson's heart, Borah proved unwilling to advance the cause in any meaningful way. The Chicagoan, stressing the need for a "counter constructive program" to satisfy the "peace furors stirred up by Wilson and the League to Enforce Peace," received nothing from the Senator beyond the promise that he would "analyze" the proposition.[40] It is interesting to note that the "Captain-General" of the Outlawrists, as Robins called Levinson, subsequently developed the habit of couching his appeals to Borah in terms of the political advantages which the latter could derive from spon-

[39] Stoner, *Levinson*, 24. The comparison between war and duelling became a standard argument for the Outlawrists. Borah himself used it on occasion. See Borah, "Outlawry of War," *Federal Council Bulletin*, VII, Number 5 (September, 1924), 18.

[40] Levinson to Borah, February 14, 1920, and Borah to Levinson, Febuary 16, 1920, both in Box 552 A–1, Borah Papers.

sorship rather than because of the plan's intrinsic merits. Either he believed the Idahoan already converted, thus rendering inspirational messages superfluous, or he considered him more amenable to the pragmatic uses of Outlawry.

Their initial encounter and exchange of correspondence during the winter of 1919–20 exemplified the relationship between Levinson and Borah for years to come. First came the approach by Levinson—an inundation of long letters, dripping with flattery, citing every imaginable reason why the Senator should move quickly and decisively to launch the Outlawry campaign. Then came Borah's reply, if one came at all, explaining why action had to be deferred for the present. When not "analyzing" the situation or throwing back criticisms of the plan for Levinson to field, Borah invariably found objective conditions inopportune. Well-known for his instant crusades, the Idahoan remained unaccountably meditative toward Outlawry. That he considered Borah "our" man for as long as he did bears greater testimony to Levinson's patience than to his wisdom.

Borah's reluctance is understandable. He never shared Levinson's view of the world as a community in which the mutual interests of all nations could be satisfied through a code of right conduct. While few nations desired war, they would resort to it before surrendering what they considered vital interests. Unfortunately, the "vital interests" of one nation often conflicted directly with those of another, as in the case of France and Germany, Japan and China, and countless other national rivalries. The leaders of all those powers knew the costs of war first hand; what could Outlawry contribute that would help to deter military solutions?

Levinson was an instrumentalist, an optimistic one. He thought the immediate objective was to win acceptance for the *idea* of Outlawry as such. If this could be done, first on a national, then on an international level, half the battle would be won in that the masses would look upon war as an unacceptable course of action whatever their leaders might say.[41] While not inconsequential, mechanical details to him were always secondary. Borah approached the matter quite differently. Although many of the criticisms he directed at the Outlawry plan were merely in order to stall for time, the Senator insisted the plan be made workable before he could give it his full support. Granting even that most nations accepted Outlawry, he asked constantly, what was to be done when one or more states committed aggression? None of the replies he received ever satisfied him.[42]

Levinson initially posited the use of counterforce as the obvious means of preventing aggressive war. Borah rejected this out of hand because every nation defended its actions by claiming they were in "defense" of some interest or other.[43] The "Captain-General" countered with the idea of punishing individuals rather than nations. Theoretically, an outraged citizenry would deliver up to an international tribunal those of its members, no matter how highly placed, who advocated a resort to arms. Borah remained skeptical.[44] As one critic

[41] Stoner, *Levinson*, 197–98.

[42] Borah to Levinson, July 29, 1922, Box 219, Borah Papers; Borah to Levinson (copy), November 29, 1922, Box 18, Robins Papers. "What are you going to do after Outlawry is established," Borah once asked Levinson, "in case Japan wantonly or otherwise attacks Siberia?" Levinson to Robins, January 13, 1923, Box 19, Robins Papers.

[43] Stoner, in *Levinson*, 189, holds that Senator Knox caused Levinson to renounce the use of force, while Vinson, in *Borah and the Outlawry of War*, 65, credits Knox and Raymond Robins. Robins himself attributed the change to Borah. Recalling their early conferences with Levinson, Robins wrote that "*You* would have none of the enforcement by force. . . . Levinson and I almost came to blows on this point, and your luminous and unhesitating judgment, against war to enforce the outlawry of war was the determining factor in changing Levinson's insistence on this point." (Robins' emphasis) Borah replied, "I recall the discussion about force. I recall it very vividly. Make a memorandum of this, Colonel." Robins to Borah, August 8, and Borah to Robins, August 12, 1929, Box 309, Borah Papers.

[44] Borah to Levinson, July 13, 1922, Box 218, Borah Papers.

put it, was it really likely that the Germans would have turned the Kaiser over to some world court had one existed?[45] Borah can hardly be faulted for entertaining serious reservations about such fancies.

Despite the Senator's elusiveness, Levinson dogged him unmercifully. Two factors stimulated his persistence. First, he considered Borah's position and ability to capture the public imagination as prerequisites to a successful campaign. Second, the Idahoan constantly led him to believe that the "heavy artillery" would soon be fired. Borah's reasons for procrastination varied but they always sounded plausible: the clarification of just one more point, pressing affairs requiring immediate action, the slight delay for the "right" moment, and always the implication that a decisive step impended. With wistful ambiguity, Levinson once described the situation precisely. "Of course," he wrote, "we firmly believe and fervently hope that Borah will continue to be our man."[46] (He might have underlined the word "hope.") Unable to admit the possibility that the Idahoan merely feigned his devotion to the cause, Levinson later began ascribing Borah's temporizing to his "Hamlet-like" nature.

It is easy to understand Levinson's reliance upon Borah; the grounds for the Senator's long but uncertain association with Outlawry have more complicated origins. Dismissing the matter as an example of his inconsistency or inability to mount a sustained effort will not do. In this case he refused even to make the grand gesture. Like a stubborn bachelor, Borah neither married Outlawry nor gave it up. Practical considerations accounted for his behavior, however, far more than did any structural flaw in his character.

Borah recognized several possibilities for Outlawry quite

---

[45] Stoner, *Levinson*, 89. The alternative, empowering the court to extradite accused nationals, was hardly more plausible and certainly repellent to Borah.

[46] Levinson to Robins, November 17, 1922, Box 18, Robins Papers.

aside from whether or not it would work. He could use it in the short run to undermine other proposals or at least to blunt their impact upon the public. From a longer view, it might well become the constructive program he needed to make him a serious contender for the presidency. As Levinson put it, "you need only one thing in this country and that is a great, paramount issue in addition to the many splendid but relatively subordinate principles you so splendidly advocate."[47] This very fact, whether or not the Outlawrists realized it, made the Senator all the more cautious. An unsuccessful campaign would do him no good, certainly, but neither would a successful one that the administration could expropriate, as had happened with his disarmament resolution. Borah wanted to make sure he carried the banner in any crusade he joined.

Perhaps the most important reason for the Senator's deference to the movement lay in his wish to retain the friendship and support of Levinson's fellow Outlawrist Raymond Robins, whose help would be invaluable if and when the Senator made his bid for the presidency. The "Colonel," as Robins liked to be called, was one of those figures in American politics whose personal influence exceeds any position he held. An intimate of most of the Republican leaders, he still enjoyed considerable prestige with what remained of the old Progressives, many of whom thought Borah a counterfeit. In addition to remarkable oratorical talents, Robins made up for what the Senator lacked in the patient ability to work with individuals and organizations. And the Colonel believed wholeheartedly in Outlawry. Borah's conduct through the better part of the 1920's indicates that when he was not using Outlawry as a smokescreen, his primary concern was to hold back on the "great campaign" until he thought it politically

[47] Levinson to Borah, January 5, 1923, Box 219, Borah Papers.

advantageous. Meanwhile he did just enough to avoid alienating Robins.[48]

Actually, Borah refused to give more than his vague approval to Outlawry until the Colonel joined Levinson in pressing him. As late as December, 1921, two years after the Chicago attorney had first preached the cause to him, the Senator had not yet found time "to go into this matter as I must before I become thoroughly identified with it."[49] On past occasions Borah had become identified with issues within two days. But he did find time at last and, capitulating to their pleas, agreed to launch the campaign in May, 1922. Although they had no way of knowing it then, this was but the first of many pledges the Senator never kept. What emerges from the tortuous negotiations which followed is the key position Robins occupied rather than that of Levinson or of Outlawry itself.[50]

Levinson, "thrilled with delight" when Borah consented to introduce a resolution for Outlawry, hoped to generate enough momentum to make it an issue in the fall elections.[51] When the Idahoan failed to carry out his promise, Levinson and Robins urged him to do so by June at the very latest. They fared no better that month as, by then, the Senator began finding faults with the resolution as it was written. Another postponement followed, this time to July 29, the eighth anniversary of the outbreak of the war. Pressing domestic affairs sidetracked the matter for July, and August as well. Whatever consolation it offered, Borah "pledged himself ab-

[48] Robins did break with Hiram Johnson over just this issue. Once, in a moment of exasperation, Levinson warned Borah that his course of action was "analogous" to this incident and might "prove fatal to Colonel's wholehearted support." He obviously believed Robins' allegiance more important to the Senator than his own. Levinson to Robins, quoting telegram Levinson had sent Borah, February 11, 1927, Box 21, Robins Papers.

[49] Borah to Levinson, December 10, 1921, Box 218, Borah Papers.

[50] For a detailed account, see Stoner's *Levinson*, Chap. 6.

[51] Levinson to Borah, May 1, 1922, Box 218, Borah Papers.

solutely" in September that he would get underway in the coming congressional session.[52] The Captain-General and his Colonel could only wait.

Since each of Borah's excuses seemed valid enough, Robins and Levinson believed he would reward their patience. Levinson expressed confidence by the middle of November that Borah would "shoot" any day. The shot never came. On November 29, Borah calmly announced he had "looked over" the resolution and had concluded "we should simplify" it.[53] One can imagine Levinson's dismay. His efforts to comply with the Senator's observation went unheeded as the Idahoan lapsed into a chilling silence. Levinson grew frantic. "Wire or write independently to Washington party," he exhorted Robins, "urging immediate action."[54] Borah acted five days later in a way which left the Outlawrists aghast. He offered instead his proposal for an economic conference without mentioning their cause. Anticipating the shock his move would produce, the Senator wired Levinson that every day. "Think if we can get this conference called," he stated, "we can force in our proposition."[55]

The Captain-General tried to make the best of a bewildering situation. Admitting that he felt uninformed as to Borah's strategy, Levinson asked for a clarification enabling him to "lend at least some aid collateral."[56] His first thoughts were

[52] Stoner, *Levinson*, 90. Apparently, Borah told neither Robins nor Levinson he had discussed an international economic conference with McDonald, Lippmann, and Cobb.

[53] Copy of letter, Borah to Levinson November 29, 1922, Box 18, Robins Papers.

[54] Levinson had read a newspaper story that Elihu Root and J. P. Morgan were making arrangements with the administration for abandonment of interest and a long extension on debt payments. Since he wished to make debt adjustment contingent upon acceptance of Outlawry, he feared "this, if carried out before our man shoots may serve to spike our guns." Levinson to Robins, December 16, 1922, *ibid.*

[55] Borah to Levinson, December 21, 1922, Box 232, Borah Papers.

[56] Levinson to Borah, December 26, 1922, *ibid.*

for the effects Borah's action would have on Robins, who disliked being toyed with. If he believed Borah to be insincere, Levinson knew Robins would have nothing further to do with the Idahoan. Concealing his own disappointment, Levinson tried to convince Robins that they had scored at least a partial victory. He forwarded Borah's telegram asserting that its contents "delighted me." Pointing out that the Senator had referred to Outlawry as "our proposition," Levinson explained this meant the Idahoan "regards himself as one of our peace partners."[57] It was the utmost he could claim under the circumstances.

Borah's promise to "force in" Outlawry might have seemed more credible had he gone all-out on his conference resolution. When he withdrew it eight days later, Robins lost his inclination to continue what looked more and more like a hoax. He had lined up a speaking tour to spread the Senator's campaign to the public; now all of it seemed in vain. Never the chronic optimist that Levinson was, Robins began urging him to dump Borah for a more likely prospect.[58]

This Levinson refused to do. He had staked everything on Borah and still believed that the reluctant Idahoan would come around. But he had little or no bargaining strength without Robins. Faced with the complete destruction of his beloved cause, Levinson tried frenziedly to repair his fences. He bombarded Robins with letters assuring him the situation never looked better and that Borah was "apparently laying a foundation from which all the charges of inconsistency, new change of heart, etc., will be successfully answered."[59] All that was necessary, Levinson wrote, was to intensify their efforts. "If you and I can only press our suit with Borah

[57] See telegram and confirming letter, Levinson to Robins, both dated December 22, 1922, Box 18, Robins Papers.

[58] Stoner, *Levinson*, 92–93.

[59] Levinson to Robins, January 8, 1923, Box 19, Robins Papers.

now," he promised, "he can literally take the world by storm."[60]

While he tried to mollify the belligerent Robins by telling him that Borah teetered on the verge of action, Levinson warned the Senator that he had better act if he valued Robins' support for his "other plans." Robins until recently had favored Hiram Johnson as the progressive Republicans' best hope, but their friendship had become strained over the Californian's refusal to back Outlawry. "You know Robins is one of the greatest organizers and political enthusiasts in the country," Levinson reminded Borah, "and I know of no greater political asset you can have than that able and energetic orator." If the Senator could convince Robins of his earnestness about the cause, it would "probably detach Robins [from Johnson] and clinch his relations with you."[61]

An impressed Borah replied he could not act immediately because the time was "not ripe." Besides, he had a few more questions about the resolution itself. He agreed nonetheless that it would be prudent to make a gesture for the Colonel's benefit, as well as his own. Since Robins already had embarked on his lecture tour, the Senator authorized Levinson to transmit a statement in which Borah endorsed Outlawry and granting Robins the right to "use my name as he pleases."[62] Sensing his argument had struck home, Levinson closed in. He advised Robins to acknowledge the message by telling the Idahoan that he, Robins, intended accompanying Levinson to Washington to plead their case for immediate action.

The Outlawrists meanwhile received help from an unexpected quarter. Since the campaign of 1920, many prominent

---

[60] Levinson to Robins, January 6, 1923, *ibid.*

[61] Levinson to Borah, January 5, 1923, Box 6, Levinson Papers, University of Chicago Library, Chicago, hereinafter cited as Levinson Papers.

[62] Levinson to Robins, January 13, 1923, Box 76, *ibid.* The quote is from Levinson's recollection of a telephone conversation with the Senator.

Republicans had spoken favorably of the Permanent Court of International Justice, or "World Court." President Harding had implied repeatedly that his projected "association of nations" might be centered around this organization.[63] The administration had refrained from any overt gesture toward membership thus far, but during January, rumors had it such a move was forthcoming. Borah interpreted this as another plot to lead the United States into a world organization by subterfuge. The Outlawry resolution, which also provided for an international court, suddenly became more attractive as an instrument to neutralize whatever plans Harding and Hughes had in mind.

Levinson and Robins journeyed to Washington early in February to beard the "Lion of Idaho." Their conversations went unrecorded; whether Robins presented any ultimata is unknown. The opportunity to "clinch" relations with the Colonel while blocking the administration's path carried sufficient appeal. On February 13, after nine months of hesitation, Borah at last presented his Outlawry resolution.[64] Levinson and Robins had secured only a partial victory, however, for he failed to accompany his resolution with the "great speech" with which they had hoped to keynote a national campaign. Borah limply explained that he had been unable to find time to prepare an appropriate address.[65]

If Borah's action lacked his usual flair for the dramatic, it served his purposes adequately. He had placated Robins who thereupon joined Levinson in promoting a vigorous propaganda campaign for Outlawry. They continued urging the Senator to more energetic leadership but for the present were satisfied that they stood by the right man. The Idahoan had also placed himself in a strategic position from which to lead

[63] C. A. Berdahl, *The Policy of the United States with Respect to the League of Nations* (Geneva, 1932), 75–76.

[64] *Congressional Record*, 67th Cong., 4th Sess., 3605.

[65] Borah to Levinson, March 6, 1923, Box 219, Borah Papers.

the fight against the World Court. When Harding officially recommended membership on February 24, Borah replied as a man who already had proposed a more comprehensive program.

Whether Harding and Hughes believed they had a genuine chance to push through court membership is unknown.[66] The President assured everyone that the administration had "definitely and decisively put aside" any thoughts of entering the League "by the side door, the back door or the cellar door," and Hughes had made up the inevitable list of reservations with which to pacify the Senate. Their conduct suggests something less than a determined effort;[67] perhaps it was only a nod toward 1924. Whatever it was, their halfhearted boomlet collapsed at the first sign of opposition and stagnated for months. Harding, in June, proposed a new plan for going into the court—one "so impossible of acceptance that Senator Borah promptly indicated his willingness to support it."[68] As usual, the Idahoan could be relied upon to favor almost anything provided he was certain it would not succeed.

Borah resumed his coy approach to Outlawry when the court issue subsided. He published two articles praising the cause in April, yet he never did locate the time to prepare the speech he had promised Levinson and Robins.[69] The long and patient work of these two men had produced inconclusive results. The Idahoan's belated presentation of the resolution fell woefully short of the bold leadership which the Outlawrists demanded of him. A truly impressive national campaign

[66] While Borah's critics argued that he merely wished to undermine the administration, Levinson and others charged the administration with using the World Court to "forestall" Outlawry. Stoner, *Levinson*, 120.

[67] New York *Times*, April 24, 1923, and Fleming, *World Organizations*, 41–44.

[68] Berdahl, *Policy of the United States*, 92.

[69] New York *Times*, April 1, 1923, and *The Locomotive Engineers Journal*, April, 1923, Reel 5, Borah Scrapbook.

required more, much more, than a few articles and a resolution.

Outlawry and Borah's association with it lay sputtering by the summer of 1923. There is nothing to indicate his preparedness to do more than he had done already. His constant theme that the time was not "ripe" must have led the Outlawrists to wonder whether such a time would ever come. On the evening of August 2, however, Warren G. Harding died suddenly; within a few hours Calvin Coolidge became President of the United States. Although Coolidge's accession seems anything but earthshaking from the larger view, its implications caused much concern at the time. No one speculated more than the Senator. The event struck him as laden with possibilities for the United States, the Republican Party, Outlawry, and, of course, William E. Borah.

CHAPTER VII

Outlawry and the Kellogg-Briand Pact

URING a period in which drab political figures abounded, Calvin Coolidge's drabness stood out. The contrast between the "eloquent Idahoan" and the "silent Vermonter," as a contemporary phrased it, could hardly have been more striking.[1] Having encountered Borah horseback riding one day, Coolidge supposedly expressed surprise at seeing the Senator and the horse travelling in the same direction.[2] If he heard of this comment, Borah's reply has eluded historians. He might have pointed out that Coolidge's hobby permitted no such surprises; neither he nor his self-exercise mechancal horse moved in any direction. Yet the two men got along well personally in spite of—more likely because of—their differences. Perhaps each recognized in the other certain attributes lacking in himself and, most important,

[1] Alexander Gumberg to Raymond Robins, March 26, 1925, Box 20, Robins Papers.

[2] James E. Watson, *As I Knew Them: The Memoirs of James E. Watson* (Indianapolis, 1936), 237.

150

each hoped to make use of the other's political strengths and weaknesses.

Coolidge had founded a successful career on two principles: avoiding controversy and never making a commitment to anything. His accomplishments were few, his mistakes even fewer. Lacking either Wilson's aura of scholarly intensity or Harding's genial expansiveness, the new President had about him the look of a testy bookkeeper awaiting an audit. His appearance deceived, however, for beneath his vapid exterior there lurked as shrewd a Yankee as ever peddled flannel sausages. He proved to be one of the few men whom Borah seriously misjudged.

When he assumed office following Harding's death, Coolidge occupied an ambiguous position within the party. Though a protégé of the late Massachusetts wheelhorse W. Murray Crane, the new President did not enjoy the Old Guard's trust. "They had planned his retirement before the death of Harding," Robins once said, "and their enforced loyalty has never been very deep." [3] His governorship of the Bay State had a quasi-liberal tinge, his nomination for the vice presidency had come almost as an afterthought by a tired, irritable convention. [4] Nor could he rely upon the party's progressive wing. Emboldened by successes in the 1922 congressional elections, the progressives found his credentials singularly unimposing. Hiram Johnson made this clear in the fall when the former Bull Mooser announced he would contest Coolidge's nomination; and in Wisconsin, "Fighting Bob" La Follette's friends for some time had been talking of a third party.

Coolidge's lack of Old Guard support had no particular significance while he remained Vice President; his succession to the presidency opened new vistas in Borah's mind, pre-

[3] Robins to Borah, September 28, 1924, Box 238, Borah Papers.
[4] Claude M. Fuess, *Calvin Coolidge: The Man from Vermont* (Boston, 1940), 187–88.

senting "an opportunity to liberalize the whole political situation."[5] The Senator's hopes rested on an assumption of Coolidge's malleability. Having gotten to know him during his tenure as Vice President, Borah had discovered few strong convictions but regarded "Silent Cal" as a progressive at heart who had not manifested his feeling thus far through sheer timidity. If the liberals could convince him that his political future lay with them—by arguing that such a move would prevent drainage to a third party, meanwhile keeping in line the regulars who would have nowhere else to go—perhaps they could lead him where he wanted to be led. Borah saw the Vermonter as a weakling, assailed by doubts, imprisoned by forces he could not control, who yearned to do the right thing. The problem was to stiffen his resolve and support him against those who would lead him astray.

Borah envisioned great possibilities if his evaluation of Coolidge proved correct. First of all, Old Guard domination of the Republican Party might be thrown off, realizing one of the Senator's treasured dreams. Second, if the President could be won over to a "sound" foreign policy, the League threat would virtually disappear along with the rest of the "international banker" control of American diplomacy.[6] Finally, although Borah would have to forego an overt bid for the presidency in 1924, he would have enhanced his position for 1928. The Senator knew his reputation stood against him but four years of cooperation with an administration sharing his basic outlook might well make him "the outstanding figure and leader of the Republican Party."[7]

[5] Borah to Robins, August 25, 1923, Box 233, Borah Papers.

[6] If the terms used on these pages (such as "liberal," "progressive," "Old Guard") are imprecise, so was Borah. Herbert Hoover can hardly be considered Old Guard yet Borah did, and he consistently equated advocacy of the League with "Wall Street." A good working definition of who the Senator thought to be a progressive is someone who shared his own (Borah's) beliefs at any given time.

[7] Levinson to Borah, October 24, 1924, Box 244, Borah Papers. Borah

Borah and Robins, each of whom had several conferences with the President during the late summer and fall, considered the prospects encouraging. While Coolidge extended no definite promises, he appeared receptive to their foreign policy ideas—recognition of Soviet Russia and Outlawry—and the need for at least a moderately progressive domestic platform.[8] His determination to seek reelection in itself heartened them. With Hiram Johnson actively campaigning for the nomination and a third party movement in the offing, Coolidge had to make an appeal for liberal support if he expected to be successful.

Coolidge's hesitancy over committing himself boldly caused little alarm; as a candidate he had to reconcile all elements of the party. Borah and Robins nevertheless looked forward to the President's annual message, scheduled for early December, as a test of his sincerity. The message, they believed, would indicate whether he merited their support in the forthcoming campaign. Coolidge in fact represented their only hope. Robins had left the door open for cooperation with the Johnson organization but the latter's definite refusal to align himself with Outlawry poisoned their friendship while Borah's relations with the Californian already had grown "cold."[9]

The Senator and Robins learned the contents of the Chief Executive's message a few days before its delivery. On the whole pleasing to Borah, it convinced him he had rightly assessed Coolidge all along. The President's address, Borah wrote, would "disclose a clear program and courage" as well

---

rarely committed himself in writing on such matters. Fortunately for this study's reconstruction of what he was trying to accomplish, Robins and Levinson often included in their letters arguments he had put forth in private conversations.

[8] See Robins to Levinson, November 20, 1923, Box 76, Levinson Papers; Levinson to Borah, November 24, 1923, Box 230, Borah Papers; and Stoner, *Levinson*, 124.

[9] Levinson to Robins, November 22, 1923, Box 19, Robins Papers.

as an overture to Soviet Russia.[10] Coolidge's favorable allusion to the World Court and failure to mention Outlawry aroused small worry in the Senator.[11] Not so Robins. The Colonel shared Borah's enthusiasm over what represented a conciliatory gesture toward Russia but expressed bitter disappointment at the President's omission of Outlawry, saying it would hurt him "beyond all calculations."[12] Robins had little choice, given Johnson's position, except to continue working on Coolidge, who had accepted Outlawry "in principle," whatever that meant.

Important in itself, Coolidge's invitation to Russia symbolized his apparent break with Hughes-Hoover foreign policy and the conservatives in general. The Secretaries of State and Commerce were by far the most powerful men in the cabinet and, though not considered Old Guard, could rely on the regular party organization while Borah and his group could not. The President's defection lasted briefly. He had underestimated the conservative reaction to what was, after all, only an offer to begin discussions, not a commitment to recognition as such. The courage Borah predicted Coolidge would show vanished in the face of a vigorous reaction. When Moscow attempted to take up the proposal, Coolidge meekly allowed Secretary of State Charles Evans Hughes to forward an offensive note denying that the United States intended any modification of policy.[13] His abject retreat shocked Borah

[10] Borah to Levinson, November 30, 1923, Box 6, Levinson Papers.

[11] Borah very likely thought Coolidge was merely indulging in a gesture toward those who favored the Court as only five days earlier Hughes had stated, "We refuse to commit ourselves in advance with respect to the employment of the power of the United States." See New York *Times*, December 2, 1923. On the day of the President's vaguely worded address, Borah told a reporter that if Coolidge "means he is against the Court unless it is divorced from the League, I am in accord with it." *Ibid.*, December 7, 1923. The Senator reintroduced his Outlawry resolution a week later but made no speech on it.

[12] Robins to Borah, December 6, 1923, Box 245, Borah Papers.

[13] Hughes's message is in *FRUS, 1923*, II, 787–88.

and Robins. Their efforts to repair the damage went unavailing as they found themselves without a shred of support from the President. Caught between the liberal recognitionists and the conservatives, "Silent Cal" prudently abandoned the former.[14]

The President's capitulation undermined his efforts to attract liberal sympathies through Borah and Robins. Although his actions tended to confirm their opinion that his faint heart rather than his inclination lay at fault, he had dampened their enthusiasm substantially. They could and did threaten to break with him, a possibility Coolidge must have weighed in allowing himself to be overruled.[15] The controversy obviously revealed that what they had to offer the Chief Executive would not compensate for antagonizing the regulars. Aside from consoling themselves by filing briefs on Coolidge's perfidy with one another, there seemed nothing further they could do.

Their despondency ended quickly when the full implications of the oil scandals broke upon the political scene. Headed by Senator Thomas J. Walsh of Montana, the investigation which led to disclosure of the frauds had been going on for some time. Since nothing of very great importance had been divulged until the middle of January, Republican leaders had dismissed it as a Democratic political stunt. Then the bottom dropped out.[16] Harding's Secretary of the Interior, Albert B. Fall, was at first the only one of cabinet rank directly involved, but subsequent testimony implicated Secretary of the Navy Edwin Denby and Attorney General Harry M. Daugherty. Fall had resigned six months previously; Denby and Daugherty were still in office. Because all three were undeniably regular, the liberals thought they had re-

[14] For details, see Chap. 8 below.

[15] Robins to Borah, January 31, 1924, Box 245, Borah Papers.

[16] See Burl Noggle, *Teapot Dome: Oil and Politics in the 1920's* (Baton Rouge, 1962), 64–95.

ceived "a bountiful subsidy from Heaven for the prosperity of their cause."[17] Whatever the source, past decisions now appeared open to question.

These developments were disconcerting indeed with elections less than a year away. Coolidge himself bore no responsibility for Harding's appointees, yet his retention of them cast a cloud over the administration. Even if he were personally honest, could the President escape the responsibility for failing to supervise his cabinet? What of the other incorruptibles, Hughes and Herbert Hoover, whose appointments to the cabinet, critics had charged, were made partly in order to "deodorize" the official family?[18] Apparently they had never entertained even the faintest suspicions about what had been going on, for they insisted their surprise matched anyone's. An aura of laxity and incompetence hovered over the administration at best; it required no great cynicism to question whether a more sordid mess had yet to be exhumed. The President could rely upon Johnson, La Follette, and the Democrats to suggest precisely that.

Borah thought the ferment stirred up by the investigation proferred unique opportunities.[19] The scandals unquestionably injured Republican prestige, especially the Old Guard's. This was emphasized when party regulars, led by the Republican National Committee, backed Denby and Daugherty unreservedly and tried to destroy the reputation of their accusers. The arguments Borah and Robins had used to persuade Coolidge to disassociate himself from the standpatters became more relevant now, and the two men personally

[17] *New Republic*, XXXVIII (March 26, 1924), 110.
[18] *Nation*, CXII (March 9, 1921), 362.
[19] Apparently, Borah did not disclose his plans. Robins was with him during this period, thus obviating the need for correspondence between them. But Robins tried to keep a running account of events for Levinson; probably overestimating his own role, the Colonel's reports on what Borah was trying to do appear accurate.

commanded a stronger bargaining position. Borah's reputation for integrity in public life loomed particularly important. Having on several occasions led fights against corruption within his own party, his cooperation would help sanctify the administration's present conduct.

The Senator stood willing to assist Coolidge—for a price. If the President moved decisively against corruption, severed relations with the Old Guard, and advocated programs palatable to Borah, he would offer his full support at the convention and in the fall campaign. Equally important from the Idahoan's point of view, he promised to launch at once a "crusade"—centered around Outlawry—to prepare the ground for a constructive platform. Borah believed his ability to attract wide publicity would take the initiative from the embattled regulars as well as divert attention from the squalid headlines.

Since Coolidge's behavior over recognition of Russia had demonstrated his propensity to wilt under pressure, the once-bitten Senator refused to bind himself on the basis of vague promises. Confident he held high cards, Borah demanded proof that the President would not scurry for cover at the first sign of resistance. His asking price was Daugherty's immediate resignation. The word "immediate" is crucial, for he intended it to constitute a positive disavowal of the regulars who had thus far supported the Attorney General. Assurances that Daugherty would be eased out at the "proper time" did not suffice.[20]

Borah resorted to pressures of his own when Coolidge hesitated to accept the offer. If the President undervalued his cooperation, perhaps an example of what he could do in opposition might be more effective. On February 23, he rose in the Senate to demand the Attorney General's dismissal forthwith. Admitting the responsibility rested with the Presi-

[20] New York *Times*, February 19, 1924.

dent, Borah added that if no action were taken, he would assist any efforts to impeach Daugherty.[21] There was every reason to accept the word of a man who already had impaled more than one Republican on charges of corruption. Coolidge attempted to avoid a collision; the next day, a Sunday, he invited Borah to the White House. Arriving with the impression that the President was ready to come to terms, the Senator left the White House "fighting mad" when he received no firm commitment. If Coolidge failed to move within forthy-eight hours, Borah concluded, he would have been "trifled with."[22]

Although the Senator's backing, or at least his silence, would be highly beneficial, Coolidge could yield too much in trying to satisfy him. However chastized its leadership, the regular organization still commanded far more strength than Borah and Robins could muster. If the President angered the Old Guard by summarily dumping the Attorney General, where would he secure a countervailing force? The Idahoan in the past had launched several crusades—his proposed economic conference for instance—only to lose interest after the first thrust. As for Robins, his influence was real but was limited to a remnant of the band which had stood at Armageddon in 1912.

Coolidge tried to elude his dilemma through a policy of what might be called creative equivocation. He reassured Borah and Robins of his fundamental agreement with their objectives and promised them he would shed Daugherty as soon as he could.[23] Naturally, Coolidge pointed out, he was not entirely free to act as he wished, but he inisisted the delay was only tactical and that he would not let them down again. Counting upon their reluctance to break off negotiations—

[21] *Congressional Record*, 68th Cong., 1st Sess., 2982–83.
[22] Robins to Levinson, February 25, 1924, Box 76, Levinson Papers.
[23] Robins to Levinson, March 4, 1924, *ibid*.

for their prospects were heady—he prevailed upon them to postpone several deadlines over a period of more than a month. Each extension was valuable. The time would come when he could jettison the Attorney General, as more and more people were urging him to do, without affronting Old-Guard sensibilities.[24] If he could coddle Borah and Robins until then, he might gain their support without personal cost.

The Colonel's accounts of the conferences involving himself, Borah, and administration leaders are revealing. They show that he and the Senator, ostensibly acting in tandem, stood far apart in emphasis, particularly as to Outlawry. When the Idahoan talked of heading a constructive campaign for the President, he counted Outlawry as only one of the issues involved. He had promised to make the "great speech" if and when Coolidge gave his specific consent and acted on Daugherty, but Borah obviously regarded Outlawry's political use as its most important feature. Robins, who preached Outlawry above everything else, rather sadly noted this and once again began doubting whether the Senator acted in good faith. Borah had the *"name"* for Outlawry, Robins told Levinson, "what he needs now is the values of the *game*."[25]

The difference in priorities became more obvious in the matter of procedure. When the President continued hedging about the Attorney General, Robins and Levinson urged the Senator to grasp the initiative. Lead off with a speech against corruption in government, they told him, and temper it with sympathy for the administration's conduct. This would "force D. out," yet make Borah "100% with the Republican party and organization."[26] Then he should follow with the

[24] New York *Times*, March 6, 1924; Herbert Hoover, *The Memoirs of Herbert Hoover* (3 vols., New York, 1951–52), II, 54.

[25] Robins to Levinson, March 6, 1924, Box 76, Levinson Papers. The emphasis is Robins'.

[26] Robins to Levinson, March 5, 1924, *ibid*. Robins added that Coolidge had asked Borah "direct" to make a speech along these lines, but the Senator refused to act until Daugherty resigned.

Outlawry speech which would thereby rally the party and furnish the inspirational program needed to repair its image. The Senator heard them out, then repeated his determination not to move before the Attorney General's ouster.

The enthusiasm for positive action shown by Robins and Levinson eventually caused friction. Despite a vested interest in Borah's personal fortunes, they accorded Outlawry the higher precedence. Borah could not agree. By nature suspicious and inclined to see pitfalls everywhere, he thought the risks too great. Assuming he made the two speeches the Outlawrists requested, assuming further that Outlawry became the "overmastering" issue as Levinson predicted, where would this leave Borah if the administration appropriated the campaign but ignored him? He would have dissipated his strength at no gain to himself. Just as Robins doubted the Senator's commitment to Outlawry, Borah began doubting Robins' commitment to him. When the Colonel continued hammering away at the need for unilateral action, Borah fell into a "grouch" and, according to Robins, appeared to think, "I may have been trying to inveigle him into a wrong position."[27]

The Senator's attitude remained unbending as the affair drew to a close. The issues could not be compromised. His earlier belief that Coolidge's lack of strength alone prevented the decisive move changed to the feeling that he had been "bunked by the Silent Lad," which indeed he had. Robins, deploring Borah's failure to try altering the situation, accurately recorded the Senator's mood. Borah saw Daugherty as the symbol of the "old reactionary crooked crowd" and himself, George W. Pepper, and others as symbolic of the "progressive liberal" group. The President's conduct regarding the Attorney General's dismissal showed "which crowd Coolidge represents and prefers."[28] Although the deadline had been

---

[27] Robins to Levinson, March 7, 1924, *ibid.*
[28] Robins to Levinson, March 9, 1924, *ibid.*

advanced several times, Borah broke off negotiations when the last one, March 10, went unheeded. "This is one of the rare nights," observed teetotaler Robins, "I would like to get drunk."

Daugherty's resignation several weeks later left unchanged Borah's opinion that Coolidge had capitulated to "the old reactionary crooked crowd."[29] The Senator, for all practical purposes, took a leave of absence from the Republican party. Despite renewed efforts by Robins and Levinson to get him back in line on Outlawry, he again discarded it as a live issue. He wrote a few articles on it and repeated his adherence to the cause, but he made no moves. To Robins' impassioned pleadings he replied, "I want what you want, possibly not so keenly nor so determinedly, and yet I feel I really want to accomplish what you want." Although he usually employed a less spartan vocabulary, the Senator's response took up where he had left off before the oil scandals broke. He repeated himself with a depressing frequency in subsequent years. Promising to "do the best I can for the cause all the time," he never found a particular time in which the situation looked "ripe"; the great speech went undelivered.[30]

When talk arose of running Borah on the same ticket with Coolidge, the Senator himself seems to have implied he might be willing.[31] That he ever seriously considered it is highly doubtful. His entire career of vociferous independence strongly suggests that the idea of being Vice President would have had little appeal to him under the best of circumstances. Though conceivably a step toward the presidency, as friends pointed out, the prospect of four years in harness must have dimmed the vision. Not only would his passion for the excitement of political combat be starved, he would, by implica-

---

[29] But see Vinson's *Borah and the Outlawry of War*, 85.
[30] Borah to Robins, April 24, 1924, Box 242, Borah Papers.
[31] Stoner, *Levinson*, 132–33.

tion, be linked with what he now called "the Coolidge gang."[32] As he told a correspondent upon turning down the offer, "after seventeen years of slavish labor in the Senate . . . I ought not to give it up for a position where I have neither voice nor vote."[33] Borah, who wanted the presidency very badly, set limits as to how far he would go to get it.

The results of the Republican convention thoroughly disgusted the Senator and Robins. The Colonel said it provided a "photograph of the combined Big Business and Old Guard elements of the Republican Party." He referred to Coolidge and Charles G. Dawes as "The Morgan Golddust Twins." Not having committed himself, Robins said, he felt free "to shoot in any direction" and requested a conference with Borah so that the shooting would be to some purpose. "I knew just how you would feel," the Senator replied, "and I am sadly demoralized myself."[34] Disinclined to support either the candidates or the platform and having his own campaign to wage in Idaho, Borah refused to have anything to do with national politics in the months following.[35] The indefatigable Robins, however, refused to stay demoralized for long.

Administration leaders approached the Colonel again in late July. They asked him to serve on the Republican organization's Advisory Committee and to use his personal influence to keep the old Progressives from going over to La Follette or sitting out the election. Robins agreed, providing "Borah got renominated by the Republican Convention [in Idaho]

[32] Robins to Levinson, May 10, 1924, Box 76, Levinson Papers.

[33] Borah to J. F. McCarthy, June 13, 1924, Box 244, Borah Papers.

[34] Robins to Borah, June 17, 1924, and Borah to Robins, June 18, 1924, Box 245, *ibid.*

[35] The Senator's excuse was that his fight in Idaho demanded all his time. He told Robins that party leaders within the state would insist that he make certain promises before supporting him. Since "I do not propose for a moment to be put on the carpet or accept any dictation from any source whatsoever," he believed he would have to "fight all the way." Borah to Robins, August 11, 1924, Box 19, Robins Papers.

and if the president seemed sound on Outlawry."[36] Robins made this tentative bargain assuming its terms were favorable enough to bring the Senator into the campaign. Disconcerted by Borah's noncommittal reply, the Colonel wired him for clarification. "Subject your approval," he said, "am disposed to join forces with Republicans. This involves active support and will be effective only with your full conference and cooperation." The Senator answered reassurringly. Borah said he thought Robins ought to "go ahead, it is perhaps the best we can do under present circumstances."[37] Confident that Borah now stood with him, the Colonel threw himself into the campaign.

Only the Senator knew what he meant by his statement to "go ahead." It did not mean, apparently, that he intended to join Robins in support of Coolidge. Robins and Levinson at first accepted his explanation that state politics required his total energies. As the weeks passed without Borah uttering a word in favor of the Republican candidate, both Outlawrists began frenetically imploring the Idahoan to speak out before it was too late.[38] Levinson resorted to a familiar argument—that Borah's continued silence endangered Robins' relations with him. Reporting the Colonel "somewhat disturbed," Levinson said that "fine reassuring" talks with Coolidge rendered Borah the only missing link in the Outlawry chain.[39]

[36] Robins to Borah, August 6, 1924, Box 243, Borah Papers. Levinson at the same time tried to convince the President how important a favorable stand on Outlawry would be to him. "With Robins will come a host of the old Roosevelt Progressives," he wrote, "and as I feel sure, the potent, active services of Senator Borah." Copy of letter, Levinson to C. Bascom Slemp (secretary to Coolidge), August 9, 1924, Box 19, Robins Papers. Levinson wrote without Borah's authorization.

[37] Robins to Borah, August 15, 1924, and Borah to Robins, August 16, 1924, Box 243, Borah Papers.

[38] Robins to Borah, September 18 and 28, 1924, Levinson to Borah, September 19 and October 3, 1924, all in Box 238, *ibid.*

[39] Levinson to Borah, September 29, 1924, *ibid.*

Borah couched his replies in placatory language at first. Apologizing for his inactivity, he repeated his earlier statements that the senatorial race in Idaho required all his time. "I am doing the best I can to serve the cause," he wrote, "that is, serve it ultimately." [40] As the incessant importunities began wearing on him, his temper grew short. [41] Finally he lost patience. To one of the Captain-General's innumerable queries, Borah irritably responded that while he regretted "you and the Colonel seem to be disappointed or dissatisfied with my work," he (Borah) had been around a long time and knew "pretty well how to get results on small capital invested." Since the Senator had not invested *any* capital, so far as Levinson could determine, the Chicagoan must have been somewhat chagrined. He nonetheless assured Borah that the Outlawrists always had his best interests at heart, and that nothing should impair their friendship. [42] Friends they remained but the Senator refused to endorse Coolidge publicly.

The Outlawrist's gloom, caused by Borah's failure to support the Republican ticket, dissipated with the election returns. Coolidge not only won handsomely, he referred to Outlawry by name as one of the issues he would take up in his next administration. Past differences were put aside, if not forgotten, and personal relationships warmed as the three men bestowed fulsome praise on one another's contributions. Shortly thereafter Henry Cabot Lodge died, whereupon Borah became chairman of the Senate Foreign Relations Committee.

[40] Borah to Levinson, September 30, 1924, *ibid.*

[41] On one occasion, a news service quoted Borah as having referred to Coolidge as "the greatest man in the political history of the United States." Robins, among others, asked him if this marked the beginning of his drive. No, the Senator answered, he had been misquoted. He had instead paid Coolidge a mild compliment on tax reduction, "one of the greatest questions of the twentieth century." The correspondence over this incident is in Box 243, *ibid.*

[42] Borah to Levinson, October 22, 1924, and Levinson to Borah, October 24, 1924, Box 244, *ibid.*

Despite so many previous disappointments, the future of Outlawry looked brighter than ever before. At this juncture Borah virtually deserted the movement.

I I

A discernible format emerged from the Senator's association with Outlawry over the years. His interest had varied in direct ratio to the prominence of other issues. He had offered the Outlawry resolution on two occasions when the administration seemed intent on pushing the World Court. He had come closest to actually launching the campaign when bargaining with it for other objectives. His many protestations of abiding faith notwithstanding, he had used the "cause" only in opposition—whether to the court, or, more recently, to the Old Guard. A new and to Borah an unsettling development had taken place which not only affected Outlawry's utility but made it potentially dangerous as well.

Diverse individuals and groups had issued peace programs during the early 1920's. Some of these plans, such as Outlawry, involved formulas excluding existing organizations. Others sought to work along with the League or the court in some fashion. One of the most important of the "League" groups orbited around Professor James T. Shotwell of Columbia University who, preferring actual membership, desired cooperation with League activities as a minimum.[43] About the only similarity between the League faction and the Outlawists thus far was the distrust each held for the other. Both sides realized the futility of internecine war among peacemakers but had difficulty effecting a compromise. Levinson scored an apparent coup for Outlawry, therefore, when he and Shotwell negotiated a tenuous alliance in the fall of 1924.[44]

[43] The terms "League" or "Shotwell" group will be used here for convenience although there was no monolithic organization bearing either of these names.

[44] For a detailed account, see Stoner's *Levinson*, Chap. 9.

The Geneva Protocol made their agreement possible. Shotwell, along with soldier-scholar-diplomat Tasker H. Bliss and David Hunter Miller, an expert in international law, had drafted the Protocol for presentation to the League in October. Basically, it provided a means of arbitrating disputes through the World Court. Those nations refusing to accept arbitration or, having done so, refusing to abide by the decision would be branded as aggressors and liable to sanctions by the Protocol's signatories. Wars of aggression, under the agreement, would become an "international crime."[45] A far cry from "real" Outlawry, it seemed to provide a basis for co-operative action.

Borah unenthusiastically consented to participate in discussions between the peace advocates which took place during November. He probably went along to counter charges (now appearing with increasing frequency) that he used Outlawry solely as a weapon of obstruction and had no real interest in promoting international agreements.[46] As soon as the movement for fusion got under way, however, he backed away from it. For almost a month following the conciliation talks, the Senator answered none of Levinson's letters. The Captain-General, consoling himself with the thought that Borah "has a settled reputation along this line," grew worried.[47] He soft-pedalled the matter of fusion with the League groups so as to avoid losing the Idahoan, yet he could not abandon the prospects of additional support for his cause.

The involved story of the efforts to achieve a working relationship between the peace groups, or "Harmony Plan," as it was called, need not be retold here. Each side treated in

[45] Vinson, *Borah and the Outlawry of War*, 97.
[46] *Ibid.*, 99.
[47] Levinson to Robins, December 23, 1924, Box 20, Robins Papers. Levinson later told John Haynes Holmes that he thought Borah had "taken offense" at the conciliation plans. Stoner, *Levinson*, 142.

a manner calculated to further its own program.[48] Borah dissociated himself from negotiations after the first conference, by declaring himself unwilling to forego criticism either of the World Court or the Geneva Protocol.[49] Meanwhile, utilizing his recently acquired position as chairman of the Foreign Relations Committee, the Idahoan blocked attempts to bring World Court membership before the Senate by threatening to hold up other legislation.[50] That he could not sidetrack the issue indefinitely reinforced his disinclination to do anything in the way of launching an Outlawry campaign. Borah previously had used the movement *against* the court; to him the Harmony Plan raised the possibility that court advocates might harvest public interest generated by Outlawry. The Senator's charity stopped short of helping those whom he believed were trying to creep into the League through the "back door."[51]

Borah resumed his old stand—with certain variations—when the Senate took up the World Court question in December, 1925. He resembled the truculent Europe-baiter of 1919 vintage while speaking of what he called the "League Court," deriding it as another effort to embroil the United States in Old World chaos. He had learned, however, that a purely negative position lacked appeal and left him vulnerable to charges of obstructionism. Now he proclaimed his unquenchable hankering for *a* world court, provided it

[48] The Shotwell group wished to add Borah's voice to the World Court campaign, or at least secure his promise not to fight it. Levinson, on the other hand, believed the court would go through in any event and was prepared to barter for the inclusion of Outlawry. *Ibid.,* 139.

[49] Regarding the Protocol, Borah said he believed it "created the most ambitious military autocracy of which I have any knowledge and they choose to call it outlawing war." Borah to Thomas Q. Harrison, March 30, 1925, copy found in Box 20, Robins Papers.

[50] Denna Frank Fleming, *The United States and the World Court* (New York, 1945), 47.

[51] Stoner, *Levinson,* 146.

had no ties with the League of Nations. If the court met his specifications, codified international law, *and* promoted Outlawry, he said he would vote for it.[52] The patent impracticality of meeting such criteria established the Senator's ploy. He wished to defeat the court while posing as a "constructive" critic, much as he had done in February, 1923. Unable to make any headway along these lines, he reverted to straight-out opposition.

Borah fretted over the World Court needlessly. Despite his efforts to defeat the proposal, the Senate adopted a resolution for membership by a vote of 76 to 17 on January 27, 1926. Though his own demands were too blatant for serious consideration, enough encumbering reservations had been added to make unlikely their acceptance by the court's existing members.[53] The administration stoked few boilers; as usual Coolidge seemed merely to be going through the motions. When the British proposed a conference to discuss the Senate reservations, Secretary of State Frank B. Kellogg replied that no American delegate would attend.[54] A conference nevertheless met, accepted the reservations in part, and requested further negotiations to secure American membership. Loathe to antagonize those senators who had concocted the disabling reservations initially, Coolidge closed the matter with

[52] Vinson, *Borah and the Outlawry of War*, 109.

[53] Borah personally aided the passage of the Fifth Reservation, which held that the court should not "without the consent of the United States entertain any request for an advisory opinion touching any dispute or question in which the United States has or claims an interest." *Congressional Record*, 69th Cong., 1st Sess., 2656–57. In support of such a reservation, by far the most stringent one, the Senator read a memorandum which, he made clear, had been prepared by John Bassett Moore. Since Moore was *at that time* a judge on the World Court, the memorandum had considerable influence. See Fleming, *World Organization*, 246–52.

[54] L. Ethan Ellis, *Frank B. Kellogg and American Foreign Relations, 1925–1929* (New Brunswick, 1961), 225–41. Aside from being wary of the Senate, Kellogg had severely modified his earlier pro-League views. See Kellogg to Coolidge, October 7, 1924, Box 256, Coolidge Papers.

a curt refusal to enter any parleys. The World Court thereupon disappeared as a live issue until 1934.[55]

Ironically, Borah's ascension to the chair of the Senate Foreign Relations Committee occurred at a time when he experienced a growing indifference toward external matters. Involving himself in no sustained projects during 1925 and 1926, save for battling the World Court, he began using the argument that diplomatic questions at most peripheral to the nation's interests should not be permitted to obscure vital domestic problems. This was reminiscent of the prewar Borah. Referring to the dangers of "lethal internationalism," he said "our first and highest obligation is here in America" and "our first concern is our own people."[56]

His attitude rested on two convictions: that Europe was bent on its own destruction whatever the United States might do, and that the American public no longer cared very much about the rest of the world. When he chose to speak out on foreign affairs, as he did sporadically, he reverted to his old practice of alternately firing shots at "decadent" Europe, "the interests," and the administration.[57] Although his personal relations with the President were cordial (once his feeling of

[55] Herbert Hoover dabbled with the court during his presidency, but probably only at the urging of Secretary of State Henry L. Stimson. Borah easily blocked Hoover's halfhearted gesture in the Committee on Foreign Relations. Afraid to push the issue, Hoover told Stimson that Borah planned on using it to "kill him [Hoover] politically." Elting M. Morison, *Turmoil and Tradition: A Study of the Life and Times of Henry L. Stimson* (Cambridge, 1960), 112.

[56] Chicago *Tribune*, April 5, 1925.

[57] Unhappy over what he considered a resurgence of American imperialism toward the South, Borah loosed some rumbles about administration policy in Nicaragua and Mexico although he did not extend himself on these matters until early in 1927. He seemed ready, during the summer of 1925, to break with the administration over China policy but Kellogg's frantic pleas apparently satisfied him. Kellogg to Borah, August 20 and 21, Borah to Kellogg, August 26, all in Box 249, and Kellogg to Borah, September 4, in Box 263, Borah Papers. See also Dorothy Borg, *American Policy and the Chinese Revolution: 1925–1928* (New York, 1947), 26–27, 72–73.

having been "bunked" subsided), Borah's conception of himself as the custodian of American virtue must have tried Coolidge's patience. The Senator, who used his chairmanship of the Foreign Relations Committee quite as much to censor Republican foreign policy as to facilitate it, weighed heavily on an administration already distinguished by its passivity.[58]

The Idahoan exhibited signs of bestirring himself late in 1926. Worn down by the Outlawrists' incessant pleading, he reluctantly agreed to offer his resolution again. He told them that he considered himself "overruled" and that he could do nothing further during the present session of Congress.[59] Borah kept his word. He made no speech and the resolution was referred to the Foreign Relations Committee without debate; Borah personally did nothing to place Outlawry before the public. Instead he focused his attention on administration policies in Latin America. Immediately after submitting the resolution, he threatened to launch an investigation of American actions in Nicaragua. He failed to go through with it but the resultant publicity consigned Outlawry to limbo.[60]

As the congressional session drew to a close, Robins and Levinson implored Borah to take action on their cause. They elicited no response. Continuing to attract wide notice via flamboyant attacks on the administration's machinations in Latin America, Borah showed no inclination to involve himself with Outlawry at the same time.[61] Robins exploded

[58] Both Ellis in *Kellogg*, and Robert H. Ferrell in *Frank B. Kellogg and Henry L. Stimson* (New York, 1963), vol. XII of *The American Secretaries of State and Their Diplomacy*, stress Borah's influence on administration policy. Perfectly familiar with the Senator's destructive potential, Coolidge and Kellogg rarely took steps without sounding him out or at least trying to assess his possible reactions.

[59] Levinson to Robins, November 23, 1926, Box 21, Robins Papers.

[60] See newspaper clippings and correspondence on this episode in Box 280, Borah Papers.

[61] Concentrating his fire on Mexican affairs, the Senator wrote directly to President Plutarco Calles regarding American oil properties there. See Borah to Calles, January 22, 1927, and Calles to Borah (translation),

once more when it became obvious that Borah intended his resolution as a sop. Advised by Levinson that the Colonel verged on breaking with him, Borah replied that as "dear and vital" as he held Robins' friendship, "my convictions must still be my guide."[62] Levinson had all he could do to prevent a rupture between them. The Outlawry crusade lay in ruins —its proselytizer refused to proselytize.

III

On April 6, tenth anniversay of American entry into the First World War, French Minister for Foreign Affairs Aristide Briand released a statement to the Associated Press which breathed life into the almost moribund Outlawry movement.[63] To further the cause of peace Briand proposed that the United States and France join in a bilateral pact to "outlaw war" between the "two great democracies" as a solemn example to the rest of the world. His offer at first aroused only mild annoyance in American officialdom and made virtually no impact on the public. But it began attracting considerable interest when Dr. Nicholas Murray Butler, president of Columbia University, addressed a letter to the New York *Times* suggesting the possible importance of Briand's démarche.[64]

The French proposal had little in common with the Outlawry program beyond using the phrase, "to outlaw war."

January 24, 1927, both in *ibid.* This unorthodox approach caused a stir exceeded only by the Senator's actions, a month later, when he proposed that the entire Senate Foreign Relations Committee travel to Mexico and Nicaragua to investigate conditions there. Ferrell, in *Kellogg and Stimson*, 54, writes that Coolidge's decision to appoint Stimson as a special presidential agent to Nicaragua came "perhaps under inspiration of this [Borah's] proposition."

[62] Levinson to Borah, February 9, 11, 12, 13, and 15, Borah to Levinson, February 11 and 13, 1927, all in Box 280, Borah Papers.

[63] Printed in full in *FRUS, 1927*, II, 611–13.

[64] Stoner, *Levinson*, 240.

Robins and Levinson, however, agreed on the possibility of parlaying Briand's offer into a boost for their cause. They believed a bilateral pact might be the cornerstone upon which universal acceptance of Outlawry could be built. If the proposal was given the proper leadership and publicity, even Coolidge, who thus far had shown agile footwork in dodging the subject, might fall in line. The key to their hopes once more was Borah. All his tergiversations could be forgiven if Robins and Levinson could persuade him to take the lead now.

The Senator reacted to the French proposal as unenthusiastically as had the administration. After first refusing to comment at all, when pressed Borah replied that Briand's message did not seem to him "anything we could really get hold of."[65] In the following weeks he appeared to see some possibilities in it, although he still emphasized his reservations. He spelled out his views in a speech made in Cleveland on May 9.[66] Let the French clarify their proposal, he said, and if they meant Outlawry as it was understood in the United States, then perhaps negotiations might proceed. He opposed a bilateral pact in any event because Outlawry's goal was adherence by all nations. Although an interim agreement by the major powers might do for a start, a treaty between only two countries violated the program's spirit.

Since Borah nursed an abiding distrust of the French, it would have been unusual had he not questioned their intentions. The Senator, always susceptible to "inside" information, received just such information soon after he had expressed qualified approval of the French proposal. He learned, in a letter written him by an American scholar in Paris, that "when the proposal is not laughed at, it is considered as a be-

[65] Borah to Sherwood Eddy, April 29, 1927, Box 282, Borah Papers.
[66] New York *Times*, May 10, 1927.

lated bid for an alliance."[67] His long-held belief in Gallic treachery confirmed and later butteressed from still another source, Borah soon began calling Briand's offer "a piece of dynamite for Outlawry."[68]

The Idahoan stood immovable for the next few months, although the Outlawrists pounded away at him through correspondence and personal talks. He insisted that what the French were proposing bore little resemblance to Outlawry because the pact would be limited to two nations and omitted both a court and codification of international law. A bilateral agreement would pervert rather than further the cause, he said, and it would be little more than a negative alliance, whatever one chose to call it. The treaty would be useless should the exigency ever arise, moreover, lacking as it did machinery to adjudicate disputes.[69] In addition to lecturing his mentors about their program, the Senator horrified them in the early fall by firing a few broadsides at French delinquency in paying war debts.

Borah underwent a remarkable metamorphosis late in October. Still hesitant, he became more warmly disposed toward the French overture. The reasons for his change in attitude are susceptible to speculation only. In a narrow sense, textual alterations suggested by Levinson mitigated his antipathy, as did the Outlawrists's insistence that should Borah fail to ex-

[67] Joseph Agan to Borah, May 7, and Borah to Agan, May 17, 1927, Box 282, Borah Papers.

[68] Dr. Charles Clayton Morrison, editor of the *Christian Century*, had criticized Briand's proposal and planned to do so again in a forthcoming book. Knowing Borah's respect for Morrison's views, Levinson and Robins tried to persuade the latter to soften his remarks. They succeeded—only to find Borah still adhered to Morrison's original estimate. Borah to Levinson, July 12 and 20, 1927, *ibid.*

[69] Borah's insistence on formal machinery at this point is interesting in view of his subsequent contributions to the Pact of Paris. In June, he had asked Secretary of State Kellogg, "What is the object of making a treaty that we will not go to war if there is no machinery to settle the questions which bring on war?" Kellogg to Coolidge, June 27, 1927. State Department Decimal Files, 711.5112 France/34.

ploit the situation, the pro-Leaguers certainly would do so. Most important, however, there was evidence of growing support for the French proposal even in the areas normally considered "isolationist."[70] The Senator's vacillation over his own candidacy for President is confusing, but the desire existed and credit for a foreign policy coup would do him no harm at the convention. He and Robins were already discussing the possibility of impaling Coolidge on the issue of a "third term."[71]

Negatively, there was little to deter the Idahoan from involving himself just then. His attitude toward administration foreign policy had grown almost benign. He had, for instance, expressed satisfaction some months earlier over the direction of American relations with China. "The influences working for intervention in China are, of course, sleepless and they sit in high places," he had written William Allen White, but "I feel that our government has sincerely rejected the intervention program, the program of force."[72] A special mission, headed by Henry L. Stimson, had helped to end civil war in Nicaragua (a war caused in part by American interference) and, more recently, Ambassador Dwight Morrow had made great strides in easing Mexican-American tensions.[73]

Borah's apprehensions further lessened as he convinced himself that the dangers in Briand's suggestion could be overcome. He still favored extending the treaty to the major

[70] Vinson, *Borah and the Outlawry of War*, 134.
[71] Robins to Borah, June 18 and July 31, 1927, Box 285, Borah Papers.
[72] Borah to White, May 12, 1927, Box 275, *ibid.*; Borg, *Chinese Revolution*, 335–36.
[73] Borah's part in Morrow's appointment has been the subject of some speculation. William Appleman Williams, in *The Tragedy of American Diplomacy* (Delta edition, New York, 1962), 120, sees his role as "significant" and the Senator's most recent biographer, Marian McKenna, uses the term "key," in *Borah*, 167. Actually, Coolidge finessed the Senator on this question; the latter did little more than agree to Morrow's selection. See record of personal interview with Raymond Robins, no date, Box 1, William Boyce Thompson Papers.

powers, yet he conceded that a series of bilateral agreements might serve the same purpose.[74] Sensing that public opinion had become aroused, he told a reporter that the situation was favorable for an Outlawry crusade.[75] They must exercise care, he warned, to direct the reservoir of good will into proper channels. He refused to introduce his resolution at this time, explaining that it might be pushed through with no thought of implementing it.

December marked the turning point on the road to the Pact of Paris. Not only did Borah swing into action, presenting his resolution in the Senate and vigorously promoting Outlawry in public, but the administration also began modifying its position. Coolidge and Secretary of State Kellogg had been unsure what to do with the French offer up to now; neither had any enthusiasm for Outlawry and, as late as mid-December, Kellogg had expressed distaste for the concept. If forced to the wall, he and the President seemed inclined to favor Senator Arthur Capper's proposal to make "aggressive" war illegal.[76] They were aware of the demand for some kind of constructive policy and initially hoped to satisfy public and senatorial opinion by renewing the Root Arbitration treaties with France and Great Britain.

Borah set two tasks for himself. The first was to convince the administration that a multilateral pact was preferable to one between two parties as there would be no implication of a passive alliance. He accomplished this when Kellogg appeared before the Senate Foreign Relations Committee to discuss the arbitration treaties. Whether the Secretary independently reached the idea of extending Briand's proposal is

---

[74] Vinson, *Borah and the Outlawry of War*, 132.

[75] New York *Times*, November 27, 1927.

[76] Kellogg to Borah, December 14, 1927, Box 282, Borah Papers. As Robert H. Ferrell points out, in *Peace in Their Time: The Origins of the Kellogg-Briand Pact* (New Haven, 1952), 117, the Capper resolution "indicated the West was awakening to the peace campaign."

uncertain; the Senator's approval was important in any case.[77] Second, Borah began preaching the gospel of Outlawry to Kellogg and persuaded the Secretary that efforts to define "aggressive" war were fruitless. Although other factors were involved, Kellogg's original petulance over the entire situation turned into a real desire to exploit its possibilities.

The most important specific contribution Borah made in subsequent months, aside from coaching the Secretary of State, lay in his advocacy of a plan which dissuaded the French from their fear of a multilateral pact. They had recoiled in horror when Kellogg first indicated American willingness to join an extended treaty. Busily loading up with as many alliances as possible, the French replied that such an agreement would undermine previous commitments.[78] Negotiations might well have broken down completely had it not been for the Senator—and the ever-resourceful Levinson.

Borrowing almost verbatim from a draft that the Chicagoan had prepared, Borah published an article in the New York *Times* providing a way out of the impasse.[79] The sense of his proposal was that a multilateral pact such as he had in mind interfered with no other agreements. Without machinery or provisions for determining aggressors, a resort to war by any of the signatories automatically would release the others from the pact; they would be free to take whatever action they wished. The French ambassador thought an agreement "might readily be reached" along the lines indicated by the Senator.[80] The Borah-Levinson article smoothed the

[77] Kellogg to Root, December 23, 1927, Box 142, Root Papers. See Ellis, *Kellogg*, 196–99.

[78] Ambassador Paul Claudel to Kellogg, January 5, Kellogg to Claudel, January 11, and Claudel to Kellogg, January 21, 1928, *FRUS, 1928*, I, 1–8.

[79] Stoner, in *Levinson*, prints Levinson's draft and Borah's article side by side, 347–50. The Senator's article appeared in the New York *Times* on February 5.

[80] Memorandum of a conversation between Kellogg and Claudel, February 27, 1928, *FRUS, 1928*, I, 11–12.

way to further achievements, although much diplomatic jockeying followed.

Before continuing with Borah's "constructive" phase, the difference between the proposed treaty and Outlawry must be emphasized. As he had observed earlier, a multilateral pact without a court or codification of law embodied the *form* of Outlawry without its *content*. Borah was always willing to support a popular cause if it violated none of his dicta against entanglement, and the project he was now promoting was as harmless as anything imaginable. Had he regarded this merely a necessary first step toward real Outlawry, as did Robins and Levinson, there would be a better case for his "conversion." His performance after the Kellogg-Briand Pact was signed precludes such an interpretation.

The Secretary consulted Borah frequently during negotiations with the various powers partly, it is clear, to avoid arousing his choler over some real or imagined slight.[81] The releasing clause had met some objections, but the question remained as to criteria for invoking the release. Strictly interpreted, Borah's suggestion might mean that only a direct assault on a nation's territorial possessions provided sufficient cause. Those nations with large empires and many "special interests" found this wholly unacceptable. By now possessed with the idea that he neared a momentous achievement, Kellogg grew terrified lest "his" project founder. Chaos would result should each power insist upon listing all the interests it wished to have included as a basis for release.

That such a situation existed revealed the plan's utter vacuity. In effect, each power would promise to resort to war

[81] Kellogg's respect—or fear—went unrequited. A few weeks after Kellogg joined the cabinet, Borah regaled a dinner party with an anecdote about his shock over the appointment and then, in one of his listener's words, "went on in his vigorous way to tell me what a boob he thought Kellogg was." Arthur Bullard to Norman H. Davis, January 16, 1925, Box 6, Davis Papers, Library of Congress.

only to protect those interests it would have fought to protect in the first place. Kellogg, wishing to sweep these messy conditions out of sight, pronounced reservations unnecessary since everyone understood they would be operative. "Of course, wherever any government has special interests, it has a right to defend them" he wrote Borah, *"whatever that degree of interest is."*[82] Kellogg denied, furthermore, that the treaty implied obligations—legal or moral. The Senator could support this kind of international agreement without hesitation.

Borah's sentiments at this time are difficult to evaluate. Any notions he had about the presidential nomination evaporated long before the convention, and he had grown correspondingly detached about identifying himself with the treaty. He adopted a fatherly tone in his replies to Kellogg's frequent and often whining letters, assuring the Secretary he was performing well, that they could handle the opposition, and that he, Borah, was satisfied the pact would not compromise American interests.[83] Shortly before leaving for Paris to sign the treaty, Kellogg apologized for having bothered him so much about it, adding that "if I had not had your backing, your encouragement and your clear mind, I should long ago have gotten discouraged."[84] Such an expression of gratitude from a Secretary of State must have made Borah wonder if he were growing soft in his later years.

The Idahoan served ably during this period—for once the administration could not complain about lack of cooperation. After the pact was signed, he stumped for it and helped get it through the Senate without amendments.[85] As there were

[82] Kellogg to Borah, July 19, 1928, Box 542, Borah Papers. (Emphasis added.)

[83] Borah to Kellogg, July 28, copy found in Box 21, Robins Papers; and Borah to Kellogg, July 30, 1928, Box 542, Borah Papers.

[84] Kellogg to Borah, August 10, 1928, Box 542, Borah Papers.

[85] Ferrell, *Peace in Their Time,* 231–39, 247–51. James Reed and

no encumbering reservations, the other powers ratified the Kellogg-Briand Treaty, or Pact of Paris—though to Kellogg's great regret—after the Coolidge administration left office. A feeling of shared victory prevailed for a time as Secretary Kellogg, the Senator, and the Outlawrists joined in heaping garlands of praise upon one another. The aura of mutual admiration dissipated into petty quarrels over the "credit" each deserved.[86] Borah remained aloof from the bickering, which reflected well on no one, while modestly describing his own contribution. He thought the ceremony held to proclaim the treaty officially (July 24, 1929) "in many respects gruesome. I thought I was at the funeral of the Pact instead of its promulgation."[87]

Borah's attitude toward the Kellogg-Briand Pact in subsequent months is revealing. Levinson badly miscalculated in thinking the Idahoan at last had the "game" of Outlawry as well as the "name" for it. His embrace proved deadly. He had admitted the worthlessness of a pact without machinery, but now, although the Outlawry program stood a long distance from completion, he refused to involve himself any further. The very encomiums he heaped upon what had been done helped to render it impossible to stimulate interest in what remained to be done.

George A. Moses upheld Senate tradition by preparing the everlasting set of reservations. The Foreign Relations Committee already had issued a report embodying similar qualifications. Borah worked with Vice President Charles G. Dawes to have the Senate simultaneously consent to the treaty and adopt the report thereby "protecting" American interests without formal reservations.

[86] See State Department Decimal Files, 711.0012, Anti-War/838 and 1043 for Kellogg's shabby efforts to minimize Levinson's role. A member of the State Department had prepared an article on the Paris Pact for the *Encyclopaedia Britannica* and submitted it under Kellogg's name. Learning that the piece, already set in type, mentioned Levinson by name, Kellogg offered to pay the costs of revising it to exclude the Chicagoan. For Levinson's part in the dispute, see Stoner, *Levinson*, 340–41.

[87] Borah to Robins, August 12, 1929, Box 22, Robins Papers.

The Outlawrists, who regarded the pact merely as the beginning of the crusade, found Borah completely unresponsive when they tried to prod him into taking the next step. Realizing finally that the Senator had abandoned the cause for good, Levinson wrote that the disappointment "was the greatest in my life" and that Borah's attitude was "gall and wormwood to me."[88] Having backed and filled for almost ten years, the gentleman from Idaho pronounced himself satisfied with the results and turned his attention to prohibition, tariffs, and the immorality of the Versailles Treaty. The crusade was over for him, its accomplishments gratifying. The "great, paramount issue" had failed to bring him the office he coveted but he had used it to help stave off what he considered a disastrous threat to the American nation. The United States stood, at the end of the decade, where it had stood at the beginning—free from the "dead hand" of commitment and, indeed, free from any obligation to a world the Senator distrusted. By employing Outlawry against the proposals of others and by exaggerating the importance of ephemeral achievements such as the Kellogg-Briand Pact, Borah had done much to prevent a break with the past. His boast that he knew "pretty well how to get results on small capital invested" held true, as the returns on Outlawry amply demonstrated.

[88] For a time Borah permitted Levinson to believe the World Court—if properly modified—might be acceptable as the tribunal the Outlawry plan called for. In the end, however, he said he "must be against it for all the reasons I have heretofore opposed it." Borah to Robins, December 19, 1929, Box 318, Borah Papers. The quotation is from Levinson's letter to Dr. F. J. Kelley, no date, copy in Box 22, Robins Papers. The text of the letter clearly indicates Levinson wrote it shortly after learning of Borah's refusal even to consider membership in the World Court.

---◄—►---

CHAPTER VIII

The Long Fight

SENATOR BORAH identified himself with many causes over the decades. He pursued none more relentlessly than his campaign in behalf of recognizing Soviet Russia. For sixteen years, in season and out, he chipped away at what he considered an utterly bankrupt evasion of responsible diplomacy. If nothing else, his extended drive undermines the view that he was constitutionally incapable of sustained interest—when, unlike the case of Outlawry, he genuinely believed in what he was doing. Nor were the ends he sought in any way unusual for him. His demand for accommodation with the Soviet government had as its most important goal the very negation of interference which nonrecognition entailed. The sole unique aspect of the Senator's conduct is that it represented one of those rare instances where he expended a great deal of capital for minimal returns.

That Borah acted according to his conception of American interests is certain. Yet it is difficult to study his speeches and correspondence over these years without concluding that the Russian question did comprise for him more than just another example of misguided diplomacy. One of his biographers suggests that his sympathy for the underdog accounts for his tenacity, which quite possibly it did. But the entire situation was congenial to his nature in other ways. By opposing the official stance of both major parties, he essayed once more that role most dear to him—the fearless dissenter crying out truth to the Philistines. And, unpopular though his sentiments were in many circles, it is not clear that his outspokenness caused him any severe political damage. Those who denounced him over this issue were unlikely to be Borah adherents anyway, while to his followers the Senator provided yet another welcome assualt against the establishment.

Borah had as his first worry at the Republican National Convention of 1920 the party's stand on the League of Nations. To liberal irreconcilables like himself, however, the division over recognition of Russia represented the same clash of forces involved in the League struggle. Warren G. Harding's nomination resolved neither matter as he managed to avoid committing himself on any question of importance. He did, however, promise Raymond Robins to reconsider American policy toward Russia in return for the latter's support in the election—a pledge the Colonel found difficult to redeem. Robins, no more pleased with Harding than was the Idahoan, agreed they had to make the best of a bad situation.[1] They failed to realize how bad the situation really was. Nonrecognition turned out to be one of Woodrow Wilson's legacies which few Republicans wished to repudiate.

Harding's pliability made his choice of a Secretary of State appear as critical for the Russian issue as it did for the League. Since Charles Evans Hughes had stated his opposi-

[1] Robins later admitted he would have supported Harding in any event, if only to rid the nation of the "witch-hunting of [A. R.] Burleson and [A. Mitchell] Palmer." Robins to J. Kespohl, September 4, 1920, Box 16, Robins Papers.

tion to recognizing the Bolsheviks in addition to advocating League membership with "proper" reservations, his appointment constituted a twofold setback for Borah and those of similar mind. Throughout his tenure of office, Hughes refused to countenance the slightest moderation of the policy set down under the previous administration. And whenever Harding or his successor, Calvin Coolidge, seemed to waver, Hughes moved forward to nudge them back in line.

Borah and Robins might well have been as dismayed by Harding's selection of Herbert C. Hoover for Secretary of Commerce. Before accepting this post, Hoover had asked for and received assurance that he would have broad powers over questions of both domestic and foreign policy. Hoover, along with Hughes, proved to be one of the dominant antirecognition figures of the administration. Adamantly against either trade with, or recognition of, the Soviet government, his strong position within the administration became evident when he, rather than the Secretary of State, made the first policy statement hostile to prospects of any change in relations. Overtures from Moscow for a resumption of normal trade relations between Russia and the United States afforded him his opportunity.

The Soviet communication at this time rested on two assumptions. First, since the Republican party represented the "business classes," Russian leaders believed the desire for trade would override the "moral" position Wilson had assumed.[2] Second, the conclusion recently of a trade agreement with Great Britain seemingly indicated that Western antagonism toward Soviet Russia had diminished. In defending this agreement, Prime Minister David Lloyd George had stated that since the Soviet regime had not collapsed as some had hoped, and since there were indications of a "mellowing"

[2] Robert Browder, *The Origins of Soviet-American Diplomacy* (Princeton, 1953), 18.

within the society, it made little sense to fossilize the status quo.[3] Communist leaders hoped this attitude also prevailed in the newly installed Republican administration.

Hoover's statement, released the day before publication of the Soviet note, corrected Moscow's misunderstanding. Nothing, he said, warranted a reconsideration of the policy formulated by President Wilson. Relations remained impossible not for lack of a trade agreement, but because under communism, Russia did not, nor would she ever, have anything to trade. The Secretary declared that Russia would be unable to "get back to production" unless she changed the foundations of her economic system. He denied that economic factors motivated the Soviet communication anyway, seeing it instead as a political move designed to bring about recognition. Given the Soviet policy of repudiation, confiscation, and continued propaganda, Hoover went on, recognition was out of the question.

To avoid a purely negative stance and to head off allusions to British policy, Hoover tried to explain how in the long run this posture would benefit the United States. The "contradictions" inherent in a communistic system, he predicted, meant that the Soviet government eventually had to collapse. When that happened, the United States would occupy the position of having been the solitary friend of the anti-Bolsheviks, the one nation which had refused to sacrifice its principles on the alter of trade. Once the opposition forces regained control of Russia, as inevitably they must, they would repay America for its loyalty by according it a favored role in the reconstruction of a liberal, democratic society with all the material advantages this implied.[4] Herbert Hoover moved in his own world of economic determinism.

Secretary of State Hughes officially rejected the Soviet pro-

[3] New York *Times*, March 23, 1921.
[4] *Ibid.*

posals several days later, casting his reply in the same terms Hoover had used. He emphasized the point that there would be no resumption of relations until the Soviet leaders gave evidence that "fundamental changes" within the economy "are contemplated."[5] Hoover released a separate statement the same day, in which he said that "nothing" could be more important than the recovery of Russia. Both men argued that the dearth of trade between the United States and Russia merely reflected economic facts rather than the absence of a formal agreement.[6]

Borah challenged the Hoover-Hughes thesis on practically all counts. He too considered Russian recovery most important, but he attacked their contentions that this could not be accomplished by the present regime. Nor did he appreciate the relevance of pontificating on the effectiveness of various economic systems. The facts indicated, he said, that trade with Soviet Russia was indeed feasible and desirable for both nations.[7] The Senator pointed out that the administration dissimulated in maintaining that all trade restrictions had been removed in March, 1920. Actually, the United States still refused the Russians credit and shipping arrangements; there was no postal service in operation; and no federal assay office would accept gold even "believed" to be of Soviet origin.[8] In a plea for "saner relations," Borah denounced as "idle" the talk about unrestricted commerce when such conditions prevailed.[9]

At this time, while the United States wallowed in the "Red scare," those who favored relations with Soviet Russia operated in a weird context. The newspapers printed stories daily

[5] *FRUS, 1921,* II, 768.

[6] New York *Times,* March 26, 1921.

[7] *Ibid.,* March 25, 1921. The United States was in the postwar recession at this time.

[8] *FRUS, 1920,* III, 717 and 725.

[9] New York *Times,* March 25, 1921.

of plots, atrocities, and revolutions, many of which bore no relation to actual events. What the Senator later called the "propaganda factories" at Riga, Revel, and Helsingfors poured anti-Bolshevik releases to American journals, which all too frequently used them without discrimination. During the weeks of discussion over the trade question, an inordinate number of these stories dealt specifically with the dangers involved in commercial relations with Russia.[10]

The administration had little to worry about from advocates of recognition within this context of extreme hostility toward "the Reds." The Hoover-Hughes position met with overwhelming approval as several important groups outside the government hastened to protest any reconsideration of policy. In addition to a vigorous appeal by Samuel Gompers, president of the American Federation of Labor, the National Civic Federation addressed a petition to the State Department urging that the United States refuse to negotiate with Soviet Russia on any level. Among the signers of this petition were William C. Redfield, former Secretary of Commerce and past president of the American Manufacturers' Association; James A. Farrell, president of the United States Steel Corporation; Darwin P. Kingsley, president of New York Life Insurance; Otto M. Kahn of Kuhn, Loeb and Company; and Lorillard Spencer, chairman of the American Legion Committee on Anti-American Activities. Several leaders of the Roman Catholic Church

---

[10] On March 24, 1921, for example, New York *Times* printed two reports from Revel on the dangers of relations with Soviet Russia. One held that a survey of those who had entered into trade agreements with the Communists found that the latter never intended to execute the contracts and simply used negotiations for propaganda purposes. Another story reported a meeting of the Soviet Revolutionary Committee which culminated in plans for a tremendous military buildup. This was to be facilitated through foreign trade; thus orders had gone out "to Soviet trade delegations for the purchase of necessary equipment abroad." How Bolshevik leaders expected to secure supplies while negotiating for propaganda purposes only was not revealed.

also issued statements against relations with the "Godless Communists."[11]

The few business and labor groups who did favor relations with Soviet Russia were in the minority and achieved little coordination.[12] Proponents of recognition found their appeals meeting with apathy, if not outright suspicion. In view of these circumstances, the Senator and Robins correctly decided against belaboring the issue until more propitious times. They did continue advocating relations with the Soviets in their correspondence and speeches; Borah also initiated a brief Senate hearing on the prospects of trade.[13] Robins broached President Harding personally to collect on their pre-election agreement but met with no success.

The debate over recognition in 1921 presaged a struggle lasting twelve years. Although the emphasis on particular points varied according to time and circumstance, neither the actors nor their lines changed fundamentally throughout the period. The most important aspect of recognition for both Borah and Robins lay in their belief that world peace stood beyond attainment as long as a nation of Russia's size and potential strength remained ostracized.[14] Treaties, agreements, and conventions, they said, had scant value providing they excluded this nation of 140 million people. "Outlawing" a country because of its economic system promoted chaos, therein establishing the foundations for future wars. The test for admittance to the "family of nations" rested not with the

[11] New York *Times,* March 25, 1921.

[12] See New York *Times,* December 29, 1920, and *Relations with Russia: Hearings on Senate Joint Resolution 164 for the Reestablishment of Trade with Russia* (Washington, 1921).

[13] *Relations with Russia.*

[14] The arguments presented in this and subsequent paragraphs have been abstracted from numerous speeches, articles, and letters either published or in the correspondence of both Robins and Borah. Almost the entire gamut of the Senator's positions can be found in a carton full of drafts and memoranda, Box 99, Borah Papers.

Soviet government but with the Western powers themselves. If they believed so strongly in the superiority of their systems, why then did they fear Bolshevik contamination? As the Senator often put it, he placed complete trust in the ability of the American people to resist the blandishments of Communist propaganda.

On the matter of Russian economic recovery, the recognitionists argued that the United States could and should participate in as large a measure as possible. Aside from contributing to European stability, such a policy would also present a genuine opportunity to mitigate the Soviet regime's harshness which so many people condemned.[15] Robins and Borah cited various benefits which would accrue to the American economy, although they used this mostly as a tactical argument to attract certain interest groups. They ridiculed the notion that the Communist regime had to collapse when, in reality, it grew stronger with each passing year. As he had written immediately after the November revolution, the Senator continued equating the failure to recognize the Bolsheviks with the failure to recognize facts, however much one disliked them.[16]

Those who protested against recognition did so on several grounds. The argument employed most frequently held that the Soviet government had demonstrated its unfitness for acceptance into the community of nations, whatever that was. Dedicated to the destruction of the existing social order everywhere, the system had to be quarantined because it stood against everything best in Western civilization.[17] The original

[15] Borah to S. S. Dale, December 2, 1922, Box 234, *ibid.*

[16] Borah, "Shall We Abandon Russia?" But see Christopher Lasch, *The American Liberals*, 214–20.

[17] The classic formulation of this position appears in Secretary of State Bainbridge Colby's letter to the Italian Foreign Minister, August 21, 1920, *FRUS, 1920*, III, 463–68. This letter was often cited during the Republican era.

reasons for nonrecognition—confiscating, repudiation, and propaganda—tended to merge into this broad "moral" argument, especially after the Soviet leaders had offered repeatedly to negotiate specific issues. Religious groups stressed the militant atheism of the Bolsheviks as an indication of their utter depravity. Finally, conservatives such as Elihu Root perceived great danger in recognizing the Communists because it would promote the view that the Russian system compared favorably with capitalism, thereby stimulating radical tendencies within the American public.[18]

Beyond the moral argument, which was most effective in shaping public opinion, some opponents of recognition offered a more sophisticated analysis. The outstanding example, Herbert Hoover, stood as a towering figure in the fight over changing policy during three Republican administrations. The Secretary unquestionably found communism repugnant in its entirety because he was, as Borah put it, "such a colossal individualist."[19] But Hoover's personal animus merely intensified a more comprehensive outlook. Long regarding Russia as one of the great undeveloped areas for capitalist penetration, he had been personally connected with a British combine whose holdings had been confiscated by the Bolsheviks. Russia under Soviet control, in Hoover's mind, bulked as a disaster to his program for an ever-expanding American economy, of which trade per se constituted only one part.

Hoover's attitude on the Russian question depended scarcely more upon commercial statistics than it did upon the fear of

---

[18] Elihu Root to Ivy Lee, March 2, 1926, attached to Lee's letter to John Bassett Moore, March 3, 1926, Box 162, Moore Papers. For a survey of American attitudes toward Russia, see Peter G. Filene, *Americans and the Soviet Experiment, 1917–1933* (Cambridge, Mass., 1967). As Filene points out, the "ingredients" making up American attitudes remained stable over the years, but "with the order of priorities revised" according to "the varying situations of war, prosperity, and depression," 274–75.

[19] Louis Fischer, *Men and Politics: An Autobiography* (New York, 1941), 213.

propaganda. Assuming the Soviet experiment succeeded, which Hoover doubted but had to accept as a possibility, American businessmen would have to conduct their transactions with a gigantic, state-controlled economic complex. Not only were there disadvantages in doing business with state monopolies which the Secretary of Commerce detested, but Soviet antagonism to large-scale private development would also limit the opportunities for broad American participation in the Russian economy.[20] Hoover's plans for the overseas expansion of America's economy could not operate successfully under such limitations. "The hope of our commerce," he wrote, "lies in the establishment of American firms abroad, distributing American goods under American direction; in the building of direct American financing and, above all, in the installation of American technology in Russian industries."[21]

As he was sincere in predicting that the Communist system had to fail because of its "inner contradictions," Hoover had no wish to postpone this collapse through trade and recognition. Thus he thought the United States ought to rule out any policies conceivably prolonging the Soviet regime's life, while remaining prepared to engage fully in the reconstruction of a non-Bolshevik society. Borah's arguments were more than simply mistaken from Hoover's standpoint, they were irrelevant. The Secretary, far from refusing to face facts, meant to change them.[22]

[20] See Joseph Brandes, *Herbert Hoover and Economic Diplomacy* (Pittsburgh, 1962), particularly Chaps. 4 and 8.

[21] Hoover to Secretary of State Hughes, December 6, 1921, *FRUS, 1921*, II, 788.

[22] Hoover's role in the American Relief Administration appears to contradict this view or else it indicates humanitarian considerations outweighed all others. While there is no need to disparage his humanitarianism, the famine in Russia brought about a happy situation whereby his philanthropy coincided with policy goals. "The relief measures already initiated," Hoover wrote in December, 1921, "are greatly increasing the

A year after the initial debate over a trade agreement, Borah found an issue with which to reopen the recognition question. He concentrated his attack once again on Boris Bakhmetev, whose status as "Ambassador of the Russian People" had survived the change in administrations and who had contributed actively to the antirecognition cause. Borah grasped the handle provided him by the arrival of General Grigori M. Semenov, former head of a Japanese-dominated White Russian government in Siberia. The Senator had obtained considerable data on the excesses committed by Semenov's regime; the latter's reputation reeked so badly that even the most ardent anti-Bolshevik groups in the United States refused to defend him.[23] Although he lacked evidence that a connection between the two existed, Borah implied as much in stating that Bakhmetev had been "among the first gentlemen whom he [Semenov] visited."[24] Playing upon Semenov's notoriety, the Senator hoped to discredit the reputation of all the Russian emigré groups centering around the ambassador.

Borah's underlying motive for raising the Bakhmetev affair was to publicize the entire Russian question. Failing in that, however, Bakhmetev's elimination as a factor in Russian-American relations would still serve some purpose. His connections, organization, and access to large sums of money permitted the ambassador to occupy a key position with the

---

status and kindliness of relations and their continuation will build a situation which, combined with other factors, will enable the Americans to undertake the leadership of the reconstruction when the proper moment arises." *Ibid.*, 789. Uttering not a word of propaganda, an American government distributing supplies under its own strict supervision demonstrated all too clearly to the Russians the difference between a capitalistic system of abundance and the Communist society which had brought them to starvation. That Hoover considered this program an anti-Bolshevik weapon can also be seen in his determination to prevent private or religious groups from sharing in relief efforts independently.

[23] See Box 214, Borah Papers.

[24] *Congressional Record*, 67th Cong., 2nd Sess., 6299.

antirecognitionists.[25] The sources of his funds also were important, for Borah hoped to demonstrate that Bakhmetev financed his activities with what remained of American loans made to the Provisional Government during the war. If the Senator could show that the large part of these funds were used against the Bolsheviks, it would weaken the case that they had repudiated legitimate debts. Finally, the Idahoan seems to have felt genuine outrage toward the aura of secrecy and intrigue surrounding Bakhmetev, which rendered him unaccountable to the public or to Congress. Reports of the ambassador's influence with State Department officials hardly assuaged Borah's anger.[26]

The Idahoan had tried repeatedly to get Bakhmetev before a Senate committee to testify about his financial operations, only to have the State Department foil each attempt by invoking diplomatic immunity. Administration officials stoutly maintained that Bakhmetev in reality served the interests of the United States in his capacity as ambassador. According to Hughes, the entire amount of funds at Bakhmetev's disposal had gone into a "liquidation account" to settle unpaid Russian debts—to the extent that the ambassador and his entourage even paid their own expenses. At the same time he denied that the fund was used for any other purposes, Hughes pointed out that the State and Treasury Departments exercised full supervision and control over all transactions.[27] In a letter to the President, written during Senator Borah's inquiry, the Secretary assured him that there were no irregularities in the disbursement of the funds in question. "It may not be out of place to recall," he added, "that the Senator who led the discussion was a member of a Senate Committee which

[25] Kennan, *The Decision to Intervene*, 322–23.

[26] See, for example, letter from Norman Hapgood, former Ambassador to Denmark, to Borah, May 5, and Borah to Hapgood, May 6, 1922, Box 214, Borah Papers.

[27] *Congressional Record*, 67th Cong., 2nd Sess., 6435.

on April 14, 1920, rendered a report to the Senate on Russian propaganda."[28] The report Hughes referred to derided the importance of Bolshevik influence in the United States, and the senator, of course, was Borah.

Lacking access to official records, the Idahoan had to make his charges from what fragmentary evidence he had been able to accumulate. What he had convinced him that the State Department sought to cover up the money's real uses.[29] According to Borah, reports thus far made public left unaccounted some $87 million. He accused Ambassador Bakhmetev not only of devoting some of this money to propaganda purposes and assisting anti-Bolshevik groups, but also of personal irregularity involving real estate speculation.[30] The Senator criticized the State Department for extending diplo-

[28] *FRUS, 1922*, II, 877. See *Senate Report 526*, 66th Cong., 2nd Sess.

[29] Borah to W. T. Rainey, June 10, 1922, Box 214, Borah Papers. Borah wrote that "a bad mess is being covered up," and that exposure would embarrass the departments in question, not to mention the administration.

[30] The writer has found no evidence to substantiate Borah's charges of personal dishonesty. It is clear, however, that the administration's reports were far from candid. They never explained why Bakhmetev defaulted on payments due the United States Government in November, 1918, but could pay interest on Russian bonds held by the J. P. Morgan Company just one year later. *Nation*, CXIV (May 17, 1922), 584. The sums Bakhmetev received from the resale of goods purchased but undelivered did not appear, nor did all the original funds go into the liquidation account. Secretary of the Treasury Andrew Mellon's letter to Hughes of June, 1922, directly contradicts the latter's assertion. *FRUS, 1922*, II, 878. Mellon's letter, dealing only with original credit of $56 million Bakhmetev had with the National City Bank of New York, refers to an exempted $9 million used for "salaries and upkeep of the Russian Embassy and consulates and other Russian institutions" which Hughes had denied. Mellon neglected to mention an additional $22 million credited to the ambassador's account in the spring of 1920; Borah assumed this came from the resale of goods. *Congressional Record*, 67th Cong., 2nd Sess., 6435. However, according to the *Wall Street Journal*, May 28, 1920, the J. P. Morgan Company received a shipment of $22 million in gold from Hong Kong, "believed to be" part of Kolchak's gold reserves sent out just prior to the latter's capture by the Bolsheviks. The identical amounts may be coincidental, no account of them became public.

matic immunity to prevent a personal accounting while refusing to release its own records because it could "not get the
permission of Bakhmetev's government."[31] Borah scoffed
that he "could not conceive of a man being an Ambassador
without a government."[32]

Although his charges failed to arouse much interest in the
broader issues, Borah did succeed in forcing Bakhmetev's
resignation and subsequent flight from the country to escape
a subpoena. The administration and Bakhmetev publicly
attributed his resignation to "personal reasons," but the latter's
offer to resign specifically mentioned the "renewed discussion"
over his status. Hughes, quickly accepting the resignation,
extended Bakhmetev's diplomatic immunity to June 30, which
enabled him to settle his affairs and leave.[33] Borah immediately prepared another subpoena effective July 1, to be served
should the Russian overstay his period of grace.[34] Raymond
Robins pronounced the Senator's attack "masterly," wryly
commenting that "history will record your wisdom even if the
State Department does not."[35]

Despite the very mild results of Borah's efforts, antirecognition leaders took the usual precautions. An article under
Hoover's name appeared in the *Manufacturing News* on May
25, citing the reasons why trade and recognition were undesirable.[36] A few weeks later Samuel Gompers directed the by
now standard "inquiry" to Secretary Hoover asking whether
the administration contemplated a shift in policy. Hoover
replied that "the obstacles to trade are purely the creation of

---

[31] *Congressional Record*, 67th Cong., 2nd Sess., 9004–9005.
[32] *Ibid.*, 6300.
[33] Bakhmetev to Hughes, April 28, 1922, and Hughes to Bakhmetev,
April 29, 1922, both in *FRUS, 1922*, II, 875–77.
[34] See Associated Press clipping headed, "Borah Still After Bakhmetev's
Scalp," in Box 214, Borah Papers.
[35] Robins to Borah, July 3, 1922, Box 219, *ibid.*
[36] Hoover's article is reprinted in the *Congressional Record*, 67th Cong.,
2nd Sess., 7911.

the Soviet authorities," adding with stern piousity, that the only gold in the Russian government's possession was "that recently taken from the churches."[37] Gompers read this message before the annual convention of the American Federation of Labor, which afterwards passed a resolution placing the federation against relations with Russia. The scope of the Russian famine seemed to verify Hoover's assertions, which were utilized in and outside Congress.[38] Borah failed to get a resolution for the recognition of Russia out of committee.

Through the summer and fall of 1922, the Senator spoke frequently in behalf of recognition at public meetings while urging his correspondents to form committees and other groups to exert pressure in this direction.[39] He also supplied certain newspapers with material on Russia—often with the agreement that his name be omitted, thus making it appear that support for recognition came from diverse sources.[40] Though assuring his followers that "the country would be swept for Russian recognition," Borah could produce little evidence of any wide interest at the time.[41]

In December, Alexander Gumberg, a friend of Robins and long-time advocate of recognition, met with the Idahoan to offer his services in the campaign. Gumberg became an important figure in coordinating the recognition forces and in providing Borah with information garnered from an intimate

[37] Max S. Hayes, delegate to the American Federation of Labor Convention, to Borah, June 23, and Borah to Hayes, June 24, 1922, Box 220, Borah Papers.

[38] The Senator answered this argument with the charge that although "our charity has perhaps saved ten million people, our policy has starved twenty million," *Congressional Record*, 67th Cong., 2nd Sess., 7910.

[39] *Nation*, CXV (October 18, 1922), 349 and Alexander Gumberg to Robins, November 14, 1922, Box 18, Robins Papers.

[40] Gumberg to Robins, November 15, 1922, *ibid*.

[41] Gumberg to Robins, November 14, 1922; *ibid*.

acquaintance with many political and business leaders. Gumberg enjoyed Robins' enthusiastic endorsement. The Colonel stated that "if I alone of all the 'wise men among the Allies' made the right guess in that confused and troubled time, it was more due to Alexander Gumberg than to any or all other reasons." Robins said he gladly accepted full responsibility for Gumberg's "ability, his integrity, his courage and his common sense."[42] The Colonel's opinion and Gumberg himself impressed Borah, who thereafter dealt with him in complete confidence.

Robins had met Gumberg when the latter served as his personal secretary during the revolutionary days in Russia. In addition to their compatibility, Gumberg probably had saved Robins' life on one occasion by facing down a mob of anarchists intent on assaulting the American.[43] Upon his return to the United States, Gumberg had dedicated himself to promoting friendly relations with Russia. According to Louis Fischer, he was an extremely attractive person, who counted among his friends such people as Robert and Philip La Follette, Burton K. Wheeler, Stuart Chase, Joseph Wood Krutch, "the whole *Nation* family," Louis Adamic, Reeve Schley of the Chase National Bank, Samuel Zemurray of the United Fruit Company, and Mark and Carl Van Doren. Dwight Morrow also became fairly close to Gumberg, consulting him on many occasions.[44] Gumberg helped form the All-Russian Textile Syndicate in 1923 and a year later the New York branch of Amtorg, a Russian-American trade organization. And since Borah had neither the time nor the inclination for

---

[42] Gumberg to Robins, December 5, 1922, Box 19, *ibid.*, and Robins to Borah, December 9, 1922, Box 234, Borah Papers.

[43] Gumberg also had "unique contacts" in Soviet circles through his brother, and helped Robins get personal interviews with Lenin and Trotsky, see Kennan, *The Decision to Intervene*, 236.

[44] Fischer, *Men and Politics*, 212–13, and Dwight Morrow to Robins, December 20, 1926, Box 21, Robins Papers.

organizational work, Robins' friend proved a welcome addition to the recognition circle.

Gumberg encouraged Borah to answer charges that the Soviet government actively persecuted religious groups in Russia. These accusations, which began appearing with alarming frequency during the spring of 1923, were extremely harmful to the case for recognition. Although some of the stories were the familiar anti-Bolshevik concoctions, the execution of a Catholic priest early in 1923 produced a strong feeling of revulsion in the United States. Gumberg disparaged reports criticizing the Soviet government, whatever their source, and convinced Borah that the execution had resulted from counterrevolutionary activities rather than from religious beliefs. The unfavorable publicity surrounding the matter prompted the Senator to try repairing the damage.

He protested, in a telegram to the editors of the *Literary Digest*, that the American press had mishandled the story.[45] Borah denied religious persecution lay behind the execution. He construed the incident as another reason for recognition by holding the unfriendliness of the Western powers responsible "for the distrust, the fear, the spirit of retaliation, which leads to harsh and cruel acts." After listing a number of things done *to* Russia, he concluded by asking that "before we charge others with cruelty and inhumanity let us practice some Christian precepts and principles ourselves." Although Gumberg pronounced the Senator's statement on the matter as one of "true liberalism," incidents of this type made it difficult for the prorecognitionists to get much sympathy for their campaign.[46]

The "moral" argument against recognition, buttressed by

---

[45] Borah to editors of the *Literary Digest*, April 4, 1923, Box 234, Borah Papers.

[46] Gumberg to Borah, April 4, 1923, *ibid.* In spite of his efforts to "correct" the matter, Gumberg reported, Borah grew "very worried" over its effects. Gumberg to Robins, May 21, 1923, Box 19, Robins Papers.

events such as the priest's execution, placed Borah at a disadvantage. While he tried to restrict the debate to questions of peace and recovery, he found himself cast as an apologist for the Soviet regime.[47] Because of this he was often accused, directly or by implication, of being a Bolshevist sympathizer. Such allegations, absurd to those who knew him, undoubtedly clouded the issues in the minds of many people.

The prospects for recognition brightened during the summer months despite the ill effects of the persecution issue. President Harding, who up to now had ignored the promise he had made to Robins at the Republican convention in 1920, at last appeared willing to make good on it. He authorized Robins to visit Russia and agreed to reconsider the situation after he read the Colonel's report.[48] In view of Harding's performance thus far, his concession in itself hardly caused wild jubilation since he was undoubtedly looking ahead to 1924. Certain other indications, however, such as personnel changes in the State Department, made it appear that some revision of policy might be underway.[49]

In addition to stirrings within the administration, the stream of business figures and congressmen visiting Russia crested during these months, reflecting an aroused interest in relations.[50] Gumberg, who kept close watch, wrote the Senator that "never since the Revolution have there been in Russia Americans as prominent in business and political life as are going there this summer. It seems," he added, "that you will

[47] See, for example, transcript of the Senator's speech in Boston, December 2, 1922, Box 234, Borah Papers. His talk followed the usual lines, but during the question period almost all queries concerned the internal affairs of Russia.

[48] Williams, *American-Russian Relations*, 204.

[49] Gumberg to Borah, June 18, 1923, Box 234, Borah Papers. Gumberg wrote that DeWitt C. Poole, head of the Russian Division, was being replaced "by someone whose attitude was not that of a Russian Monarchist." Gumberg regarded this a "hopeful" sign.

[50] *Ibid.*

have plently of support on your Russian position in the next Congress."[51] Gumberg continued to supply Borah with names and positions of the various people making the trip. These goings on did not elude the antirecognition leaders who responded according to custom. Although Gompers addressed his protest to Hughes instead of Hoover this time, he received the usual reply that the administration anticipated no change in policy.[52]

I I

President Harding's death on August 2 resulted in the cancellation of Robins' mission, but, almost immediately, signs appeared that Calvin Coolidge might be more amenable to recognition. Borah met with the new President on this matter and came away encouraged. An article appearing in the New York *Times* headed, "Coolidge Will Give Russia 'Once Over,' " and a similar one in the *World*, led Gumberg to think they came from "responsible quarters." Hopeful, he did not anticipate an easy victory. "Past experience," he noted, had shown that whenever such rumors came out "all the Washington Russian princesses would use their special influence and in general all the dark forces praying for a Czar would work overtime."[53] By October, however, even Gumberg had grown more sanguine. He reported to Borah that recognitionist James P. Goodrich, after having breakfasted with Hoover and Will Hays, "was as optimistic now about the Russian situation as he had ever been."[54]

The antirecognition forces correspondingly stepped up their protests. When Burton K. Wheeler returned from Rus-

[51] Gumberg to Borah, July 5, 1923, *ibid.*
[52] Gompers to Hughes, July 9, 1923, and Hughes to Gompers, July 19, 1923, both in *FRUS, 1923*, II, 758–59.
[53] Gumberg to Borah, August 22, 1923, Box 234, Borah Papers.
[54] Gumberg to Borah, October 25, 1923, *ibid.* Goodrich, an ex-Governor of Indiana, had worked with the American Relief Administration.

sia, he announced that "there is absolutely no reason in the world why the United States should not recognize Russia."[55] Using this statement as a basis for registering his organization's disapproval, the National Civic Federation's president, Alton B. Parker, released a public letter addressed to Wheeler. In addition to the usual points against recognition, Parker's letter asked Wheeler how he could have been the "guest" of a government which openly promoted communism and atheism. Wheeler replied that he personally had nothing to fear from Communist propaganda, nor did he think the American public in any great danger of being seduced by it.[56]

Immediately before Coolidge's annual address to Congress on December 6, Robins talked with both Will Hays and the President on several matters, including the Russian question. Remembering Harding's evasive tactics after their previous agreement, the Colonel demanded evidence of Coolidge's intentions before agreeing to support him in 1924. The outcome of these meetings satisfied Robins; he and Borah felt confident the President's message would be an important step toward recognition. Both men used what influence they had to prepare a favorable reception for Coolidge's anticipated statement and to head off the furor they knew it would incur. Certainly they realized Hoover and Hughes would not accede to any real change without a fight. They appeared to have scored a triumph, however, when the message indicated that policy toward Russia might be revised in the near future.[57]

Though studded with qualifications, Coolidge's address clearly implied that the United States would show more receptiveness to negotiations than it had in the past. "I do not propose to make merchandise of any American principles," he stated; but he went on to say that whenever "there appear

[55] Fischer, *Men and Politics*, 211.
[56] *Nation*, CXVII (November 28, 1923), 384.
[57] Robins to Borah, December 6 and 15, 1923, both in Box 234, Borah Papers, and Williams, *American-Russian Relations*, 205.

works meet for repentence," the United States stood ready to go to the "economic and moral rescue of Russia." Although this could have meant much or nothing of itself, his specific reference to Russian debts contracted only under "the Republic" seemed to mark a retreat from earlier preconditions. Borah commented to a reporter that he was "in accord" with the President's message; the New York *Times* editorialized that "a truce" impended between Russia and the United States.[58]

Soviet leaders interpreted the presidential message as an invitation to begin negotiations. On December 16, Soviet Foreign Minister Georgi Chicherin addressed a note to Coolidge offering to open discussions between the two nations on the basis of "your message to Congress."[59] Chicherin cast his note in terms of settling *both* Russian and American claims, the former arising out of damages suffered during the intervention.

Secretary Hughes answered on December 18 with a stinging rebuke to the Russian request. Delivered through an intermediary, his note stated that there could be no negotiations until such time as the Soviets had modified their position drastically. "The American government . . . is not proposing to barter away its principles," he wrote, paraphrasing Coolidge's words, but the terms he specified showed that he differed greatly with the President as to what constituted the sale of American principles.[60] Beginning with a denial that the Russians had any claims to damages caused by the intervention, Hughes went on to demand that they make all the concessions before discussions could start. The Secretary's reply was un-

[58] All quotes in this paragraph from the New York *Times*, December 7, 1923.

[59] *FRUS, 1923*, II, 787. Robins had cabled Moscow suggesting the kind of answer he thought they should make to Coolidge's address. See Stoner, *Levinson*, 125.

[60] *FRUS, 1923*, II, 788.

acceptable on its face; Chicherin said later it had "amazed" him in view of Coolidge's "reasonable and conciliatory" message.[61]

Hughes's action staggered those privy to the talks with Coolidge, for they believed the President really had come around on the matter.[62] Salmon O. Levinson, who was with Borah when Hughes's note appeared, wrote to Robins that the Senator was "dumbfounded" but determined to "fight it." Levinson also urged that the Colonel broach Will Hays to find out what had gone wrong.[63] The answer was obvious. Hoover and Hughes commanded enough backing to nullify Coolidge's temporary capitulation to Borah and Robins. As the President later acknowledged, he had no choice except to recant when faced with the combined power of his two cabinet members.[64]

The antirecognition forces, in and outside the administration, realized this had posed the most serious challenge to the status quo. Simultaneously with his note to Chicherin, Hughes released incriminating documents "intercepted" from leaders of the Communist International showing that they intended to "raise the red flag on the White House" in the near future. He included with the papers an editorial translated from *Izvestia* establishing a close connection between the In-

[61] James P. Goodrich to Coolidge, November 24, 1925, Series 1, CF156A Coolidge Papers. Goodrich had recently returned from Russia where he had discussed recognition with Chicherin.

[62] In reply to protests over the administration's inconsistency, the President's secretary, C. Bascom Slemp, wrote that Coolidge and Hughes were in basic accord although they had expressed themselves "in somewhat different terms." See Jerome Davis to Coolidge, December 22, John Haynes Holmes to Coolidge, December 24, 1923, and Slemp to Davis, January 19, 1924, all in *ibid*.

[63] Levinson to Robins, December 19, 1923, Box 19, Robins Papers.

[64] But see Pusey, *Hughes*, II, 234. On the basis of an interview with Hughes in 1946, Pusey writes that Coolidge wanted to send out Hughes's note over his own name, but the Secretary generously offered to "shoulder the storm" that would result. In view of Coolidge's message of December 6 and his later statements, this account lacks credibility.

ternational and the Soviet government.[65] As Gumberg had predicted, the outcries from the National Civic Federation and other groups reached a crescendo.

Gompers rose in shrill indignation. In a statement released on December 18, he recorded once again his "unqualified opposition" to any relations with "Soviet terrorism." Now he attacked Borah directly, alleging collusion with the Communists. Gompers stated that the Soviet note had come only after the Senator had "professed" to see the opportunity in Coolidge's message. "Immediately following Senator Borah's well-timed suggestions," he went on, "Commissar Chicherin addressed his note. Senator Borah and Bolshevist Chicherin both understand perfectly that any compromise with Soviet terrorism is a victory for the Soviets. Outlaws and brigands commonly act on that principle."[66]

Borah tried to carry the fight to the admininstration through the press and in the Senate. Attacking the authenticity of the documents which Hughes had released, he disparaged generally the emphasis upon Communist propaganda. He referred to it as "miserable fustian and futile trash," and added, "it will instill in them [Americans] a greater love for orderly and regulated liberty. But our people cannot well withstand another world war." Criticizing the prevailing atmosphere of terror and suspicion, he challenged the administration to present the documents before an impartial court for verification as to their authenticity.[67] The Senator used material supplied mostly by Gumberg to cite the various people who, having returned from Russia, urged recognition as in the best interests of the United States. He offered all the familiar

[65] *FRUS, 1923*, II, 788–92.

[66] New York *Times*, December 19, 1923.

[67] *Congressional Record*, 68th Cong., 1st Sess., 584–85, and William E. Borah, "Borah States the Case for Russia," New York *Times*, December 30, 1923.

arguments for recognition from its importance for world peace to trade potentials.

Senators William H. King and Henry Cabot Lodge spoke for the antirecognition forces. King, playing in low key, reported on his own trip to Russia without indulging in wholesale condemnation.[68] But he attacked Borah's position on two counts. King first asserted that the International and the Soviet government were virtually identical, which tended to verify Hughes's emphasis on the significance of the documents. Second, King maintained that Borah erred in claiming that the Russians met their obligations to those nations with whom they traded. He said most of the powers found broken contracts the rule, and that he had learned the Soviets invariably used commercial negotiations to advance their propaganda.

Lodge did not so restrain himself. In addition to his own lurid comments on the threat of Bolshevik contamination, he had read into the *Congressional Record* a report prepared by the United Mine Workers of America, a union which itself had come under attack for alleged Communist leanings. "Imported revolution is knocking at the door," the report began, and it further announced there were six thousand active Communist leaders and over a million "members, adherents and sympathizers" working for the destruction of the American society. It specifically cited the existence of a "plot" to bring about recognition which, if carried out, would earn the Communists their greatest victory "short of the overthrow of the Federal Government itself."[69] And the latter, according to Hughes's captured "documents," the Bolsheviks had under advisement.

Borah's resolution for the recognition of Russia never had a chance. Even though he sought to keep the issue alive by

[68] *Senate Document 126*, 68th Cong., 1st Sess., "Conditions in Russia."
[69] Quotations in this paragraph are from *Congressional Record*, 68th Cong., 1st Sess., 592–614.

initiating hearings by the Senate Foreign Relations Committee, the impetus was lost.[70] He and Robins, so optimistic when Coolidge addressed the Congress, found themselves overwhelmed by the forces within the administration, the Senate, and the public at large. Leaving aside the advisability of recognition as an economic or diplomatic question, the antirecognitionists had succeeded in presenting the case as a problem of national security, thereby assuring the results they desired.

When the Senator, Robins, and the others asked that the United States recognize and cooperate with a society purportedly threatening the republic's very existence, they asked a great deal. The severity of the "red scare" had abated, yet it left a very exploitable backlog of fear and distrust. Clearly, Hughes had this in mind when he issued the incriminating documents, and Borah's attack on their authenticity placed him once again in the position of defending the Communists. It is ironic but understandable that some of the most rabid supporters of nonrecognition, such as the American Federation of Labor and the United Mine Workers, had themselves been damaged by the atmosphere of the times. Threatened by accusations of subversion (and afraid that their own organizations might be subverted), they responded by shouting louder than anyone else about the Bolshevik conspiracy.

Borah and Robins, already beaten, nevertheless intended pushing matters to a conclusion. They made recognition one of their demands during negotiations with Coolidge following the Teapot Dome revelations. As discussed in an earlier chap-

[70] See *Senate Miscellaneous Document 31*, 68th Cong., 1st Sess. Borah requested (January 14) that the Secretary of State submit to the Senate all reports made by those who had been in Russia over the past six years. He was trying to draw attention to the one Robins had given Wilson in 1918. On February 1, Coolidge advised the Senate that the State Department had no record of any reports other than from military personnel and two letters from Goodrich. The report in question can be found in *FRUS, The Lansing Papers* (2 vols., Washington, D.C., 1939), II, 365–72.

ter, the President held back even with the oil scandals hovering over him and the discussions fell through.[71] Perhaps to forestall any resurgence of the Russian question in Coolidge's second administration, his new Secretary of State, Frank B. Kellogg, released another set of "intercepted" documents a month after the inauguration. These papers revealed Communist plans to invest large sums of money in converting American Negroes. Kellogg became very fond of citing the Bolshevik menace for his own purposes.[72]

A few brief flurries of interest excepted, the Russian question received little attention between the spring of 1924 and the onset of depression in 1929.[73] Hopes of arousing wide sentiment for a change in policy withered during the prosperous years of the late 1920's. The case for recognition seemed less convincing than ever before in terms of either domestic or international needs. Given the lack of public interest, Borah's role became secondary with most of the effective work being done by Gumberg who concentrated on cultivating business support for an "enlightened" policy.[74]

[71] See Chap. 7.

[72] Copy of letter, Kellogg to the President, April 3, 1925, Box 258, Borah Papers; and see Ellis, *Kellogg*, 40, 70, 71.

[73] A very mild renewal of concern began late in 1925. Coolidge apparently did little more than check with certain business leaders to determine whether their positions had changed. They had not. See reply to Coolidge's inquiry, George A. Ranney of the International Harvester Company to Coolidge, December 2, 1925, Series I, CF156A, Coolidge Papers. In the spring of 1926, Ivy Lee initiated a minor campaign for recognition. Although connected with Standard Oil at this time, he insisted that he merely acted out of personal interest, a plea few believed. See Lee letters to the New York Chamber of Commerce, Box 271, Borah Papers, and Lee's correspondence with Elihu Root and John Basset Moore, in Box 162, Moore Papers. At the time of the Paris Pact in 1928, there was a stir as to whether Russia's signing the Pact would imply recognition.

[74] In conjunction with Reeve Schley, vice-president of the Chase National Bank and president of the American-Russian Chamber of Commerce, Gumberg promoted many luncheons and conferences with business leaders to urge trade and recognition. See file marked "Reeve Schley," in Alexander Gumberg Papers, State Historical Society of Wisconsin, Madi-

The Senator often had used the argument that the United States would benefit economically from a resumption of commercial relations. Yet, as he noted in 1925, figures on trade between the two nations began revealing an ominous situation. The obstacles to commerce imposed by the United States made it virtually impossible for all but the larger corporations to do business with Russia. As a result, these firms might actively be engaged in trade relations with the "outlaw" while remaining noncommittal, or actually hostile, toward recognition.[75] Meanwhile, the smaller businessmen, who needed postal and exchange facilities, had no access to the Russian market.

The patent hypocrisy of this irked the Senator who repeatedly chastized those who "talked one way to one group of people and another way to another group." He pointed out that the two Secretaries of State who had taken the most moral positions against the Soviets when in office, Robert Lansing and Charles Evans Hughes, reappeared as counselors to oil interests negotiating for Russian concessions. Borah said that Hughes, as Secretary of State, had "warned all men to stay away from these people, who were irresponsible and with whom it was dangerous to do business." As a Standard Oil Company attorney, Borah went on, Hughes must have lacked his usual effectiveness in persuading the firm "to

---

son, and Gumberg memorandum to Borah, December 11, 1925, Box 271, Borah Papers.

[75] Russian leaders attempted to exploit this situation by offering concessions contingent upon the resumption of relations. This, they reasoned, would place the "interests" behind recognition, thereby generating pressure against the administration. The scheme worked in getting individual corporations on the "right" side, but met with little success at the State Department. When Robert Lansing showed up representing Sinclair Oil, E. L. MacMurren told him frankly that the Bolsheviks ought to sue the company for "non-performance" in the attempt to "pull their [the Russians] political chestnuts out of the fire for them." MacMurren memorandum of conference with Robert Lansing, March 20, 1925, State Department Decimal Files, 861b.6363/123.

hold back from the great peril." Now that the world had been warned to stay away, the Senator concluded, the oil companies "have bravely gone in and taken the risk and have secured such concessions and contracts and advantages as will enable them to lay a solid foundation for a world monopoly on oil."[76] Borah's feelings toward "big business" were in no way tempered by this spectacle.

The combination of the Manchurian crisis and the onset of the Great Depression stimulated a renewal of the recognition compaign. For more than a decade Borah and Robins had said that since the interests of the Soviet Union and the United States coincided in Asia, friendly relations with that power would provide an effective ally in containing Japanese aggression. The Senator often remarked that the policies of nonrecognition, antagonism toward Chinese nationalism, *and* opposition to Japanese expansion placed the United States in an awkward spot. Washington, in practice, had acted as the protector of Russian interests—or as a "moral trustee" as Hughes phrased it—even while failing to recognize the Soviet regime.[77] Borah urged dropping this fiction, substituting in its place the frank admission of mutual American-Russian aims in the Far East.[78]

As in 1921–22, the depression gave life to the economic argument for recognition. Worsening conditions made trade with Soviet Russia appear far more attractive and urgent than before. J. D. Mooney, president of the General Motors Export Company, typified this reaction. Congratulating the Senator on a speech for recognition, Mooney wrote that it

[76] All quotes in this paragraph from Borah to C. J. Carlson, April 3, 1929, Box 303, Borah Papers.

[77] Pusey, *Hughes*, II, 525.

[78] Pauline Tompkins, in *American-Russian Relations in the Far East* (New York, 1949), details Washington's struggle to safeguard the interests of "the Russian people" until such time as a "legitimate" government appeared.

was "good old-fashioned common sense to say, in effect, that
if our neighbor across the street is prosperous there is a better
chance that he will buy some of our own goods and contribute thereby to our own prosperity . . . this home-town reasoning exists internationally, and it exists specifically as between the United States and Russia."[79] Mooney presumably
thought the folksy approach appropriate toward a senator
from Idaho; in any event Borah replied that this attitude "delighted" him.[80]

The recognition stalwarts of old now found themselves accompanied by various individuals, groups, and newspapers in
demanding that the administration reverse its policy. Though
Borah, Robins, and Gumberg remained active, the trend clearly involved more than just another "campaign." President
Hoover saw the files which he kept on protests for recognition
fatten at an alarming rate.[81] That the man who had so con-
fidently predicted the downfall of the Soviet system because
of its "inconsistencies" would turn to that same regime in an
effort to shore up his own society was, perhaps, too much to
expect. Steadfastly refusing to acknowledge that recent developments in any way altered the fundamentals of recognition, Hoover proceeded on a steady course.

The drive for recognition during Hoover's administration
culminated in Borah's appeal to Secretary of State Stimson,
on August 25, 1932, which asked for a reconsideration of
Russian policy in light of the current situation. While there
is reason to believe that Stimson personally favored recognition, he couched his reply to Borah in pure Hooverese.[82]

[79] Mooney to Borah, December 29, 1930, Box 238, Borah Papers.
[80] Borah to Mooney, December 31, 1930, *ibid.*
[81] Browder, *The Origins of Soviet-American Diplomacy*, 40–41.
[82] Fischer, *Men and Politics*, 213. Borah told Fischer he had talked with
Stimson in the summer of 1932 and that Stimson would have recognized
Russia "but for President Hoover." Fischer received the same impression
from an interview with the Secretary on February 3, 1933. See also

He wrote that although some advantages might be had from such a step during "this emergency," should the United States reverse its stand "the whole world, and particularly Japan, would jump to the conclusion that our action had been dictated solely by political expediency." The loss would be so grievous to America's moral position, he went on, "that we could not take the risk of it."[83]

The Senator probably wielded less influence during these years than at any previous time in the Republican era. His relations with President Hoover had become overtly antagonistic and, in the latter's thinking, may have made Borah a liability rather than an asset to the recognition cause.[84] His usual strength in getting publicity for his views suffered because of sensational charges that he had received Soviet money in payment for his services.[85] Discredited by responsible public leaders, such accusations nonetheless impaired his credibility.

The antirecognitionists were not disposed to lose by default. Reliable groups, such as the American Federation of Labor and the National Civic Federation, took up the challenge as did many prominent individuals—Elihu Root and Bainbridge Colby to name but a few. And, though sentiment for recognition had spread rapidly within the business community, nothing resembling a consensus was obtained. Those industries believing themselves threatened by Russian competition grew particularly vociferous in denouncing the resumption of relations.[86] Since Hoover betrayed no signs of

---

Richard N. Current, *Secretary Stimson, A Study in Statecraft* (New Brunswick, 1954), 110.

[83] Stimson to Borah, September 8, 1932, *FRUS, 1933*, II, 778.

[84] Almost immediately after Hoover's inauguration, Borah fell out with him over farm policy and other matters. See Levinson to Robins, May 11, 1929, Box 22, Robins Papers. As a result, Levinson wrote, the Senator "might as well throw his Russian resolution into the Potomac."

[85] See McKenna, *Borah*, 297–300 for details.

[86] Borah to O. M. Hans, May 19, 1931, Box 249, Borah Papers. See

yielding, proponents of recognition started feeling out the Democratic candidate in 1932, Franklin D. Roosevelt.[87]

Roosevelt straddled the Russian question by pledging to give it his careful attention. Domestic conditions reduced other matters to trivia, but there were indications that he would be favorably inclined. Borah, Robins, and Gumberg kept each other informed during the period between the election and inauguration; the sources of all three pointed toward the President-elect's "soundness."[88] They feared, however, that the issue would be swept aside by the press of events, which in fact it was. Robins and Gumberg exerted every effort to coordinate support for their project; Robins received a "hurry up" call from "the friends of Russian recognition" to visit Washington shortly after the inauguration. But Roosevelt moved cautiously, and even when recognition was finally accorded in November, 1933, the debt question remained in abeyance.[89]

Borah, the man who for sixteen years had championed the cause and done most to keep it before the public, stood inconspicuous at the time of its achievement. He wired the President that "it was a fine, big, courageous thing to do," but his exultation must have been tempered by Roosevelt's failure to do more than to perfunctorily acknowledge his message.[90] Most important, the outcome of his labor brought small returns on expended effort. The United States had long since lost any chance—assuming that one ever existed—to influence Russian development, and recognition by this time

---

also Gumberg to Robins, July 24, 1931, Box 24, Robins Papers, enclosure headed "Joint Conference on Unfair Russian Competition."

[87] Browder, *The Origins of Soviet-American Diplomacy*, 76.

[88] See especially Borah to Gumberg, November 11, 1932, Box 332, Borah Papers.

[89] For the negotiations and ensuing difficulties, see Donald G. Bishop, *The Roosevelt-Litvinov Agreements: The American View* (Syracuse, 1965).

[90] Borah to Roosevelt, November 19, 1933, *Borah Scrapbook*, X.

had small importance as a factor in world affairs. Even the predicted economic benefits never materialized—partly because of continued impediments laid down by the United States and partly because of the depression in world trade.[91]

The effects of rapprochement with Soviet Russia during its formative years can only be guessed. Although Borah most certainly exaggerated the benefits which recognition would confer, it is difficult to conceive of a policy less viable than the one actually followed. As the Senator claimed all along, the Hoover-Hughes attempt to destroy or to force drastic modifications of the Soviet regime rested upon unwarranted political and economic assumptions. Tampering in revolutionary situations all over the world, Borah thought, was a hazardous pasttime with no chance of success. These upheavals contained their own "inevitable logic" which outside pressures were powerless to alter significantly, while engaging in such practices entailed involvements the Senator wished to avoid. His long campaign for recognition was another manifestation of his dedication to the diplomacy of abstinence which he had persistently advocated toward Latin America, China, and everywhere else in the world. To this kind of isolationism, Borah freely admitted.

[91] Due to the failure to settle the debt question, opponents of relations with Russia succeeded in having the Johnson Act applied against the Soviet Union. The Johnson Act forbade granting credits to any nation which had defaulted on its debts. See Browder, *The Origins of American-Soviet Diplomacy*, 179. Until 1931, the removal of obstructions would have materially aided the growth of trade. After this time the Soviet Union found it increasingly difficult to exchange her raw materials with any nation and had little except gold to export to the United States.

CHAPTER IX

Borah's Last Stand

THE Democratic victory in November, 1932, incidental-
ly cost Borah his chairmanship of the Senate Foreign Relations Committee, a strategic post he had enjoyed since the
death of Henry Cabot Lodge in 1924. The loss was symbolic.
Age (he was sixty-eight in 1933), failing health, and, above
all, the times, diminished his power. A decade inaugurated
by the Manchurian conflict and ending in the midst of another
world war proved inhospitable to the kinds of peace programs
with which Borah had identified himself during the 1920's.
Still capable of a crusade or two, formidable under certain
circumstances, the Idahoan became more a given factor than
an independent force. Whereas Republican Presidents and
Secretaries of State had found it necessary to seek his bene-
dictions—and often wilted before his displeasure—the new
administration, as Robins put it, tended "to leave him alone
and take what comes from his cooperation or opposition as
all in a day's work."[1]

[1] Robins to Levinson, March 13, 1933, Box 24, Robins Papers.

The Senator's influence on domestic affairs waned accordingly, especially during the New Deal's early years. His homilies on thrift and morality in government, which had seemed relevant in the Coolidge era, now bordered on the macabre when offered as remedies for the worst depression in the nation's history. Because he became ill during the latter part of the "first hundred days," Borah did not participate in the consideration of several key bills. Little matter. His strength lay in his ability to perceive, appeal to, and to focus public attitudes; for success he needed defined issues and time to mount one of his campaigns. The atmosphere of crisis and uncertainty prevailing in the spring and summer of 1933, coupled with the general belief that at last "something" was being done to meet the emergency, left him without effective voice. The Lion of Idaho for the moment was just another senator of the minority party.

His biographer has pointed out that Borah voted with the administration on eleven of seventeen major bills during the 1930's, a score he rarely approached under his own party's leadership.[2] The gravity of conditions undoubtedly minimized his normal inclination to dissent, and he had admitted the need for more forceful steps by the federal government than Hoover had been willing to advocate. Although later critical of the manner in which they were administered, the Senator usually voted for measures providing work and relief and against those he believed promoted collectivism, threatened the balanced government provided for in the Constitution, or benefited the financial and industrial interests at the expense of the agricultural community. These criteria led him to denounce some of the administration's most fundamental legislation.

Before its destruction at the hands of the Supreme Court, Borah regarded the National Recovery Administration as the

[2] McKenna, *Borah*, 320.

New Deal's most dangerous innovation. Allowing businessmen to draw up their own codes of conduct while suspending antitrust laws, he warned, meant delivering almost complete control over the national economy to the forces of monopoly. He saw this as a surrender of the last restraints upon the malevolent forces responsible for the depression in the first place.[3] The Agricultural Adjustment Act, providing for crop and livestock control, seemed to him just as wrongheaded although he reluctantly voted for it under the mistaken impression it would assure "cost of production" minimums for farmers.[4] To a man who always had argued that underconsumption, not overproduction, caused agricultural surpluses, destroying animals and produce amounted to insanity in its terminal phase. Without a more equitable distribution of income, he complained, it was hypocritical to talk of surpluses when so many people lacked adequate food and clothing. Borah castigated the failure to opt for more fundamental solutions as a shameful capitulation to the entrenched interests.

Later, when the New Deal began emphasizing reform instead of recovery, the Senator applauded most of the assaults upon what he considered business extravagances. He also initiated his last great crusade on a domestic issue, however, when Roosevelt attempted to "pack" the Supreme Court early in 1937. Fearing that the Court would disembowel the New Deal and emboldened by the preceding November election, FDR sought to increase the Court's size with his own appointees under the guise of lightening the work load of older Justices. There can be little question that this represented to Borah more than an opportunity to embarrass the administration; he always had resisted executive encroachment against

[3] Borah to George L. Record, June 19, 1933, Box 348, Borah Papers.

[4] Johnson, *Borah of Idaho*, 475. When a conference agreement between the Senate and House dropped this provision, Borah voted against adoption of the conference report.

the prerogatives of the Court and Congress. Despite his advanced years and precarious physical condition, he drove himself without letup throughout the struggle.

Borah appeared at his best in such situations. He had the "great issue," he fought on the side of the angels in defending tradition, and his talent for portraying convincingly the nightmarish consequences of measures he disliked showed to good advantage. He conducted an exhausting assault on Roosevelt's project through public appearances, radio speeches, articles, and personal correspondence. In the Senate, where his position on the Judiciary Committee assured him a base of attack, he performed as one of the opposition's key strategists. The Idahoan's most precious asset in the Senate was his lifelong avoidance of party discipline; he "cashed in" on his reputation, as Robins phrased it, which helped to raise the dispute above partisan lines.[5] Contemporary observers and more recent scholars rightly assign him a crucial role in defeating the Court-packing scheme.

But the Senator had predicted a revolt against Democratic leadership long before Roosevelt's ill-advised venture. His assumptions led him to make his most determined thrust for the presidency in 1936.[6] The New Deal had barely gotten underway before the Idahoan began confiding to friends that it would eventually arouse a wave of reaction as strong as had Hoover's penchant for inactivity. Pleased to see what he regarded as the utter repudiation of Old Guardism in 1932— he had refused to say whether he would vote for Hoover, let alone campaign for him[7]—Borah thought the public likewise

---

[5] Robins to Levinson, August 5, 1937, Box 28, Robins Papers. See also William K. Hutchinson, "News Articles on the Life and Works of William E. Borah," *Senate Documents 150*, 76th Cong., 3rd Sess., 7–17.

[6] Robins to Levinson, March 17 and 19, 1933, Box 25; November 22, 1933, July 5, December 21, 1934, Box 26, Robins Papers. These letters report conversations between Robins and Borah.

[7] Telegrams, United Press to Borah, Borah to United Press, October 26, 1932, Box 337, Borah Papers.

would turn against the Democratic administration once its collectivist tendencies became evident. The stage then would be set, he said, for the emergence of a movement—nominally Republican but attractive to disillusioned Democrats—promising clean, progressive government, conducted within strict constitutional limitations. Chronically fuzzy about what progressive government stood for other than progressivism (he favored a "statement of principles" in lieu of a platform), there existed no doubt in his mind that the logical choice to head the movement was William E. Borah.

Already considered a bit long in the tooth to be an acceptable candidate, the Senator's knowledge that time ran against him undoubtedly colored his perception of the public mood. So strongly did he believe in his assessment, however, that he began planning a purge of the party's "undesirable" elements many months before the convention met.[8] He seemed to think he depended less upon the party's endorsement than it depended upon riding in on his coattails. The prize was to be bestowed upon him by popular demand, on his own terms, and over the heads of party leaders—such was the stuff of which his dreams had long been made. Robins, who usually had a keen political sense when not involved personally, wondered whether it might not be wiser to secure the nomination first before reorganizing the party.

The Senator's vision dissipated in the face of reality. He still enjoyed a wide if disorganized popularity, and it was true that many stalwart Republicans had been discredited along with Hoover. But few of the regulars had grown so distraught as to accept the old maverick who had plagued them all these years, nor did an aroused public overwhelm them. Scoring impressively in some western primaries, Borah went into the convention with a modest number of delegates pledged to him

[8] Copy of Letter, Borah to Levinson, December 22, 1934, found in Box 26, Robins Papers.

and a legion of enemies determined to stop him.[9] It soon became obvious he had no real chance to win, nor did he succeed later in swinging the convention to Senator Arthur Vandenberg of Michigan.[10] As a gesture to gain his support in November, the victorious forces of Alfred M. Landon, the nominee, accommodated Borah in drawing up the platform. Some thought even this was more than he deserved. "Why anyone should want to 'placate' Borah," complained a longtime foe, "is beyond my understanding. He is a hopeless publicity hunter and that is his beginning and end."[11]

The Idahoan had departed from custom in 1928 when he campaigned actively for Herbert Hoover, the first Republican nominee he had so blessed since 1916, and the last. Accusing Landon of reneging on the platform compromise, the Senator confined himself exclusively to his own campaign in Idaho. Rumors even began circulating that he might bolt to FDR in exchange for the latter's help in the state election, but Borah came out for no one.[12] He solemnly went his own way, and not surprisingly he registered a by-now standard landside victory. All things considered, he had not done badly. Painful as his defeat at the convention must have been to him, he at least escaped the humiliation which Landon suffered in November. The "great reaction," which Borah had prophesied, netted the GOP only Maine and Vermont; however, in all fairness it should be remembered that he had based his predictions upon a more stimulating alternative than the uninspiring Landon—had Borah himself received the nomination he might have carried Idaho as well. When some of

[9] For details, see McKenna, *Borah*, 322–36.

[10] Frank Gannett to Borah June 16 and 20, Borah to Gannett, June 23, 1936, Box 393, Borah Papers.

[11] Nicholas Murray Butler to William Allen White, September 14, 1936, Box 234, White Papers.

[12] James McGregor Burns, *Roosevelt: The Lion and the Fox* (New York, 1956), 279.

the faithful began a "Borah for President" move in 1939, the Senator had the good sense to discourage them immediately.[13] The old giant was, by that time, little more than a relic of bygone days.

Borah found New Deal diplomacy relatively palatable—at least in the beginning. Roosevelt's attitude toward Soviet Russia and his apparent interest in tying debt adjustment to disarmament foreshadowed several areas of compatability. The Senator had preached what amounted to a "Good Neighbor" policy toward Latin America long before FDR popularized the phrase. Although presaged during the Coolidge-Hoover era and sometimes perverted in application—as in Cuba when State Department officials first tried to bolster the dictatorship of Gerardo Machado, then tried to undermine the reform government of Ramón Grau San Martín—Rooseveltian diplomacy ran along lines the Idahoan had advocated for years.[14] Borah never concerned himself overmuch with the broader implications of American penetration into the region; he asked merely that it not be accompanied by the use of force. Finally, the Tydings-McDuffie Act of 1934, providing for the eventual independence of the Philippines, satisfied partially a long-time Borah demand. His only regret, he said, was that the act failed to grant independence immediately.

Some of the administration's policies digested less easily. Secretary of State Cordell Hull's program of reciprocal trade agreements incurred the Senator's angriest protests. Hull believed fervently in such arrangements, claiming they would help lift the United States from the slough of depression by

[13] New York *Times*, September 25, 30, 1939.
[14] Lloyd C. Gardner, *Economic Aspects of New Deal Diplomacy* (Madison, 1964), 53–57. Henry W. Berger, "Laissez Faire for Latin America: Borah Defines the Monroe Doctrine," *Idaho Yesterdays*, IX (Summer, 1965), 10–17. And see San Martín to Borah, October 2, Borah to San Martín, October 6, 1933, Box 350, Borah Papers.

providing a major stimulus to world trade. Borah himself persistently stressed the importance of foreign markets, but he thought reciprocity in practice sacrificed the farmers' interests to those of the manufacturers. Just as he had argued against reciprocity with Canada during the Taft administration, the Senator declared that business profited from increased sales at the cost to the farmer of dumping cheaper foreign produce on an already glutted American agricultural market. Even were this not true, Borah said, he opposed such legislation because it unconstitutionally delegated congressional powers to the Chief Executive.[15] An insufficient number of congressmen agreed with him to prevent adoption of the administration's Reciprocal Trade Agreements Bill in 1934.

Borah enjoyed more success when the administration, late in that year, attempted to revive interest in joining the World Court. Roosevelt's motives for disinterring the court issue at this time are obscure. Probably doing no more than gesturing toward a campaign pledge, he showed commendable restraint if he had any real enthusiasm over the World Court. Aside from sending Congress a brief message advocating membership and discussing the matter with a few senators personally, the President apparently exerted minimal influence to secure passage.[16]

Borah joyfully, if somewhat creakily, manned the parapets along with the rest of the isolationists. Indicting the World Court on various specific counts, he concentrated on stigmatizing it as a political instead of a judicial body, whose sole purpose consisted of providing a veneer of legality for decisions already made by the League itself. The Idahoan's text rang familiar—he had recited it often enough—but circumstances necessitated one revision. During the 1920's he

[15] See folder on "Tariff Agreements," Box 375, Borah Papers.
[16] Robert A. Divine, *The Illusion of Neutrality* (Chicago, 1962), 83.

had portrayed the League as a concert of imperialistic plunderers bent upon world domination. Its performance thus far rendered that accusation unserviceable and forced the Senator to recast his argument. Now he complained that the United States ought not align itself with an organization so completely discredited because of its helplessness.[17] The League's metamorphosis from dragon to dodo had no effect on Borah's dour forecast that participation in the World Court meant surrendering American sovereignty to a cabal of foreigners.

The Senate mercifully disposed of the World Court Bill without prolonged debate. Neither Borah nor anyone else said much which had not been said many time before, and with greater enthusiasm. The vote, taken on January 29, 1935, showed 52 senators for, 36 against it—7 short of the two-thirds necessary for passage. The Idahoan had pronounced the World Court issue "dead as a stinking mackerel" in 1932; his premature description applied more suitably three years later.

Many accounts have stressed the importance of Father Charles E. Coughlin and William Randolph Hearst in defeating the World Court proposal. Both conducted vituperative campaigns against it in public; Hearst financed as well a platoon of lobbyists to harass senators personally. Their efforts produced results as a flood of anti-World Court mail descended upon Washington in the days before voting began. Although Borah's warm telegrams of congratulation to both radio priest and publisher appear to certify their contribution, he privately denied that their efforts materially affected the outcome.[18] He told Robins that enough support to defeat the measure had been lined up well before the publicity campaign began, and that the early support, with two exceptions,

---

[17] *Congressional Record*, 74th Cong., 1st Sess., 434ff., 695ff., 879ff.
[18] Borah to William Randolph Hearst, Borah to Father Charles Coughlin, January 30, Hearst to Borah, February 4, 1935, Box 391, Borah Papers.

held firm to the end.[19] By this time "adreaming" of the presidency again, the Idahoan had few compunctions about sharing the laurels with those whose backing he wished to secure.

I I

The World Court fight in reality amounted to little more than an exercise in nostalgia, despite the exaggerations of both sides. The critical—and the most hotly debated—diplomatic issue throughout the 1930's involved the question of American behavior toward recurrent hostilities in Europe and the Far East. As each confrontation brought closer the threat of war, the American people and their leaders searched for a formula which would enable this nation to avoid another major conflict. Unanimity existed over the formula's ultimate purpose; bitter disagreement arose concerning its ingredients and proper application.[20]

The largest group through most of the decade consisted of those Americans who believed the only practical way the United States could immunize itself lay in forswearing any steps which might antagonize one of the participants in a dispute. They advocated instead complete impartiality toward all belligerents regardless of actual or assumed culpability. Others, in the minority but sporadically backed by the Democratic administration, called for a more active policy. Abstaining from such questions, they said, merely encouraged international lawlessness. The minority group felt that the nation could best serve its interests by working with other powers to designate and to deter aggression whenever it occurred since allowing hostilities to go unchecked might delay, but would not prevent, ultimate involvement. Both groups put forward legislation purporting to insure American "neutral-

---

[19] Robins to Levinson, February 15, 1935, Box 26, Robins Papers.

[20] The best account of the long, complex struggle can be found in Divine's *The Illusion of Neutrality*.

ity." Their definitions of the term placed the matter beyond reconciliation.

Borah stood unhesitatingly with those who considered participation in collective efforts futile and dangerous. He denied that he advocated withdrawal since he continued urging revision of the Versailles Treaty, disarmament, economic conferences, and the like. When confrontations did occur, however, he said the United States should avoid even the hint of favoring one side over the other, much less designate and attempt to coerce "guilty" parties. To head off such efforts, he and other isolationists supported neutrality legislation—at first limited to an arms embargo but later expanded to prohibit loans and travel on belligerent's shipping—which would go into effect mandatorily upon the outbreak of hostilities, applying equally to all disputants.[21] They bitterly and successfully opposed the collective security advocates who wished to grant the President discretion over when and against whom the legislation would be invoked. Beginning with the Neutrality Act of 1935, their view in substance prevailed until late 1939.

Graduations existed within the broad category of isolationists. Many thought bans on shipping armaments barely touched the problem. In modern war, they pointed out, all commodities had military value insofar as they added to a nation's resources. Germany had resorted to unrestricted submarine warfare during World War I not because of the traffic in munitions, but because American exports in the aggregate had sustained the Allied war effort. Some therefore wished to embargo *all* trade to belligerents while others, notably

[21] His attitude pertained only to situations possibly involving large powers. In the waning days of the Hoover administration, Borah sponsored a bill giving the President the right to designate against whom an arms embargo would be applied. He did so because the administration had assured him it would involve the legislation exclusively to the Chaco War then in progress between Bolivia and Paraguay. *Ibid.*, 35–36. Borah to Levinson, March 1, 1933, Box 320, Borah Papers. *Congressional Record*, 72nd Cong., 2nd Sess., 3590.

those from agrarian states, would have banned a wide range of manufactured goods but exempted foodstuffs.[22]

Not so Borah and Hiram Johnson. These two old "bitter-enders," now reconciled with each other if not with the world, headed a small-but-vocal faction which denounced any curtailment of trade beyond that in armaments as a cowardly surrender of neutral rights. Protesting that the economy could ill afford such indulgences, they argued that the United States could carry on nonmilitary trade in relative safety provided it stood ready to defend its traditional claims. Belligerents almost certainly would observe the rules so long as this nation adhered to international law and demonstrated its willingness to fight if necessary. If they did not? Well, as the Senator so often put it there were "other" things which Americans prized more highly than peace. "I think," he said on one occasion, "we talk too much in these times about peace, peace."[23] And he stated his preparedness to vote for war again in behalf of neutral rights.[24]

Borah's repeated denunciations of war have obscured the strain of militance which permeated his rhetoric throughout the period. He sought no part in quarrels between other powers—he never had—but when it came to matters he believed impinged upon national interests or honor, he remained as pugnacious as ever. For all his alleged "conversions," the Idahoan in reality had moved not an inch from where he stood in 1917. His otherwise befuddling performance over the neutrality question becomes understandable only if it is recognized that he feared the political consequences of war, its "logic" in his terms, far more than he did war itself.

[22] See Wayne S. Cole, *Senator Gerald P. Nye and American Foreign Relations* (Minneapolis, 1962), Chap. 7.

[23] Borah to Dr. G. George Fox, November 28, 1938, Box 683, Borah Papers. For an earlier expression of this view, see Senate Committee on Foreign Relations, *Neutrality Hearings*, 74th Cong., 2nd Sess., 31.

[24] *Congressional Record*, 75th Cong., 1st Sess., 1681.

Borah personally contributed to a later misreading of his thinking during the 1930's by a statement he made concerning American participation in the First World War. He said, in an oft-quoted interview, that of all the votes he had cast in the Senate, he regretted most the one favoring American entry.[25] Since he had condemned almost every aspect of American diplomacy during and immediately following it, his statement taken broadly was perfectly appropriate. Most scholars, however, construing his remark in its narrowest sense, place the Senator among those who believed that some combination of sinister forces had led the United States into a war it never should have fought.[26] The facts bear out the contrary. Unlike many of the other isolationists, the Idahoan did not think American entry a mistake, and he said so openly and consistently.

The United States went into the war, Borah claimed, because this nation found intolerable the threat of a German-dominated Europe—strategically, economically, and politically.[27] Having gone in to preserve the national interests, the Wilson administration had betrayed those interests through falsely identifying American goals with those of the Allies and by pursuing the chimera of attaining world peace through an association of nations. The results had been the infamous Versailles Treaty, to which the Senator attributed most of

[25] Johnson, *Borah of Idaho*, 202.

[26] Professor Johnson drew no such conclusion then or later. He does not recall, after thirty years, the precise context in which Borah made the statement, but he thinks the latter may have meant his remark as a broad one indicating his objection to war "on general principles and as a futility, but not as a specific repudiation of his vote for the war. I do not believe," continues Dr. Johnson, "that Borah ever thought that his vote for the war was morally wrong." Letter to the author, December 19, 1966.

[27] Detailed statements of this interpretation can be found in *Congressional Record*, 75th Cong., 1st Sess., 1682, 3696. As late as October, 1939, Borah said he had never changed his mind on American entry, see below. His "threat of a German victory" thesis came after the fact, however. At the time he justified his vote solely on the basis of neutrality violations.

Europe's distress, and the only-narrowly-defeated campaign to bring the United States into the League. The real danger now, in Borah's opinion, was that there appeared every possibility of repeating the cycle, this time with perhaps even more catastrophic results.

Borah hoped the United States might steer clear of all wars, certainly, but his fundamental concern lay in preventing the consummation of what he regarded as fatal to American independence and well-being—a coalition with Great Britain and France formalized by a resurrected world organization. He believed that the former Allies schemed endlessly to create such an arrangement and that powerful forces within the United States had similar designs. Borah was already suspicious by 1933, and practically everything done subsequently only confirmed his apprehension that Roosevelt's ultimate goal was to complete the job Woodrow Wilson began. The Idahoan's preoccupation with this "plot" so dominated his thinking, especially after 1935, as to become almost his sole criterion for judging any specific policy.

The degree to which the reality, or appearance, of cooperation with Great Britain and France, rather than the threat of war itself, pervaded Borah's outlook is exemplified by his contrasting views toward the Ethiopian question in 1935 and the onset of civil war in Spain the following year. In the former case, he supported the administration when it invoked, in addition to the arms embargo demanded by law, a "moral embargo" on other goods but did so *before* any European powers or the League acted.[28] Repeating his admonition that the United States must abjure the business of designating aggressors, Borah commended the President's good sense in remaining neutral—this despite the fact that Roosevelt's actions had the deliberate intent of curbing Italy.

[28] Divine, *The Illusion of Neutrality*, 130. See also Borah to J. David Stern, November 26, 1936, Box 377, Borah Papers.

The Spanish civil war was another matter. There, Great Britain and France adopted policies of noninterference in hopes of keeping the struggle localized, even though Italy, Germany, and Russia intervened almost from the start. Borah should have complimented the administration once again when it agreed to an impartial embargo (written specifically for the Spanish situation) on all war materials. The Idahoan instead sniffed suspiciously. Did Roosevelt plan to use the embargo as its framers intended—a way to avoid entanglement—or as a means through which he could bring the United States into a working partnership with the former allies? Borah joined Senator Gerald P. Nye in raising the specter of collusion; as for himself, he declared, "I am no more desirous of cooperating with Great Britain than I am with Italy."[29] He voted for the measure with great misgivings and began denouncing it almost immediately.

But what could he say? Impartial neutrality, after all, was precisely what he had demanded right along. His desire to avoid even the hint of collective action overrode all other considerations. The embargo was wrong, he said, because it applied only to the contending factions in Spain whereas everyone knew "that Germany and Italy are, and have been, carrying on war in every and all meanings of that term."[30] Frankly abandoning his maxim that the United States could not for itself determine aggression, he asked for an extension of the embargo to include the two "fascist" states. In other words—do something, no matter what, to distinguish American policy from that of the French and British. Apparently he gave little thought to what reactions Italy and Germany might have to such a move.

[29] *Congressional Record*, 75th Cong., 1st Sess., 77; Cole, *Nye and American Foreign Relations*, 112.

[30] Borah to Clyde R. Miller, June 2, 1937, Box 405, Borah Papers. See also Borah to Eugene Davidson, April 21, 1938, Box 417, and Borah to Elizabeth Smith, January 13, 1939, Box 426, *ibid.*

Borah's conspiracy theory caused him to gyrate wildly over particular issues. His argument that belligerents would refrain from interfering with neutral trade provided Washington stood behind it, for instance, assumed the existence of naval forces possessing enough strength to act as a deterrent. It also assumed using the fleet solely for protection. Conscious that a weak navy made his own position on the safety of neutral commerce untenable, the Senator nevertheless opposed the administration's program for renewed building. He did so because he believed Roosevelt was less interested in protecting neutral trade than in maintaining a fleet conforming to the needs of an as yet unwritten Anglo-American "understanding."[31] Thus the Idahoan labored in the twilight area of plumping for a navy which would be strong—but not too strong—capable of defensive operations only. He was, in short, unable to stand for anything a calculating administration might use to further its ends.

And so it went. He did another headstand in 1936–37 during the debates over "cash and carry." The architects of this proposal hoped to circumvent the danger which wartime trade involved by having belligerents take full title to, and provide shipping for, all American goods purchased. Because the plan would benefit those nations having large navies, the Idahoan saw in it both a craven effort to profit by war without incurring risks and a treacherous scheme for aiding Great Britain when the need arose.[32] He knew where his duty lay even if it was not at the door of consistency. *Of course* belligerents believing thmselves harmed by neutral trade would retaliate, he announced, regardless of what the United States might do. The question was *where* attacks would occur. If exports were carried in American ships, an aggrieved power

---

[31] McKenna, *Borah*, 353.

[32] Memorandum, Box 544, Borah Papers; *Congressional Record*, 75th Cong., 1st Sess., 1678, 1681.

would try to sink them, but such action would take place hundreds, perhaps thousands, of miles from our shores. The "cash and carry" scheme, Borah warned, would force that same nation to interdict trade through strikes against industrial centers and port cities. Offering the prospects of American skies darkened by clouds of bombers, the Senator neglected to explain why a belligerent's response would depend exclusively upon which ships carried the trade.[33] He used, and discarded, his arguments according to the needs of the job at hand.

The importance Borah attached to the threat of rapprochement with Great Britain and France also accounts for the comparative tolerance he displayed toward Asian affairs through most of these years. Having concluded after the Manchurian incident that the former Allies had "written off" the Far East as an area of vital concern, the Senator displayed far less hostility to deviations from the rigid impartiality he demanded in European matters.[34] Thus he denounced talk of applying an arms embargo against both China and Japan in 1932–33, on the grounds it would benefit Japan who was prepared to wage war and discriminate against China who was not.[35] He supported FDR for the same reasons in 1937 when the latter, taking advantage of a clause in the existing neutrality law, refrained from invoking an impartial embargo against the two powers by refusing to "find" a state of war existing between them (despite the actual fighting).[36] Insofar as Roosevelt's famous "quarantine" speech of October 5, 1937, referred to Japan, Borah stated that he had no quarrel with it nor found the President's words in any way offensive. The Idahoan said he believed Roosevelt to be acting in the

[33] *Congressional Record*, 75th Cong., 1st Sess., 1678, 1679.
[34] See radio speech, February 22, 1936. Reprinted in Borah's *Bedrock: Views on Basic National Problems* (Washington, 1936), 204–205.
[35] Borah to Levinson, March 1, 1933, Box 320, Borah Papers.
[36] Divine, *The Illusion of Neutrality*, 200–10.

interests of peace and that he, Borah, had no wish to quibble over "the technical observance of the neutrality law."[37] The President himself seems to have been somewhat uncertain about what a "quarantine" implied, as Dorothy Borg has pointed out. Perhaps his subsequent denial that he meant economic sanctions reassured the Senator.[38] It is difficult, nonetheless, to imagine Borah behaving so generously over a European question.

Given his assumption that Great Britain and France might discuss the Far East but would decline to act, Borah exuded an almost boundless tolerance. He responded with disdain instead of alarm when the League of Nations Assembly, on October 6, simultaneously condemned Japan's actions and proposed a Nine Power Conference to discuss Far Eastern matters. He disliked cooperating with the "impotent" League, of course, and in any case he thought it "too late to suppose Japan will yield to peaceful means."[39] But the Senator also made clear his doubts that anything would be done unless the United States took on the responsibility—a possibility he discounted at the time. Borah seriously opposed neither American participation in the conference, which opened on November 9, nor the watery resolutions coming out of it. In only one instance, when rumors began circulating that the American representative, Norman H. Davis, had begun work on a proposal for collective sanctions, did the Idahoan bestir himself, and then without enthusiasm. Answering a query by the Hearst press, he said he would ask for Davis' recall if the stories were true.[40] They were not. When the second session

[37] Borah to John A. Heffernan, November 9, Borah to Mrs. Thomas E. Kinney, November 18, 1937, both in Box 405, Borah Papers.

[38] *The United States and the Far Eastern Crisis of 1933–38: From the Manchurian Incident Through the Initial State of the Undeclared Sino-Japanese War* (Cambridge, 1964), 381–86.

[39] Telegram, Borah to Philadelphia *Inquirer*, October 7, 1937, Box 405, Borah Papers.

[40] Borg, *Far Eastern Crisis*, 433. But see Divine's *The Illusion of Neu-*

of Congress met while the conference still sat, Borah had nothing at all to say about it, devoting himself instead to farm problems and to an antilynching bill he opposed.

The Senator's permissiveness toward Far Eastern policy died slowly and in a roundabout fashion. He expressed only mild concern when Japanese aircraft sank the American gunboat *Panay* in December; he suggested it might be relevant to determine the exact nature of the *Panay*'s mission when the attack occurred.[41] He saw no real cause for excitement. Having taken on at least as much as she could handle in China, Borah said, Japan would avoid war with the United States unless given insupportable provocation. His attitude changed in the following months because of his growing conviction that the Japanese "menace" was a decoy behind which the internationalists connived to implement their European plans. Thus, during the debates over naval expansion in the spring of 1938, he called talk of war with Japan "sheer folly" since that nation required a navy three times its present size before contemplating war with the United States.[42] Sarcastically referring to Japan as the "mother" of the American navy, he repeated his charges that the advocates of a large navy really intended using the fleet to augment British strength in Europe.[43] He broadened his conspiracy theory as time went on until at last it accounted for almost every foreign policy decision. By late 1938, the Senator began criticizing Roosevelt for not invoking an embargo against China and Japan —a course he had acclaimed only a year earlier.[44]

Granting the Idahoan's fear of entanglement with the for-

---

trality, 214, for Davis' suggestion to Hull that the neutrality legislation be repealed.

[41] *Congressional Record*, 75th Cong., 2nd Sess., 1356.

[42] Borah to Theodore B. Mitzner, April 4, Box 420, Borah to Samuel McCrea Cavert, April 26, 1938, Box 426, Borah Papers.

[43] *Congressional Record*, 75th Cong., 3rd Sess., 5781-82.

[44] Borah to Margaret Maser, December 30, 1938, Box 417, Borah Papers.

mer Allies and a resuscitated world organization, could he not see that Nazi Germany and Adolph Hitler posed a far greater danger than had the Kaiser? Many people thought so at the time. If true, the threat to American interests was as serious as in 1917 when, as Borah said, the United States rightfully intervened. However clear the answer may be in retrospect, it was not so to the Senator then. Hitler's actions were portentous to be sure. But did they really mean that he intended to dominate all of Europe? Or was this instead a fiction promulgated by the British and French, who in actuality sought American backing only to prevent Germany from redressing the grievances of Versailles? Hitler couched his demands in just such language, and German militance seemed understandable to the Senator because of the treatment she had received since the war's end. Since he was always prone to let his hopes govern his judgment, Borah fervently argued this was the case until contrary evidence became overwhelming.

Before the Munich conference in September, 1938, the Idahoan habitually interpreted German actions as the "inevitable working out" of the situation created in 1919. He described the steps Hitler had taken as consistent with the goals any great power might set for itself. As late as the spring of 1938, Borah employed his "logic of events" thesis to explain the significance of the German occupation of Austria.[45] He recalled that when the two nations had tried to form a customs union during 1931, the plan had been wrecked by the vindictive British and French working through what he considered an utterly subservient World Court. Stymied when

[45] *Congressional Record*, 75th Cong., 3rd Sess., 5780. "It was natural," he wrote, "for Hitler to take Austria. Austria was really a German state and the Versailles peacemakers had ruined, crippled and dismembered it, and it could not stand alone. I do not think the fact that he took Austria is nearly as serious as generally supposed." Borah to Mrs. D. F. Bacon, March 21, 1938, Box 417, Borah Papers.

they had undertaken a "natural" connection through peaceful means, the Germans regrettably but understandably had effected the union by force. What could anyone expect?

Hitler's demands upon Czechoslovakia, in the fall of that year, rendered Borah's "logic of events" interpretation untenable even for him. The Czech incident revealed beyond question that the German threat was something more than the figment of British and French imaginations. That the Senator himself regarded Munich a major disaster he revealed in a letter to Walter Lippmann in October. The Munich Pact did not merely "surrender a piece of territory nor stab to death a small nation," he said, it involved "the economic system of a whole continent."[46] Borah as usual held the former Allies responsible for the tragedy. Since their repressive impositions had brought on present conditions, he pointed out, Great Britain and France should set them in order. He denied the United States shared this obligation.

Looking on while Europe fell under German hegemony, or becoming enmeshed with Britain and France if they did resist, posed stupefying alternatives for the Senator. He responded in a manner not unlike that species of bird which, when threatened, simply goes on pecking the ground until the danger passes—or it is slain. He suggested nothing through the end of the decade beyond his original prescription for neutral conduct. There was one exception. Shortly after Munich, the Idahoan proposed that he meet personally with Hitler in hopes of modifying the latter's conduct or, as Borah put it, getting him to "relax a bit."[47] The administration fortunately squelched this project and in the process reaffirmed his suspicion that Roosevelt had little real interest in accommodation. No longer believing the President acted in the interests of peace, the Senator henceforth resisted all action.

[46] Borah to Lippmann, October 18, 1938, Box 683, Borah Papers.
[47] Hutchinson, "News Articles," 31.

Borah's growing apprehensions about Germany failed to mitigate his fear of involvement with the former Allies. After Munich he began emphasizing an allegation with which he had only flirted before—that the French and British cooperated willingly in the dismemberment of Europe.[48] Professing his inability to see any difference between Hitler's actions and acquiescence to those actions, the Senator went further; he said that the Western powers in reality stood "behind" the dictator rather than wobbled before him. Because French and British conservatives regarded Bolshevism as a greater menace than the Nazis, he said, they collaborated with Hitler to create an anti-Communist bulwark or, at the very least, to direct German aggression against the East instead of the West.[49] They were quite willing to betray allies, ignore treaty obligations, and delude their own countrymen in pursuing these ends.

Borah's indictment had some foundation. It is equally true that he had a vested interest in denigrating France and Great Britain as a matter of course. By consistently attributing to them only the most sordid of motives, he worked to destroy any sympathy for their plight which the American people might entertain. At best his campaign might prevent the United States from becoming involved in European matters deliberately and unnecessarily—which is where he thought administration policy was headed. Even he had to admit, however, that the time might come when a choice no longer existed. His goal in that distressing event was to have created a public mood whereby American leaders could justify their actions solely in terms of the national interests, instead of some fictitious ideological crusade such as Wilson had palmed off twenty years before.[50]

[48] Borah to J. C. Fenton, December 26, 1938, Box 417, Borah Papers.
[49] Hutchinson, "News Articles," 38.
[50] Borah to Pat McCarran, August 31, Borah to International News

But if the British and French worked in cahoots with Germany, willingly or otherwise, surely this lessened the probability of a European war in which the United States might become enmeshed. Perhaps in the short run, the Senator conceded, but not ultimately. He predicted that the British public in time would repudiate Prime Minister Neville Chamberlain's "appeasement" policies in favor of more forceful leadership. When this happened, Anthony Eden (who had resigned from the cabinet in protest), or someone like him, would emerge to preside over a British confrontation with Germany. Then, "Look out," said Borah, for he believed Eden's militance rested largely on the assumption that "Roosevelt would stand by Britain in any war with the dictators."[51] Such a hypothesis permitted the Senator to disparage Anglo-French treachery on a day-to-day basis while holding to the theory that war was inevitable.

To the Idahoan's great dismay, more and more Americans became convinced, in the months following Munich, that the United States did have an interest in bolstering the Western democracies against the Nazis. The heretofore indecisive administration abetted this trend, and in turn it grew sufficiently encouraged to push more forcefully for revision of the neutrality legislation—particularly the repeal of the arms embargo. Borah and a great many other prominent Americans denounced repeal as the first step toward a *de facto* alliance, only to find support for Roosevelt's position increasing. Still strong, isolationist sentiment began waning; the process was speeded along by developments such as Hitler's seizure of all of Czechoslovakia in the spring of 1939.[52] No one in the

Service, September 1, 1939, both in Box 426, Borah Papers. *Congressional Record*, 76th Cong., 2nd Sess., Appendix, 79–80.

[51] Hutchinson, "News Articles," 44.

[52] Divine, *The Illusion of Neutrality*, 229–57. But see *FRUS, 1939*, I, 656–57, for Hull's fear of appearing before the Foreign Relations Committee at that time.

administration advocated direct involvement, of course; the President reassuringly denied isolationist accusations that his proposal constituted a threat to American neutrality.

Shifting public attitudes compelled the Senator to regroup his defenses. In upholding the need for rigid neutrality legislation, he had customarily described Europe in most pessimistic terms—a tinderbox which the tiniest spark could set ablaze.[53] He undoubtedly would have gone on doing so had popular opinion remained fixed. Now, when the threat of war strengthened the President's hand instead of weakening it, Borah's immediate problem was to prevent exploitation of real or trumped-up crises for the purpose of revising the laws. Under the circumstances he had only one recourse—to continue stressing the danger of war as a general proposition while denying, in any given instance, that an emergency existed. The Idahoan hewed to this tactic—it was just that—until, and in a sense even after, the conflict began, thereby causing himself to be remembered, if for nothing else, as the man who predicted there would be no war in Europe less than two months before World War II erupted.

Borah uttered his famous "prophecy" during the White House conference of July 18, 1939. A few days earlier, the Senate Foreign Relations Committee (still heavily manned by isolationists) apparently had defeated Roosevelt's campaign for repeal by voting to delay reconsideration of the neutrality laws until the next session of Congress. Hopeful that repeal might give pause to Hitler if accomplished in time, FDR summoned the meeting in an eleventh-hour attempt to change the verdict. Those present, in addition to FDR, Vice

[53] In January, 1939, Borah wrote that he thought war might break out in Europe that spring. Borah to J. Wesley Holden, January 11, 1939, Box 426, Borah Papers. By April he was saying, "The world is really at war now." Senate Foreign Relations Committee, *Neutrality, Peace Legislation and Our Foreign Policy: Hearings*, 76th Cong., 1st Sess. (1939), IX, 268.

President John Nance Garner and Secretary of State Cordell Hull, were Majority Leader Alben Barkley; Minority Leader Charles L. McNary; Minority Whip Warren Austin; Chairman of the Senate Foreign Relations Committee Key Pittman; and the committee's ranking Republican member, Borah. Roosevelt hoped to override the committee's decision by conveying to these leaders his own sense of urgency concerning Europe. He erred badly in thinking he stood even a chance with the obdurate Senator from Idaho.

Published versions of the session agree in substance.[54] FDR opened with an appeal for neutrality revision, then he deferred to Hull who proceeded to disclose the State Department's evaluation of European affairs, doing his best to convince his listeners that war loomed near. Partway through the Secretary's discourse Borah interrupted, saying he thought the State Department exaggerated the threat. When Hull replied that he might change his opinion if he consulted the cables flowing daily into the State Department, the Senator declared that he placed more faith in "other" sources then in his possession which indicated that there would be no fighting in Europe in the near future. Hull, known for his temper, grew extremely agitated over what he considered a slur on his department's efficiency. Ignoring Borah's protest that he had intended no slight, the Secretary broke off his talk and refused to answer further questions. After a poll of the individuals present, Garner reported to the President that he could not obtain enough votes with which to reopen the question successfully. Roosevelt adjourned the meeting and, with great regret, announced publicly that nothing further could be done until the next session of Congress.

[54] Cordell Hull, *The Memoirs of Cordell Hull* (2 vols., New York, 1948), I, 649–50; Joseph Alsop and Robert Kintner, *American White Paper* (New York, 1940), 58–59; William L. Langer and S. Everett Gleason, *The Challenge to Isolation, 1937–1940* (New York, 1952), 143–44.

Borah's performance in the meeting was, and is, criticized for the wrong reasons. Subsequent events made him appear ridiculous—the old windbag parading his everlasting "inside dope" in the face of near unanimity among those who knew what they were talking about. He looked even more foolish following the later discovery that his "other sources" consisted primarily of a sensational left-wing British journal to which he subscribed.[55] But all this misses the point because of the implication that he would have acted differently had he allowed himself to be convinced by Secretary Hull or, perhaps, if he read another magazine. Actually, since he wished to retain the arms embargo whatever the circumstances, *especially* if war impended, he would have argued exactly as he did had he looked at and believed every dispatch in the State Department's files.

Soon after Germany attacked Poland in September, a newspaperman queried Borah about his earlier prognostication. The Senator denied that he had been mistaken given the facts then available. The Russo-German Pact unconsummated at the time of the White House Conference, he said, explained the present situation, signifying as it did Hitler's unwillingness to go on serving as a cat's-paw against the Soviets. Great Britain and France, realizing their game was at an end, had at last taken a stand in protection of their own interests.[56] That war had come for whatever reasons only intensified the Senator's determination to prevent revision of the neutrality laws.

Borah knew the administration would renew its drive to get rid of the arms embargo, this time with every prospect of success. He tried blunting the thrust, temporarily anyway, by again expressing doubt that conditions were as serious as some people made them out. Two weeks after the war began, he

[55] McKenna, *Borah*, 364.
[56] New York *Times*, September 12, 1939.

suggested a plot so cynical that even he, a man who took European duplicity for granted, had at first failed to recognize it as such. Noting the absence of any large-scale battles such as had characterized the early weeks of World War I, Borah claimed there was "something phoney" going on and speculated as to why the combatants were "pulling their punches." Perhaps, he suggested, Great Britain and France had declared war on Germany merely as a face-saving gesture. Then, after a decent interval during which they could boast of "having discharged their duty to Poland," they would negotiate terms with Hitler as they had known all along they would do.[57] His was a convenient theory indeed, as it embraced not only a swipe against the former allies but also a view of the war which denied it presented any real danger to the United States. Only Borah could have interpreted recent events in such a way as to assert that "the chances are increased for peace."[58]

Although the "phoney war" theme achieved a measure of popularity within those circles predisposed to grasp at straws, the Senator himself used it sparingly. Like another decoy of his—that British control of the seas could defeat Germany without help from the United States—efforts to minimize the war's implications for America did confuse issues, as he intended, yet diluted his most telling argument. He wished above all to identify neutrality revision as a step leading inexorably to complete involvement in the European conflict. Belittling that conflict as "phoney," or as one which naval forces alone could decide, weakened his case that unimaginable disaster lay ahead. He sought to evoke horror, not complacency. His major speeches, therefore, unlike the confections he spun out before reporters, concentrated heavily on depicting Europe as a gigantic "slaughter pen" into which the

[57] *Ibid.*, September 19, 1939; Hutchinson, "News Articles," 42.
[58] New York *Times*, September 19, 1939.

administration conspired to pour the flower of American manhood.

Roosevelt summoned Congress into a special session which opened on September 21. Congressional leaders had advised him against trying to secure outright revocation of the neutrality legislation.[59] Enough support existed to lift the embargo, they said, only if the sales of arms together with all other commodities were placed on a "cash-and-carry" basis, leaving the rest of the laws untouched. Sentiment for aiding Great Britain and France had by no means eliminated the very strong determination to stay out of war. Wary of suffering another defeat as he had during the summer, Roosevelt concentrated on the obtainable.

Two hours after the President asked Congress for repeal of the arms embargo, Borah and twenty-three other senators met in Hiram Johnson's office. The consensus there ran against compromise; most of the group vowed to fight *any* neutrality revision "from Hell to breakfast" as one of them phrased it. Forming what they called a "vigilante committee," the dissidents strove to coordinate their efforts for maximum effectiveness by planning among other things a vast letter-writing campaign to show how strongly public opinion ran against tampering with neutrality.[60] For some of the veterans it was a repetition of the battle against the League two decades earlier. This time they served in a losing cause.

Administration leaders moved to hold off debate for the time being, thus permitting the Foreign Relations Committee time to report out the most satisfactory bill. No one objected. Borah and the others apparently welcomed the postponement themselves. No longer possessing enough strength to block Chairman Key Pittman anyway, they hoped popular senti-

[59] *Ibid.*, September 21, 1939; Divine, *The Illusion of Neutrality*, 290–95.
[60] New York *Times*, September 22, 23, 1939.

ment would mobilize behind them during the interim. The debate got underway on October 2.

After Pittman presented the administration's case for repeal, Borah led off for the opposition.[61] He first questioned why they should be discussing the issue at all. In 1935, he pointed out, there had been overwhelming approval for mandatory, impartial neutrality laws including an embargo on arms. Why? Because most Americans regarded such legislation as the best possible way to stay out of foreign wars— an assumption the administration presumably shared since it had raised no objection. That war had come subsequently left the situation unchanged as it applied to the United States. The neutrality laws never had been designed to *prevent* hostilities between other powers, only to keep the United States out of them. Those who proposed revision really sought to abandon neutrality. This the Europeans understood full well. Repealing the arms embargo, Borah said, meant to the Germans that the United States was "going" into the war, and to the British that we were "coming" in. He believed their interpretations were correct, administration disclaimers notwithstanding.

The Idahoan focused next on the nature of the war itself. He examined, and found wanting, the view that it represented a conflict between the forces of "democracy" and "totalitarianism." Were this true, he said, he personally would go beyond "cash-and-carry" to favor providing, free of charge, the wherewithal necessary for defending freedom. But power politics rather than ideology had brought on the war. Great Britain and France had shown themselves perfectly willing to do business with dictators—provided their own vital interests remained untouched. Having decided to fight, they naturally concealed their motives behind sanctimonious

[61] *Congressional Record*, 76th Cong., 2nd Sess., 66–74.

rhetoric as they had in 1914. Borah found it unconvincing. What masqueraded as a crusade against Nazism, he said, really amounted to a war over the division of territory. And if the administration persisted in its course, the time would come when American troops would have to fight in behalf of such an ignoble cause.

The Senator closed on a belligerent note. Senator Pittman had attempted to make him appear inconsistent by citing his speech favoring American entry into World War I. Borah said he never "had any occasion or thought to modify" the sentiments he had expressed at the time, nor had he now. "I am not a pacifist," he declared. Should any European power "deign" to notice his remarks, he wanted it clearly understood that he would vote for war again sooner than allow encroachments by either side upon American neutrality. Only one consideration influenced him, he concluded, and that was America—"America with peace if possible but, America." He sat down amidst wild applause.

Stirring though it may have been to those who heard it, Borah's speech had no discernible effect other than further weakening an already sick man. He faltered badly toward the end, observers noted, with his voice at times all but deserting him.[62] Beyond an occasional brief comment or question, he abstained from deliberations on the floor thereafter although they lasted almost a month. Not that it mattered. Despite the isolationists' very strenuous efforts—radio speeches, letter-writing campaigns, mass rallies—administration estimates proved remarkably accurate. On October 27, the Senate by a crunching majority passed the Pittman bill removing the embargo on arms. The group which had met in Johnson's office on the first day gained a scant half-dozen allies; there were thirty dissenting votes. Important in itself, repeal to Borah merely portended the unfolding of a "general

[62] *Borah*, McKenna, 366.

program" aimed at projecting the United States into "the European balance of power system."[63] He was disconsolate.

Several developments during the weeks following adjournment confirmed Borah's opinion that the administration intended launching fresh asasults against neutrality whenever the opportunities arose. Soviet Russia's attack on Finland late in November at first elicited only official expressions of sympathy for the beleagured Finns. It soon became known, however, that Roosevelt intended requesting loans for Finland after the regular session of Congress began. Although Borah himself pronounced the Rusian invasion barbaric, saying he hoped Americans would participate in *private* endeavors to help Finland, he deplored any overt steps by the government.[64] Nor was that all. Key Pittman had begun working a bill which provided for an embargo on war goods to Japan and which, if passed, would go into effect when the existing commercial treaty expired late in January. Borah thought Roosevelt's unilateral abrogation of the treaty the previous July insulting enough to Japan; he regarded a discriminatory embargo as disastrous.[65]

An apparently rejuvenated Borah took his place in the Senate as the regular session convened. Having recovered much of his strength since the exhausting fight over neutrality legislation, he performed vigorously in committee and on the Senate floor. The opposition to proposals concerning Finland and Japan appeared substantial, affording the Idahoan cause for optimism. Indeed, he and Arthur Vandenberg began planning a campaign aimed at mending relations with Japan by

[63] Borah to Jess Hawley, October 31, 1939, Box 426, Borah Papers.

[64] Borah to E. H. Hanson, January 5, Borah to Dean Driscoll, January 9, 1940, both in Box 434, Borah Papers.

[65] Borah had not opposed the move at the time. Langer and Gleason, *The Challenge to Isolation*, 158. For his later view, see Borah to Ned David Miller, December 2, 1939, Box 427, Borah Papers.

building support for a new commercial treaty. The state of the economy demanded some such arrangement, they argued, which could be implemented without implying that the United States condoned Japanese actions in China.[66] But for the Senator from Idaho time had run out. On the morning of January 16, he suffered a massive cerebral hemorrhage. He died three days later without regaining consciousness.

[66] McKenna, *Borah*, 367.

An Overview

THE achievements of American foreign policy between the wars were unimpressive. Whatever the drawbacks of international organizations formed after 1918, the United States neither worked within them nor showed a capacity for independent leadership. Individuals and groups urged greater participation, of course, but the mood of the times ran against them. Perhaps the choices available could not have materially altered subsequent developments. To the men involved, meaningful alternatives did exist; some believed American influence could help construct a peaceful world. Senator Borah contributed signally to neutralizing that influence. Endlessly professing his yearning for international cooperation, he opposed every serious effort to bring it about. In so doing he sometimes fostered illusions he did not himself share, and he did it well enough to fool his chroniclers as well as his contemporaries. His was a unique talent.

For all his invocations of the Founding Fathers, Borah's distaste for collective action encompassed more than a blind reverence for tradition or a presumption of American inviolability. He had become aware, by the end of World War I, that European conditions directly affected the economic and political interests of the United States. He perceived the issues rather sharply for all his tendency in the direction of superficialities. His weakness lay in his inability to translate his perceptions into a viable approach to foreign policy. He was paralyzed in this regard by a set of assumptions which permeated his outlook and denied him the slightest latitude.

America existed in a world of rapacious nation-states, ran his premise, whose behavior warranted the affection one might hold for a swarm of barracuda. He considered especially treacherous the major European powers, believing them driven by the narrowest conception of immediate advantage. Had he ever doubted this concept, the Versailles Treaty proved to him beyond question that France and Great Britain subordinated everything to the drive for national aggrandizement. Becoming associated with them for any reason, he anticipated, meant dragging the United States into everlasting European convulsions. Elsewhere in the world these same nations, trying to maintain their empires through force of arms, avidly sought American backing to preserve the status quo—an aspiration he thought immoral and futile as well. He found utterly repellent the idea of stationing the United States alongside those attempting to hold back the tides of world revolution.

Granting his views a core of truth, there remained the matter of which path the United States should take. Would it not have been better, after all, to employ American strength as a moderating influence rather than to back away from the problems? Borah disagreed for two reasons. Despite its best intentions, he believed, the United States would find itself drawn inexorably into tangles beyond extrication. His "logic of events" interpretation of history caused him to shrink from any step which might, and probably would, lead to unanticipated consequences. Equally important, he distrusted his own government whoever stood at the helm—the "international bankers" and the "interests" prowled behind every President and Secretary of State. Such reasoning left him unable to function as anything but an obstructionist in fact, however much he denied the name.

If Borah represents an exaggerated symbol of "isolationism," his association with the various conferences, peace movements, and treaties of the 1920's appears at first paradoxical. So deeply pessimistic about individuals and nations, how could he also be the naive "utopian" who believed in preventing world conflict by signing properly worded agreements? His expressed attitudes about foreign policy, taken at face value, point to a mind singularly lacking in coherence. Borah was a man in whom there were contradictions, certainly, but an even more pronounced consistency underlay his conduct over the years.

The Senator had shown a penchant for using one issue to becloud another even before the world war. Henry Cabot Lodge's artful strategy in fighting *the* League, but not *a* league, must have impressed him, however, for he adopted it as his own. Obstructionism *qua* obstructionism, he came to see, earned miniscule dividends. Repetitious opposition to all proposals lessened one's effectiveness against a specific proposal. And, harboring political ambitions himself, Borah soon realized that his association with the "Battalion of Death" categorized him as a mere spoiler. He therefore cultivated the facade of a constructive leader ardently promoting international cooperation of a nature preferable to that existing organizations could offer.

Comparing his rhetoric with his actions—especially the timing of those actions—leads to the conclusion that Borah regarded as tactical weapons most, if not all, his "constructive" propositions. His enthusiasm varied according to the dangers he apprehended from those who skulked around the "back door" to entanglement with the League. Each time a threat arose he hurried forward suggesting conferences, world courts, and toothless treaties—only to abandon them as soon as the peril receded. He tried to confuse issues, blur distinctions, and attack other proposals from the vantage point of already having offered alternative programs. As Hiram Johnson once said of him, Borah habitually carried on his person "a pocketful of red herring." All else failing, he inevitably reverted to the irreconcilable of 1919.

The end of Borah's "positive" phase coincided roughly with the stock market crash. Already at odds with President Hoover, the Senator found his goods unsalable at a time when economic catastrophe occupied most people's minds and when events abroad made a mockery of peace pacts and campaigns to banish war. The Democratic landslide in 1932 nudged him farther from the seat of influence he had once held. Now less significant in the total spectrum, the Idahoan yet functioned as a spokesman for the majority in opposing collective security efforts through most of the decade. The public, stimulated by influences such as the Nye investigations of the munitions industry, decried involvement of any kind. Even here Borah could draw little comfort, for everything the administration did seemed to him motivated by the desire to place the United States in the center of the European maelstrom.

Cracks appeared in the neutrality wall with the advent of "cash and carry," a scheme the Senator attributed to pro-British intrigue. Then, as the threat of war drew closer, isolationist sentiment began contracting as more and more people accepted the idea of aiding the Western democracies—if only by making it possible for them to purchase materials for their own defense. Borah reacted as he had always reacted in such circumstances; he scattered his herring generously, here arguing one proposition, there another, now predicting the imminence of war, then its implausibility. Pursuing his goals with a single-minded devotion, he used whatever lay at hand to achieve them. And beneath it all—the sundry "conversions" in the 1920's, the frenzied thrusting and parrying in the 1930's—his thinking remained essentially constant. The Borah of 1939 was, basically, indistinguishable from the Borah of 1917.

The Senator's debilitating prejudices hampered him less in those areas where he saw no threat of entanglement. Although it is impossible to calculate his influence with any precision, his unremitting opposition to interventionist policies in Latin America and the Far East placed him ahead of his times. Perfectly in keeping with his brand of isolationism, he demanded that the United States deal on a level of equality with all nations regardless of their size or strength. Gunboats and marine detachments he looked upon as remnants of a bygone era. To this it must be added that his attitude seldom went very far beyond the idea of acting "honorably." The consequences of American economic activities rarely concerned him provided the interests involved did not ask for special privilege or physical intervention by the United States government.

His lengthy campaign in behalf of recognizing Soviet Russia, aside from casting further doubt on his alleged erraticism, raised an interesting and difficult question: What *is* the appropriate response to a government whose tenets and actions run contrary to one's own conception of the "good society?" Borah thought world peace impossible so long as such a large and potentially powerful nation remained an outcast. Doubtless overestimating the extent to which the United States might have influenced Soviet evolution, he refused to believe that ostracism afforded a sane answer. For, beneath their many lines of argumentation, the antirecognitionists offered nothing more than the hope that some ineffable "contradiction" within the Communist society would destroy it. As the Senator predicted, such a notion provided a rickety basis for the conduct of diplomacy, whatever psychic reassurances it bestowed.

By the time of his death, Borah no longer commanded the attention once paid him as a matter of course; the days when newspaper editors considered his statements more important than those of a President had passed with another age. Had he lived a few years more, it is entirely unlikely that he would have exercised any perceptible influence on the course of history. He would have had the misfortune, however, of seeing virtually all of his fears realized. President Roosevelt did lead the United States into an ever-closer relationship with France and Great Britain; subsequent measures against the Japanese did provoke them to war; and the movement for another world organization—the United Nations—this time did prevail. As Borah himself might have insisted—ruefully—the "logic of events" since 1919 foretold precisely such results.

A Selective Guide
to Sources

The William E. Borah Papers, located in the Manuscript Division of the Library of Congress (hereafter abbreviated as LC), are indispensible for any study of the Senator. Most of the more than seven hundred boxes contain his correspondence (letters received and copies of letters sent), and are arranged chronologically. There are some cartons marked "foreign relations," but a great deal of relevant material is filed elsewhere. Folders within each container are in alphabetical order by correspondent and by subject. The collection, fullest through the 1920's, thins out for later years. Age and health, as well as the fact that many people with whom he corresponded most frequently had died or retired from political life, probably accounts for this. With the collection are fifty-five reels of microfilm taken from Borah's scrapbooks which are at the University of Idaho in Moscow, Idaho. These scrapbooks consist of newspaper clippings primarily, but contain some letters.

Second in importance to the Borah collection are the Raymond Robins Papers at the State Historical Society of Wisconsin, and the Salmon O. Levinson Papers at the University of Chicago Library. Both men corresponded frequently with the Senator and between themselves. Their letters are particularly informative for those periods when one of them was in Washington with Borah, reporting to the other. The Borah-Levinson relationship cooled perceptibly when the former refused to pursue Outlawry after the Kellogg-Briand Pact, although they did exchange some letters thereafter. In 1932, Robins suffered the first of a series of debilitating ailments and accidents which progressively restricted his activities.

The Alexander Gumberg Papers in the State Historical Society of Wisconsin are helpful, especially on the matter of recognizing Soviet Russia, as are the John Bassett Moore Papers (LC). Borah corresponded on a variety of subjects, mostly the League of Nations and the World Court, with Albert Beveridge (LC). There is a series of interesting letters about Borah, written by Hiram Johnson, in the Harold L. Ickes Papers (LC). Much of the material is gossipy, however, and this writer found no way of verifying it. The Hermann Hagedorn Papers (LC) includes ten boxes of notes, transcripts of interviews, and other documents amassed for Hagedorn's biography of William Boyce Thompson. Raymond Robins and others supplied Hagedorn with personal recollections which include a number of references to Borah.

Other collections consulted proved of small value in understanding Borah, but they provided background material and, in some cases, "negative" information. The Elihu Root Papers (LC), for instance, reveal how small a part Borah played in formulating Republican strategy toward the League of Nations. The Papers of Woodrow Wilson, Robert Lansing, and Breckenridge Long, all in LC, yielded material on the League and on Russia, as did the E. M. House Collection (which includes the papers of Frank Polk, Gordon Auchincloss, William C. Bullitt, and others), in the Sterling Library, Yale University. The Charles Evans Hughes Papers (LC), particularly the Beerits memoranda, provide a rich source for administration activities in the early 1920's, although there are only scattered references to Borah himself. Other collections used include those of Philander C. Knox, Calvin Coolidge, Norman H. Davis, William Allen White, George D. Norris, Key Pittman, and Cordell Hull.

At the time research was done on this manuscript, several sources which might have been of value, such as the Robert M. Lafollette Papers (LC) and those of Arthur M. Vandenberg at Ann Arbor, Michigan, were closed to scholars.

Material located at the National Archives, Washington, D.C., crucial for administration policies, proved less helpful for this study. Although the writer by no means investigated all of the State Department correspondence for a period of over thirty-three years, he did go through a number of Decimal Files for those subjects in which Borah interested himself. The files are made up almost entirely of letters and cables to and from representatives abroad, memoranda on interviews with foreign officials, et cetera; rarely do they shed light on what a particular Senator has done or might do.

Papers of the Senate Committee on Foreign Relations, also in the Archives, were of some help, particularly for the period when Borah was committee chairman. Mostly consisting of petitions, protests, bills, and the like, there are also letters between the chairman and administration officials.

PRINTED SOURCES

(Autobiographies, Memoirs, and Collected Letters are cited in the footnotes)

The *Congressional Record*, a primary source for any Senator's public speeches, is especially fruitful in Borah's case, for he had something to say about practically everything. In those areas where the State Department Decimal Files were not consulted, use was made of *Papers Relating to the Foreign Relations of the United States*. This series, consisting of several volumes per year, as well as separate collections for specific subjects, contains a fairly generous sampling of State Department documents. Senate Committee on Foreign Relations *Hearings* proved valuable, often as much for Borah's questions as for his statements. These are cited individually in the footnotes, along with other printed *Senate Documents*. One, "News Articles on the Life and Works of William E. Borah," by William K. Hutchinson, printed as *Senate Document 150*, 76th Congress, 3rd Session (Washington, 1940), bears special mention. Hutchinson's collection of pieces, based on his friendship with Borah over a span of nineteen years, frequently is adulatory but provides information not found in other sources.

There are two published collections of Borah's speeches: Horace Green (ed.), *American Problems: A Selection of Speeches and Prophecies by William E. Borah* (New York, 1924), and Borah's *Bedrock: Views on Basic National Problems* (Washington, 1936). The series *Vital Speeches of the Day*, vols. I–V, contain a number of Borah's speeches.

NEWSPAPERS AND PERIODICALS

The New York *Times* (and its index) was indispensible for this study. The *Times's* practice of quoting the reactions of prominent officials whenever an important issue arose helped greatly, because Borah usually was one of those whose statements appear. The New York *Tribune* (*Herald Tribune* after 1924), the Chicago *Tribune*, and the Idaho *Statesman*, were also used. The *Literary Digest* provides a convenient sampling of contemporary editorial opinion.

Century, Current History, Foreign Affairs, Outlook, the *Nation,* and the *New Republic* were consulted most frequently, especially the latter two whose interests often parallelled Borah's. Contemporary periodicals printed a large number of articles about the Senator over the years, most of which are without insight. Some exceptions are: a series of pieces by Charles Merz which appeared in the *New Republic*, XXXIX (May 26, June 3, June 10, 1925); Walter Lippmann's "Concerning Senator Borah," *Foreign Affairs*, IX (January, 1926); Henry Pringle, "The Real Senator Borah," *World's Work,* LVII (December, 1928); and Allan Nevins, "Borah and World Politics," *Current History*, XXXVII (February, 1933).

SECONDARY SOURCES

The number of books and articles treating various aspects of American foreign policy between the years 1907–40 is almost beyond counting. Those having to do with American entry into World War I, the League of Nations, isolationism, peace movements, neutrality during the 1930's, and American relations with Russia, usually mention Borah at the very least. Works used directly in this study are cited separately in the footnotes. Others undoubtedly influenced the writer but must go unmentioned. The following note on sources is restricted to those studies which either pertain wholly, or in large part, to Borah, provide information about him unavailable elsewhere, or otherwise have special relevance.

There are two biographies of the Senator: Claudius O. Johnson's *Borah of Idaho* (New York, 1936), and Marian C. McKenna's *Borah* (Ann Arbor, 1961). Johnson's book, based on personal interviews with Borah, as well as the use of his papers, is detailed and generally accurate, though with a pronounced tendency to consider issues from Borah's standpoint. More critical, but in some ways less satisfying, McKenna's volume has the advantage of dealing with Borah's last years. Many of McKenna's conclusions, particularly on foreign policy questions, rely almost completely upon the work of others.

More limited in scope, though less so than the title implies, is John Chalmers Vinson's *William E. Borah and the Outlawry of War* (Athens, Ga., 1957). Although this writer disagrees with a number of Vinsons's interpretations, such as the matter of Borah's "conversion" to whole-hearted support of Outlawry, Vinson's book is a scholarly, thoughtful study, of far more sophistication than either of the biographies.

John Milton Cooper Jr., in "William E. Borah, Political Thespian," *Pacific Northwest Quarterly*, LVI (October, 1965), presents a brilliant portrait of the Senator, but one which bears too heavily upon its theme. Printed along with his piece are two critiques—very much worth reading—by Merle W. Wells and Claudius O. Johnson, and Cooper's reply to them. Although a review article, based on McKenna's biography, John Braeman offers an interesting analysis of the Senator as a "traditionalist" progressive, in "Seven Progressives," *Business History Review*, XXXV (1961). Written almost entirely from secondary sources, but of some value, is Charles W. Toth, "Isolationism and the Emergence of Borah: An Appeal to American Tradition," *Western Political Quarterly*, XIV (June, 1961).

Analyses of Borah from the "New Left" point of view can be found in two works by William Appleman Williams, "The Legend of Isolationism in the 1920's," *Science and Society*, XVIII (Winter, 1954) and *The Tragedy of American Diplomacy* (revised Delta Edition, New York, 1962), and Orde S. Pinckney's "William E. Borah: Critic of American Foreign Policy," *Studies on the Left*, I (1960). Both authors stress those of Borah's opinions which coincide with their own, and attribute to him conceptualizations he would have been surprised to learn that he held.

SPECIAL STUDIES

Two articles by Waldo W. Braden, "Some Illinois Influences on the Life of William E. Borah," *Journal of the Illinois Historical Society*, XL (June, 1947) and "William E. Borah's Years in Idaho in the 1880's," *Kansas Historical Quarterly*, XXXII (November, 1947), treat Borah's early years. Selig Adler's *The Isolationist Impulse* (New York, 1957) contains material on the Senator's work with "hyphenate" groups during the fight over the League, but it must be read with care because Adler invariably uses emotively loaded terms whenever he refers to Borah. Henry W. Berger, "Laissez Faire for Latin America: Borah Defines the Monroe Doctrine," *Idaho Yesterdays* (Summer, 1965), is excellent for Borah's attitude toward Latin America. William Appleman Williams' *American-Russian Relations, 1781–1947* (New York, 1952) is useful for the fight over recognition of Russia. Also helpful, although somewhat misleading as to Borah's position, is Christopher Lasch, *The American Liberals and the Russian Revolution* (New York, 1962).

John Chalmers Vinson's *Referendum for Isolation* (Athens, Ga., 1961) and *The Parchment Peace: The United States Senate and the Washington Conference* (Athens, Ga., 1955), careful studies of the League fight and the Washington Conference, contain useful assessments of Borah. Older works, such as Thomas A. Bailey's *Wilson and the Peacemakers* (New York, 1947) and Denna F. Fleming's *The United States and the League of Nations* (New York, 1932), yield some data but treat the Senator with barely disguised contempt.

John S. Stoner, in *S. O. Levinson and the Pact of Paris* (Chicago, 1943) deals with Borah in considerable detail, with a bias favorable to Levinson. Robert H. Ferrell's judicious *Peace in Their Time: The Origins of the Kellogg-Briand Pact* (New Haven, 1952), is generous to all participants. Ferrell's *Frank B. Kellogg and Henry L. Stimson*, vol. XII of *The American Secretaries of State and Their Diplomacy* (New York, 1963), and especially L. Ethan Ellis' *Frank B. Kellogg and American Foreign Relations, 1925–1929* (New Brunswick, 1961), evaluate Borah's strong influence on the Coolidge administration. That the Senator, though formidable, figured less importantly during the Hoover years can be seen in that part of Ferrell's book devoted to Stimson, and in his *American Diplomacy in the Great Depression* (New Haven, 1957).

For Borah's part in the neutrality controversy during the 1930's, see Robert A. Devine's extremely thorough *The Illusion of Neutrality* (Chicago, 1962). Less valuable for this study, because the bulk of the work deals with the period after Borah's death, is William L. Langer and Everett S. Gleason, *The Challenge to Isolation: 1937–1940.* Manfred Jonas, in *Isolationism in America, 1935–1941* (Ithaca, 1966), includes pertinent material about Borah in the 1930's, although the overall treatment of him is perfunctory.